BRANDY OF THE*DAMNED*

COLIN WILSON

on music

Foruli Classics

**Foruli
Classics**

Published by Foruli Classics

First published as *Colin Wilson on Music* by Pan Books Ltd 1967
This edition published by Foruli Classics 2014

ISBN 978-1-905792-54-2

Cover copyright © Foruli Ltd 2014
Text copyright © Colin Wilson 1964, 1967

A CIP catalogue record for this book is available from the British Library

Cover by Andy Vella at Velladesign (www.velladesign.com)

Printed by Lightning Source

Foruli Classics is an imprint of Foruli Ltd, London

www.foruliclassics.com

To my friend Dan Danziger of Washington,
to whom I owe my first acquaintance
with American music

CONTENTS

CONTENTS

INTRODUCTION

Purely personal: on being a musical eclectic

As a glance down the list of chapters in this book will show, I am a musical eclectic in the fullest sense of the word. I like dozens of composers and hundreds of pieces of music; on the other hand, I have no very positive dislikes. As this certainly distinguishes me from anyone else who has ever written about music, I feel that a word of explanation is necessary.

Perhaps I should begin by mentioning two blind spots. Unlike J. D. M. Rorke, the author of *A Musical Pilgrim's Progress*, I have never had a 'Chopin phase'; the music of Chopin has never meant a great deal to me. I can listen to it with interest if I am, say, comparing the technique of Richter with that of Paderewski or de Pachmann; but I have never yet played a Chopin record when I have been alone and felt like music.

The case of Bach is slightly different. I take Schweitzer's word for it that Bach has something to say to me if I will only listen carefully enough, and I am quite capable of listening to Bach with a book about him open on my knee to tell me what I am supposed to be listening for. Many things of his give me a certain pleasure: the pastoral interlude from the Christmas Oratorio, the slow movement of the double violin concerto, the final ricercar of *The Musical Offering* (particularly in Webern's transcription); yet I never feel the sudden conviction: 'Ah, here is a great composer' which I am capable of feeling for many composers whom I do not particularly enjoy. I will listen to Bach as happily as to Buxtehude or Locatelli; but I cannot pretend that I place him on my list of great composers.

As to the development of my musical taste, there is very little to be said. It was easy for people of my generation to discover that they liked music—certainly easier than for people born in the previous two decades, and probably easier than for the generation born during the Second World War, who tend to devote their spare time to television. The reason is that I was born in 1931, at the beginning of the era of the 'talkies'. Most films rely heavily on background music, and in the 1940s background music became an extremely important part of the film, particularly in the heavy dramas. In *Odd Man Out*—surely one of the best films ever made in England—the music takes over completely in the second half, to the almost complete exclusion of dialogue. The drama is intensified by the music; but, oddly enough, one's musical appreciation is also intensified by the drama. The schoolboy of fifty years ago probably had to rely on 'descriptive music'—Beethoven's 'Pastoral' Symphony, *The Sorcerer's Apprentice*, *The Flight of the Bumble Bee*—to give him his initial 'shock of recognition'. My generation found it easier, since they were able to associate their first musical experiences—the Warsaw Concerto, the *Glass Mountain* music, *The Way to the Stars*—with an experience that was in itself dramatic, the war. From there to Disney's *Fantasia* was only a short step; and after that, the way was open: through Holst's *Planets*, the piano concertos of Rachmaninov and Schumann, the Beethoven Fifth Symphony and Violin Concerto, Stravinsky's *Firebird* and *Rite of Spring*. This was certainly the royal road to the appreciation of music.

The purists will no doubt object that this is a most damaging admission, that music should be appreciated as music, not because it is associated with a romantic film. I cannot agree. Surely all music is dramatic in essence. Surely the interest with which we follow the development even of a piece we know well is like the interest with which we re-read a favourite novel. This, at all events, is the way in which I have always reacted to music. A symphony is a stage play with the parts written for instruments instead of for actors; a piano sonata is a story told by one voice, like Cocteau's *La Voix Humaine*. If this is the wrong way to feel about music, I am sorry; but it is the way I feel. Perhaps it also explains why I cannot get excited about Bach and Chopin; this is a matter in which I am deficient in self-knowledge. I will return to this later.

I was fortunate in another way. By the time I was twenty the long-playing record had appeared.* Even in those days, before the cheap LP, the price compared very favourably with the old 78 rpm. (At the time of writing—Christmas 1963—a full-length LP can be bought for as little as 10s, the price of a single 12-inch disk of pre-war days.) I was unable to afford a gramophone in

*1951.

those days, but I had friends who were better off; in particular, John Crabbe of Leicester, who would play me whole operas of Wagner and Puccini. Finally, in 1956, the publication of my first book suddenly made enough money for me to feel that I could afford to start a record collection. I think that this was undoubtedly the keenest pleasure brought about by 'overnight success'—to read about a work that interested me, and to be able to walk into a record shop and buy it immediately. When I moved to Cornwall in 1957, I had 500 records; since then, I've accumulated another 4,000. I can say of records what George Saintsbury said of wine: 'There is no money among that which I have spent since I began to earn my living, of the expenditure of which I am less ashamed, or which gave me better value in return.' (I also enjoy good wine, but if it ever came to a choice between wine and music, I would turn teetotal without a second thought.)

In my early teens I listened to a great many concerts on the radio. Haydn and Mozart meant little to me, and I listened to Beethoven's symphonies with a sense of performing a duty that would make me feel virtuous later. But radio performances of Stravinsky's *Firebird*, Falla's *Three-cornered Hat*, Franck's *Symphonic Variations* excited me so much that when, at the age of eighteen, I bought a few 78s to play on our 'wind-up' gramophone at home, these were the first items I collected. (I also paid Franck the somewhat dubious compliment of calling the first version of my novel *Ritual in the Dark*, 'Symphonic Variations'.) Other records bought or borrowed at this time were the 'Liebestod' sung by Flagstad, the final dances of the *Rite of Spring*, Beethoven's *Egmont* Overture, and Rachmaninov's 'Paganini' Variations.

Then, at about the age of sixteen or seventeen, I began to develop musical snobbery. Since I had heard *Swan Lake* and the Unfinished Symphony of Schubert so many times, I concluded that they must be bad music, since otherwise they would not be so popular. Another aversion, oddly enough, was Beethoven. It must not be supposed that I arrived at these conclusions out of extra-musical prejudice; it really seemed to me, on listening to these composers, that their music was bad: that is to say, it produced a definite aversion in me, *judged by ear alone*. Beethoven seemed to be a series of thumps and bangs; his music

11

made me think of an actor whose voice is so harsh that he can only speak in a shout. And yet even now, when my friend Burnett James has injected into me a little of his own boundless admiration—and perhaps a little of his understanding—of Beethoven, I am not entirely apologetic about my opinion at eighteen. I think I sensed that Beethoven's music is a triumph of the will rather than an outpouring of vital and lyrical impulse. Even a minor composer like Puccini can sometimes be swept away by sheer musical ecstasy, and one gets the feeling that the' music is bubbling from him with the spontaneity of bird song. In Beethoven I never hear this; I feel that he wrote music in the spirit that Napoleon soldiered—out of a determination to be a great musician. He *is* great; but it seemed to me at eighteen that he thumped the table with his fist far too often. The opening phrase of the Fifth Symphony or the Hammerclavier Sonata sound to me as if he is saying: 'Now you listen to me . . .'

In my own defence, I hasten to add that I never clung dogmatically to these opinions. My aim has always been to widen my musical taste in every possible way, to get the most out of the realm of music which is, after all, a free gift. I like music in the way that some people like human beings—any human beings. I personally do not find most human beings very interesting. (I agree that this is a failing, but it is a necessary one for a writer of ideas.) In the same way, I do not particularly enjoy travel; a few days of it is enough to make me wish myself back home. But in these matters a principle of economy seems important if I am not to waste too much time and energy. Where music is concerned, I cannot see any point in applying Occam's Razor; my aim is to multiply possible sources of enjoyment. So, in due course, I returned to Schubert and Tchaikovsky, and deliberately set out to enjoy what could be enjoyed. Later still, I applied the same principle to Falla, Delius, and Elgar (encouraged again by Burnett James). At first, it seemed to me that I was merely anxious to give myself the widest possible range of musical enjoyment. Later, I came to see that a more important principle was involved.

This principle must be made quite clear at this point, for it will recur in one form or another in every chapter in the present volume. It could be called the fallacy of intolerance. Let me offer an example. In an excellent and stimulating little book,* the American music critic B. H. Haggin describes his reaction to Brahms: how for years he accepted that Brahms was one of the greatest of all composers, and then was one day playing a movement of the 'Cello Sonata, op. 99, when he realized that this was 'not real creative activity, but the pretence and pose of such activity'. After this, he found more and more of this 'faking' in Brahms, and he ends by admitting that he nowadays finds only two or three works of Brahms at all bearable.

All this sounds fair enough. Haggin may well be right about Brahms's faking. But even so, ought we to congratulate him on his sudden insight, or commiserate with him? It only means that he has lost a whole world of enjoyment, just as Beethoven lost a world when he went deaf.

It will be objected that Haggin only came to see what was 'really there'. Is this so, or is it only another disguised fallacy? When a child gets enjoyment out of a Christmas card with silver snow and reindeer, is he deceived because the card is artistically valueless?

I am not trying to defend a relativity theory of art—the beauty is what you put there, etc. On the contrary, I believe that aesthetic values are objective; the beauty is really 'out there'. But Blake was right when he said that if the doors of perception were cleansed everything would appear infinite. Works of art give us brief flashes of a 'being', an 'is-ness', which is nothing to do with us or our minds; our perceptions keep it out rather than let it in. If a child gets a glimpse of beauty from a poor work of art, the artist is not to be accused of faking; the child is to be congratulated that his perceptions are less closed-up than our own.

This probably sounds like casuistry. But consider this matter. If a man explains that he ceased liking Wagner at the age of twenty, and that his favourite composer is now Bartók, he is implying that his change of heart is a kind of mathematical progression, a pure gain in perception. What he is forgetting is that all such changes involve gaining certain things and losing others. Again, Haggin tells how he came to 'see through' Wagner at Bayreuth, finding *The Ring* tawdry and bombastic, even though he could appreciate intellectually its 'prodigious

*The Listener's Musical Companion, New York, 1956.

13

musical power'. But any lover of *The Ring* will confirm that getting to know it entailed a certain amount of hard work. (I can remember my own preparations for making a first acquaintance with *The Ring*, broadcast on the Third Programme, which entailed a reading of Shaw's *Perfect Wagnerite*, Newman's *Wagner Nights*, and the making of a list of the leitmotivs in alphabetical order to consult as they came up.) One might say that one's involvement in *The Ring* is almost as complicated an act as driving a car. It involves a certain 'suspension of disbelief'; it may even involve definitely placing certain of one's critical faculties in abeyance, as when one goes to watch children act a play at school. All this, then, might at least suggest that if a composer's spell suddenly ceases to work, it may be, to some extent, due to an increasing laziness on the part of the listener, or simply to a deterioration in his power of projecting sympathy into the artist's conception.

I should add that although I have conscientiously collected all Wagner's operas on record, including even an atrocious abridged *Rienzi*, he no longer exercises the same spell as when I was twenty; and I find it difficult to understand how Thomas Mann could have remained a Wagnerite to the end of his life. Still, I am also aware of an occasional tendency to dismiss Wagner altogether—to dismiss it as German bombast and dullness—which I immediately subject to critical scrutiny or correct by reading Mann's essay. I excuse my loss of interest in Wagner by reflecting that I have made the acquaintance of some hundreds of composers since I was twenty. But I firmly refuse to join the ranks of those who believe the world would be a better place without Wagner's music. This would be surrendering to unreason. What is more, if I decline to allow my intellect to surrender to it, I don't see why I shouldn't exercise the same discipline over my emotions, and deliberately induce in myself the state of mind in which I enjoy Wagner. Men are too much slaves to their moods and emotions.

I remember being irritated and shocked when a few years ago an introverted poet accused me of using music as a form of escapism. Perhaps he simply meant that I am inclined to play music to visitors to avoid conversation. Still, his comment made me reconsider the question. I suppose the obvious explanation is that, like anyone else, I find music a release into an intenser form of existence. But it would not be true to say, for example, that I turn to music for an emotional experience to counterbalance the 'intellectual' experience of writing books about ideas. For, as often as not, my approach to music is intellectual. I read about music almost as much as I listen to it. This combined exercise of mind and feeling is very similar to the pleasure I get from reading philosophy—or writing it, for that matter. Consequently, for me, the sitting-room is the place to listen to music, rather than the concert hall. I realize that the quality of the experience is different in the concert hall, not to mention the quality of the sound. But in my sitting-room I can allow my musical caprices to carry me where they will; I can jump from a Beethoven quartet to Puccini, from Schoenberg to Scriabin (although these two have more in common than appears on the surface), or even from Stravinsky to Bix Beiderbecke. In the concert hall, I probably have to put up with yet another rendering of the Tchaikovsky Fifth, a Berlioz overture, and the Mendelssohn Violin Concerto. Admittedly, a concert can take fire in a way that a recording never can, and sweep the audience into close participation; it can also drag hopelessly.

I had an argument about this with Victor Gollancz some years ago. I asked him which room in the house he used for listening to records, and he said that he had never possessed a gramophone; for him, the pleasure of music was also the pleasure of sitting in an audience and feeling that the experience was being shared. He seemed shocked when I said that I much preferred the gramophone to 'live' music. Obviously our temperaments differ in some basic respect: but perhaps this is no place to go into that. On only one point would I concede that there is much to be said for his view; I agree that it is in many ways preferable to listen to opera in an opera house, simply because the stage action is, after all, part of the drama. But even there, I am not sure. I found that *Carmen*, *Tristan and Isolde*, and *Otello* gained considerably from being heard in the opera house; but a performance of *Rosenkavalier* only made me aware of something that I had not realized from listening to it on record—that the opera is at least twice too long. Strauss is certainly one of those composers who have a great deal to gain from the gramophone. The bitterness of critics like Wallace Brockway and Herbert

15

Weinstock, who have so many harsh things to say of Strauss in their *Men of Music*, may be the result of sitting through tone-poems that last for three-quarters of an hour, or operas that seem to drag on interminably without very much taking place on stage. The gramophone is the ideal way of getting acquainted with the 'Alpine' Symphony, or with *Capriccio* or *Arabella*; played in twenty-minute chunks, these works leave no ill-feeling behind.

Then, of course, there is the music which is for gramophone alone: old opera recordings, classic jazz, performances by great conductors of the past. Nowadays, this list is being extended by experimental works that would be almost impossible to perform in a concert hall—works like Stockhausen's *Gesang der Jünglinge* or Badings's *Capriccio* for violin and two sound tracks. I know of people for whom only this last group would hold any interest. They are sound enthusiasts, and they feel that sound is an important part of the quality of the performance. To some extent, this is obviously true; but it can lead to para-doxical results. It means, for example, that they would prefer to hear Tchaikovsky's *Manfred* Symphony played in 'glittering stereo' by Carmen Dragon and the Hollywood Bowl Symphony Orchestra rather than in the astounding Toscanini performance, whose sound is acceptable but certainly not 'glittering'.

As for myself, it still seems to me that the greatest perfor-mance of Otello's 'Niun mi tema' is the one recorded by Tamagno in 1906, accompanied by a piano. This may seem an extreme kind of judgement, considering the quality of the singing—not to mention the sound—in the 'complete performances' by Ramon Vinay and Mario del Monaco. I can only suggest that the reader tests the matter for himself.

For me, this kind of discovery is one of the greatest pleasures of a record collection. Music is a kind of travel, perambulating in time as well as space. I find something extraordinarily satis-fying in listening to a recording of a Tchaikovsky aria made in St Petersburg in the 1890s, and sung by the Figners, whom Tchaikovsky chose to play the lead in his *Queen of Spades*. (It is not generally known that the first opera recordings were issued in St Petersburg in 1888—nearly two decades before the recording industry got under weigh in Europe and America.)

I find the same kind of satisfaction in comparing the ways in which Melba, Tetrazzini, Zinka Milanov, Callas, and Joan Sutherland negotiate the difficult bit in 'Casta Diva'. Here music takes on some of the excitement of history, and gives a glimpse of what Hermann Hesse meant by his 'bead game' (in the novel of that title) that somehow combines all the arts and sciences.

There is one more pleasure in a record collection that I should mention here for completeness, although it is the most obvious of all: simply discovering new music. Beecham spent much time in music libraries rediscovering some of the forgotten French and Belgian composers of the previous century: Grétry, Méhul, Dalayrac, Isouard. (His recordings of some of their shorter pieces are still available.) Musically untrained listeners cannot hope to discover new music in this way; but the gramophone offers an excellent alternative. The concert-goer gets used to the same old fare of symphonies by Beethoven, Schubert, Brahms, and Franck, and 'showpiece' overtures by Bizet, Mendelssohn, Berlioz, and Wagner; he must sometimes suspect that there is no 'popular' music outside the two dozen composers that he hears so regularly. One could surprise him by giving a gramophone concert of equally enjoyable and accessible music by composers who are never played in England. One might begin with the overture to Ganne's *Saltimbanques* (as a kind of equivalent to the *Carmen* overture that launches so many programmes), followed by the introduction to d'Albert's *Tief-land*. For the symphony, the choice is wide: there are excellent and little-known symphonies by Lalo, Chausson, Max Bruch, Fibich, Szymanovsky, Balakirev, and Goldmark. (The latter's *Rustic Wedding* Symphony was a favourite of Beecham's.) The concerto could be by Spohr, Glazounov, Rubinstein, Ridky, Goldmark, Glière, Medtner, or Busoni. (The latter's Piano Concerto is perhaps impracticable—it plays for an hour and requires a men's chorus—but his Violin Concerto is an acceptable alternative.) The once popular Scriabin has not been played in English concert halls for forty years or more; but modern audiences might be agreeably surprised by his Piano Concerto, and there is no reason why his 'controversial' symphonies—decadent and ecstatic affairs—should sound unusual to an audience that can accept Delius.

17

CHORDS AND DISCORDS

I am not contending that concert promoters should include these works—no doubt concert economics forbid it—but only that, in this respect, the gramophone is greatly preferable to the concert hall.

My first point is made: that musical eclecticism may be a discipline rather than a self-indulgence. Rilke said that the poet's problem is to keep himself as wide open as he can, even if, like a flower in the sunlight, he may find it impossible to close up again.

My 'eclecticism' may raise certain problems for the reader of this book. Where a writer has very positive likes and dislikes, you know where you are. If you read Haggin, you know that Schoenberg and 'modern music' generally are unacceptable. If you read Constant Lambert, you know where you stand on jazz, popular music, and 'Les Six'. If you read Hans Keller or Donald Mitchell, you expect to be in the midst of the Schoenberg-Stravinsky mystique, which may unbend to the extent of admitting that Britten possesses genius, but would obviously not dream of discussing Delius or Sibelius. I have many reservations to make about most composers, including Delius and Schoenberg, but this does not prevent me from listening to both of them with a certain pleasure. If I therefore take a sideswipe at the Schoenberg mystique, or refer to Webern as a minor composer (a judgement, incidentally, which is endorsed by Donald Mitchell), it must not be assumed that I side with Haggin on the subject of 'modern music', any more than I side with Hans Keller if I comment that Constant Lambert overrated Sibelius.

In fact, this book was written for pleasure, not because I have any important thesis about music that I want to communicate. Its aim is not to teach anybody anything—I probably know less about music than any critic in England—but simply to communicate some of the results of twenty years of enthusiastic listening to music. There are times when I have wished that I was a musician, and there are some ways in which, even now, I would rather be a musician than a writer. Since I shall never give the world anything of musical value, I may as well accept second best, and try to repay music by communicating to others some of the pleasure it has given me.

18

I have left till last a subject that is really the main point of this preface. For years now, in every book of ideas I have written, I have laboured the importance of 'existential criticism'; I want to do so here again.

The alternative to existential criticism is academic criticism —criticism that concerns itself solely with the value of the *work*, as if it could be determined as precisely as the weight of a pound of butter. For me, no work of art can be clearly separated from the personality of the artist and his life. Academic criticism, for example, would compare the symphonies of Haydn with those of Beethoven, observing the changes in form and musical procedure brought about by Beethoven. But it would ignore the most fundamental fact: that Beethoven's whole personality and attitude to life were completely unlike those of Haydn. In the same way, ordinary literary criticism might examine the work of F. Scott Fitzgerald, and make all kinds of observations about his talent, his artistic honesty, his social background and influence on his age, etc., and yet completely ignore the most fundamental thing about him: his basic lack of confidence in face of life, his defeatism. Nothing useful could be said about Beethoven without taking into account his aggressive attitude to life, his determination to be a conqueror, an emperor of the realm of the spirit; and nothing useful can be said about Fitzgerald without recognizing that his attitude to existence was the reverse of Beethoven's.

Consequently, when I write about Schoenberg, I am far less concerned with the implications of the twelve-tone system than with Schoenberg's mind and personality. An artist's theories are relatively unimportant compared with his basic attitude to life. Delius' theories about life were mixed up with a half-digested Nietzscheanism and paganism; but his music reveals the inner Delius—weak, over-sensitive, unsure of himself, afraid of life. Other musicians have immense skill in keeping their true personalities out of their work, in throwing up a smoke-screen of theory; Hindemith and Stravinsky are examples. In that case, the critic's task is not to take the artist at his own valuation, but to try to get down to the fundamentals of his personality.

The essence of existential criticism was expressed in an article on Puccini by Francis Toye: 'Puccini was not a great composer because he was not a great man.' Ultimately, the critic's task is to determine how far an artist *is* a great man. Within the past few days I have seen Britten, Stravinsky, and Schoenberg all referred to as 'great composers' in newspaper articles by reputable critics. Evidently these critics were not of Francis Toye's opinion. Or perhaps they would object that greatness does not have to be of the obvious spiritual kind discernible in Beethoven: that it can be an altogether subtler kind of strength. To me, this is beside the point. An artist's work is not like a scientist's, entirely independent of his personality. A complete fool or weakling might stumble on an important scientific or mathematical discovery, and his importance to science will be judged solely by the discovery. But the essence of a work of art is that it is the expression of the artist's personal truth, and the only important question about the work is of the value and intensity of the artist's truth. Only a critic who judged music superficially would dream of calling either Britten, Schoenberg, or Stravinsky 'great'.

All the essays in this volume are an attempt to write existential criticism.

1

THE ROMANTIC
HALF-CENTURY

*The flute is not an instrument that has a good moral effect—
it is too exciting.*—Aristotle, Politics, viii. 6. 5.

T HERE is a time-honoured and convenient tradition among writers on music of positing some unlikely situation—such as shipwreck on a desert island with a gramophone and record library—of which I now propose to avail myself. It is brought to my mind by an article by Neville Cardus, in which he says that if he were marooned on a desert island and allowed only one composer he would choose Brahms. I personally would find such a choice impossible. I would be inclined to plump for Mozart or Beethoven; but the preliminary indecisions would be so painful and protracted that I would probably end by taking nothing at all. It would be pleasanter to make a clean break. And yet if I were allowed to choose some *period* in music (of, say, fifty years), then there would be no hesitation at all; I would choose the second half of the nineteenth century; or better still, the period 1860–1910. I will not say that this period covers my favourite music; I prefer Mozart's operas to anything written in the nineteenth century. But it contains more music that arouses my sympathetic interest than any other fifty years of musical history.

I say 'sympathetic interest' deliberately, for this is exactly the feeling. There is an extraordinary intensity about so many of those late romantic composers, a pure distillation of some unique spirit. To gather what I mean, in the crudest sense, one has only to listen to any good recording of Liszt opera tran-

scriptions for piano;* or better still, to the Second Hungarian
Rhapsody as played by Horowitz at his twenty-fifth anniversary
concert in Carnegie Hall. One sniffs at the mention of this
Rhapsody; even a musical ignoramus could hum most of it
from memory. And yet as Horowitz strikes those thunderous
opening chords one is suddenly seated in some bare concert hall
of the 1860s, with the master himself at the piano—that powerful and ugly face that is so striking that most writers describe
it as handsome, the immense flowing mane, the large bony
hands, the total composure. What a man that was! What a way
to live! This man was the nineteenth-century counterpart of
the pop idol of today, and his audiences sometimes became as
hysterical as any teen-ager doting on Elvis Presley. But will
our children of the twenty-first century know what the 1950s
saw in Frank Sinatra, Johnny Ray? Will they, supposing the
opportunity is offered them, be able to distinguish between
records of the 'idols' and of the hundred or so who never quite
make the top twenty? Yet when we listen to Liszt well played,
it is all still there, like some perfume preserved in an airtight
bottle. There is no loss of impact whatever. We hear that Liszt
made a transcription of the 'Liebestod' from *Tristan and Isolde*
and we smile; it might have done for provincial audiences of
the 1880s, who never had a chance to hear a real orchestra; but
most of us can turn on the complete *Tristan* in the sitting-room,
probably in stereo. Then we play Brendel's recording of the
transcribed 'Liebestod', and the smile vanishes. It is incredible
that the piano can do so much; not only does it lose nothing, it
seems to gain something; Wagner is magnificent, but he does
sound a little thick sometimes; even Flagstad gasps like an
exhausted swimmer as the waves close over her voice. In the
piano version, all is clarity and brilliance; and yet the piano can
sound like an orchestra as those waves of sound burst at the end.
(Brendel is sensible enough to see that it needs to be taken
slightly more slowly than in the orchestral version, giving the
breaking waves a sense of inevitability, stateliness.) It is unbelievable, yet it works. The same is true of the *Norma* transcription. I imagine that Liszt would begin his concerts with
things like the Second Rhapsody, to stagger his audience with
what can be done with the piano; he is like a great actor who

*There is a superb set on Vox PL 10580, played by Alfred Brendel.

can play anything from Othello to Sir Andrew Aguecheek, l'Aiglon to Cyrano. There would follow the tougher fare— Mozart or Beethoven, perhaps Schumann—and then into the barnstorming stuff. These opera transcriptions are the true ancestors of the 'pop classics' of the forties—the 'Warsaw' Concerto, the *Cornish Rhapsody*, the *Glass Mountain*: they are melodious and dramatic, and require a minimum of musical concentration. There is a tradition that Liszt used to choose the climactic moment to swoon over the keyboard. If there is any truth in this—and one hopes there is—then I doubt whether he *chose* the moment; the swoons were probably genuine. Liszt was sensitive to the emotions of his audience; he saw himself as they saw him. And what did they see? A giant who had challenged his rival Thalberg to battle on the concert platform and carried the victory effortlessly; who had run away with one of the most beautiful women in Europe, a married countess with three children (and gave her two more, one of whom became Wagner's wife); who was universally known for his amours, and yet who was *persona grata* with the Church; whose tours of Europe were (to quote Ralph Hill) an orgy of hero-worship; who was a national hero in his own country; who was universally known for his generosity towards other musicians. . . . What seems most amazing in retrospect is how Liszt managed to carry such a load of adoration, of non-stop frenzy, and still remain a decent, generous, and in some respects even a modest man. For all his theatricality, there was a touch of the saint in Liszt's composition. And this was the man who now sat before his dazzled audience and played them music in a way that seemed to give it an immense, religious kind of significance. And as Norma's 'Qual cor tradisti' or Isolde's 'Mild und leise' rose to its climax, some of those impressionable young ladies, who had left their half-finished George Sand novels at home, no doubt felt that such a moment would never recur in their lifetimes. The emotional pressure in the room must have been strong enough to stifle a lizard.

I do not here propose to talk at length about Liszt. Clearly, he is not a great composer, and I have musical friends in whom the *Dante* Symphony and the *Années de Pèlerinage* produce acute nausea. The two symphonies (particularly the *Dante* Symphony) contain some magnificent moments, and admirers of

Liszt will always prefer *Les Préludes* and *Orpheus* to *Till Eulenspiegel* and *Don Juan*. Still, it is surprising that a man of Liszt's artistic personality produced no really memorable orchestral music—certainly very little that survives in the concert hall today. It is men like the taciturn and thin-skinned Wagner, or the modest bourgeois Richard Strauss, who produced the music that is the true counterpart of Liszt's extraordinary life. Liszt's greatness was diffused between his life and his music; Wagner's was concentrated in his music. And yet there is something admirable in the Liszt ideal. It would be a sad business if this life-art opposition were a law of nature. One likes to think that in a really great man, the life would somehow become the material of the art, although this would no doubt be easier for a novelist than for a musician. I personally find that it adds a dimension to the musical personality of Mr Humphrey Searle to know that he is an admirer of Liszt. I believe Searle's Second Symphony to be one of the finest English symphonies of this century, while the Webernian squeaks and silences of his Fourth leave me cold and baffled. Yet a man who is an admirer of Liszt can never go far wrong; he is sure to emerge from his musical Thebaid sooner or later.

Liszt, I say, provides an example of the whole-heartedness that I find so attractive about the second half of the nineteenth century. This was a strange century. As Thomas Mann points out, a century of giganticism: of the *Comédie humaine*, the Rougon Macquart cycle, of Hegel's System, and Wagner's *Ring*: we might even add: of the Chicago exhibition and the Crystal Palace. And in the two musical giants of the 1870s and '80s, Wagner and Brahms, I see symbols of the two great emotions of the nineteenth century—adventurousness and love of security. There is something uncompromising about Wagner's music; it seems to shout 'All or nothing'—ecstasy or death. Thomas Mann's essay 'The Sufferings and Greatness of Richard Wagner' is, to my mind, the finest thing written about him, and it catches admirably that suicidal quality. Wagner felt that art was his destiny, and yet he believed that the artist is a Prometheus; for carrying a touch of the god-fire among human beings ('human, all *too* human', groaned Nietzsche) he pays with an eternity of torment. At one point he even proposed to go to a famous watering-place to cure himself of his artistic faculty, believing that it was a form of sickness.

Brahms, on the other hand, is caught admirably in that contemporary caricature that shows him on his way to drink with cronies at the Red Hedgehog. It shows a short, fat little man with stumpy legs, his plump belly stuck out, hands behind his back, a cigar in his mouth, and heavy, clumsy shoes on his feet, accompanied by a fat hedgehog that looks more like a pregnant rat, and that might be his *alter ego*.* This is the man who adored women, yet who was too cautious to marry, who (unlike Wagner) was able to live well on his income from composing, who covered up a gentle and melancholy disposition with a brusque manner.

It is easy to get sick of the music of Wagner. Few people manage to retain their early enthusiasm for it. The trouble, to some extent, is that Wagner wrote little but opera. With Beethoven, one can graduate from the orchestral music to the chamber music and piano sonatas; there is always something new. But once you know one Wagner opera thoroughly, there can be no fresh surprises from the others. There is great magnificence, but it is all of a kind, like the same mountain scenery going on for hundreds of miles. Still, it is worth the exercise of 'bracketing out' one's awareness of Wagner as the artistic idol of a generation, and making the attempt to approach his music as he must have approached it when its inspiration first came to him. To view him in retrospect is the worst way; it is far more rewarding to look at him from the point of view of Rossini and Weber; then one can truly appreciate his immense greatness. What is so admirable is that he was a lone fighter, a true 'outsider', who refused to be defeated. In some respects, his character was appalling. He had little sense of honour where either women or money were concerned; his autobiography is almost unreadable because of its humourless conceit: it is less autobiography than autohagiography. Speaking of an uncle on page one, he writes pompously: 'We shall meet him again at a critical turning-point in the story of my youth.' One almost expects him to write 'The Story of My Youth' in capitals. This is the tone of the master lecturing to disciples, assuming that every word is being received with rapt

*Reproduced in Hanslick's *Selected Criticisms*, Gollancz, 1950, p. 242.

attention; in fact, he writes as if he is his own most enthusiastic disciple. Yet when one considers what he had to say, and what he was up against, it becomes comprehensible. For some reason, all the great innovating artists arouse a fury of petty spite. It is surprising that so many of them succeed in winning through, and not at all surprising that most of them feel permanent resentment against the world.

Why is this? It would be pleasant to think that it is because their contemporaries see only their worst qualities; but I am afraid the explanation is less flattering to human nature. Men hate greatness unless it is at a safe distance—preferably dead, or so moribund that it can be taken for granted as a landmark. It is true that men must 'love the best when they recognize it'; the problem is that human beings *want* to refuse to recognize it for as long as they can, like a man who stays in bed until the last possible moment on a winter morning. They stick to the idea that it is charlatanism for as long as possible; after which they enthusiastically acknowledge it, vying with others to sing its praises. And as soon as the admiration has had time to wear a little thin, they usually take a retrospective look and decide that perhaps they *did* go a little too far after all. So a man like Sibelius spends the first twenty years of his creative life struggling against the current; then for twenty years he receives ample acknowledgement; then there is a swing back into disparagement for the last twenty-five years. It is a discouraging business. The devices of human self-delusion would require an encyclopaedia to record them all.

It seems to be a particular kind of talent that excites this reaction, and this needs a little more explaining. I have said elsewhere that it would almost seem as if the year 1800 is a dividing line in human history. Up till that time man thought of himself as a 'creature'; he believed it would be presumption to 'scan' God, because 'the proper study of mankind is man'. It was science that brought about the revolution that we call romanticism, for science made men aware that God was an unnecessary hypothesis. When Byron's Manfred stood on a hilltop and shook his fist at God he was performing one of the most important symbolic acts in human history. The romantic had found out that man is not the limited creature he had always taken himself to be; unbelievable ecstasies and insights were

26

possible to him; he was more like a god than ever he realized, a 'god in exile' in Heine's phrase. In that case, what was to prevent him from becoming more godlike in every way? If he was no clod to grub in the earth, why could he not assume his new rank in the universe immediately? Why was he so limited? Why this absurd paradox, that he could have such tremendous glimpses of immortality and ecstasy, and then find himself again a slave of the trivial? The romantic 'outsider' seemed born for catastrophe because of his dual nature, half god, half worm. To the great question: Master or slave? half his experience answered conclusively, 'Master'; the other half, 'Slave'.

I believe, and I have expressed my reasons at length elsewhere, that the romantic 'outsider' was an evolutionary experiment. This is not to say that I believe the 'life force' took special pains to create him; his historical position did that—the death of God and of 'universal purpose', and the rise of science. To begin with, the experiment was totally unsuccessful; the 'outsiders' discovered they were human, all too human; they were not yet ready to face an empty universe in which self-pity would be an absurd self-indulgence. And yet, whether they liked it or not, the great change had taken place. Man had always taken it for granted that there was as much difference between himself and the lower animals as between the lower animals and dead matter. This conceit was somewhat premature, and the nineteenth century brought this home. History said, in effect: 'If you are so godlike, then go ahead and *be* a god', and man was confronted by his own inadequacy, his boredom and lack of purpose. Yet the change *had* taken place; there could be no turning back; things could never be the same again. The ultimatum had been presented; sooner or later, the consequences would have to be faced; in the words of Sir Julian Huxley, man had to become the managing director of evolution whether he wanted the position or not.

Yet, as Dostoevsky pointed out in *The Grand Inquisitor*, men do not want freedom; it is too heavy a burden. Dostoevsky was partly wrong; statistics appear to show that about five per cent of the human race seems to possess that additional enterprise and purpose that constitute the evolutionary drive. This five per cent *does* want freedom.

Still, the arguments of the Grand Inquisitor apply. In fact,

CHORDS AND DISCORDS

Christ was not crucified by a Grand Inquisitor but by ordinary men—the other ninety-five per cent—the decent men who 'must needs love greatness when they see it', but who, like Nelson, are adept at clapping the telescope to the blind eye. They find the 'all or nothing' quality antipathetic.

In our own century the romantic problem is still unsolved, although existentialism has made an even more determined attempt to solve it (and I myself have made certain suggestions in that direction). But some of that flavour of magnificent abandonment has gone. The works of Sartre, Camus, and Heidegger are exciting in many ways, but there is an element of dryness, of caution, that was not present in Schiller, Novalis, Hoffmann—and Wagner.

All these men possessed the new dimension of freedom—the evolutionary dimension. Or rather, I should say, they were aware that it *could* be possessed, and that man is at the beginning of a new stage in his destiny.

Having said this, we can now see Wagner in true perspective, and understand the progress of his work. And a most fascinating study it makes: the rise and fall of the spirit of freedom in Wagner. Listening to his early operas *Die Feen* and *Das Liebesverbot* (both of which were broadcast by the B.B.C. in 1963), one can hear nothing of the revolutionary Wagner; they are reminiscent of Weber, Marschner, even at moments of Rossini. And there is something dull and earthy about Weber and Marschner, for all their supernatural devices; they are of the world and its preoccupations and emotions; there is no 'evolutionary' dimension. *Rienzi* is a better opera than is generally recognized, and long passages might have been written by the later Wagner. Still, that overture with its brass-band music, rather reminiscent of an old song called 'The Galloping Major', is dangerously accomplished; it has a note of individuality, but not enough to frighten the philistines; at this point Wagner might easily have gone on to become another Meyerbeer. It has a note of complacency, like Elgar at his worst. Luckily, German legend was waiting to save Wagner from becoming a carbon copy of Meyerbeer. *The Flying Dutchman* has never been a favourite of mine; it is still too close to Weber and Marschner; it is at once too supernatural and too human. But in *Tannhäuser* Wagner had made contact with his true subject. The plot is largely derived from a story by Ludwig Tieck,* who in Wagner's day was a story-teller of immense popularity; his reputation was comparable to that of Hoffmann or Jean Paul. For the first time, Wagner had come to grips with the 'spirit of the age', with the real wine of romanticism. (The story, *Trusty Eckhart*, can be found translated in Carlyle's miscellanies.) The result is that the music has a different sound. It is still recognizably the musician of *Rienzi* and *The Flying Dutchman*, and yet there is a new sense of purpose, a new kind of ecstasy and power. *Lohengrin* is a temporary relapse, except for its prelude, into the style and subject-matter of Marschner and Weber. But now comes the germ of the idea for *The Ring of the Nibelung*, and from then on there is no looking back.

At its best, *The Ring* is the music of human aspiration, the music of evolution. I personally must admit that I became too familiar with *The Ring* in my early twenties, due mainly to B.B.C. broadcasts from Bayreuth, so that I now listen to it a great deal less than, let us say, to *The Magic Flute*—which is to say, I suppose, that it now gives me less pleasure. But I do not propose to pander to the heresy that declares that *The Magic Flute* is greater music than Wagner because 'more human'; this is only another evasion. I do not believe it is greater. It costs me more effort to enjoy Wagner because I have to go through a process of 'bracketing out' my preconceptions about the music and the man; but if I happen to be playing Wagner to some young person who is just discovering him, and is intoxicated by the music, I can again enjoy it as if hearing it for the first time. Whatever my present taste, I believe that *The Ring* contains some of the greatest music ever written. I may not be able to enjoy it as freely as before, as George Saintsbury was unable to drink wine in his sixties because of gout; but like Saintsbury, I shall not cease to sing the praises of the wine. The best parts of *The Ring* are music of courage and of power, an act of faith and of praise of life. It is a pity that the finest parts are also the parts that are played in 'bleeding chunks' at every symphony concert, so that the music loses its impact—the 'Ride of the Valkyries', the 'Magic Fire' music, the 'Rhine Journey' (which even now never fails to make my hair tingle), the 'Funeral Music', 'Forest

---

*I feel that Ernest Newman allows insufficient importance to Tieck in his account of *Tannhäuser* in *Wagner Nights*.

Murmurs'. Yet there are other extracts, only slightly less familiar, that can renew the impact: The opening scene of *The Rhinegold* and its last fifteen minutes from the storm music, the 'moonlight' music from the first scene of *The Valkyrie*, the tremendous 'Heil dir, Sonne' from the third act of *Siegfried* (which used to be available on a splendid recording with Flagstad and Set Svanholm). This is the true Wagner, the 'all or nothing' Wagner, shaking his fist at the heavens; it makes the flesh tingle like Byron's lines:

> The mountains look on Marathon—
> And Marathon looks on the sea;
> And musing there an hour alone,
> I dream'd that Greece might still be free.

This is not the strained heroics of *Robert the Devil* or *The Vampire*; there is something purposive about it, a more grim form of heroism that knows what it wants and intends to get it. This is the strength of the best of Wagner's music. It has not yet developed into the almost suicidal 'all or nothing' of Scriabin's *Poem of Fire*, although it comes close to it in *Tristan and Isolde*. (And yet we might say that *Tristan* is counterweighted with the *The Mastersingers*, with humour and earthiness— German beer music, as Nietzsche called it.) It is the true music of courage and evolution.

Already in *Tristan* Wagner is finding the long struggle too much for him—otherwise, perhaps, he might have had the sense to see that internal logic of *The Ring* demanded that it should end with Siegfried's triumph, not his death—and prepares to capitulate. I cannot agree with critics like Newman that the Christianity of *Parsifal* is already present in *Lohengrin*; at least, Newman is missing Nietzsche's real point. Wagner's achievement was immense; but he would have had to be ten times as great as he was to see his way out of the defeatism of the nineteenth century; besides, in spite of his strength, he was a man of his age, sensitive to its values. It took the intellect—and the insularity—of Shaw to reject conclusively the 'non-purposive' hypothesis underlying nineteenth-century thought. Wagner was inclined to accept it intellectually; so the death of Tristan and Isolde is a gesture of protest against it, as if he had commented: 'If life is really as pointless and as purposeless as you say, then I prefer death.' *Parsifal* revealed a chastened and exhausted Wagner—I was tempted to write 'a brain-washed Wagner'. For the whole point of the nineteenth-century revolution was that it rejected the old form of 'redemptionist' religion, and declared in effect: 'Unless I can save myself, then I am unsaveable.' Romanticism was not irreligious, for religion is very close indeed to the spirit of romanticism, and there is not all that much difference between the spirit of Schiller and that of Cardinal Newman; Newman's Catholicism was only another form of the romantic protest against science. But it was emphatically unchristian in the old Wesleyan sense of an authoritative, lawgiving Christianity; its Christianity tended to be a matter of sentiment, like Pater's. To my mind, and my ear, *Parsifal* reveals a Wagner who has betrayed his evolutionary intuition. This is not to say that I am indifferent to it, as I am relatively indifferent to *The Dutchman*; its over-ripe mysticism, its smell of rising incense, sometimes appeal to me as Scriabin's *Poem of Ecstasy* or Delius' Violin Concerto appeals. But it somehow brings to mind Arthur Koestler's Rubashov, in *Darkness at Noon*, who is finally persuaded, by many subtle pressures, to renounce his own vision and accuse himself of being a traitor. I doubt whether Wagner would have written *Parsifal* if he had not spent a lifetime fighting fools, armouring himself against stupidity and malice. A man who has finally achieved a degree of success and worn himself out in the process feels a desire to be at peace with the world, to show a new, resigned aspect of himself to his enemies. (If D. H. Lawrence had ended up as a grand old man sitting in his own Bayreuth in New Mexico, I suspect that he would have produced some novel of reconciliation, perhaps even a Christian novel.)

This, then, seems to me the essence of Wagner; he was the greatest revolutionary spirit since Beethoven. Berlioz might have come close to it, but he was too wrapped up in Gallic frenzy and self-pity. The forces against Wagner were too great for continuous development on the scale of Beethoven. In a profound sense, Beethoven was a fierce evolutionist, a pure romantic. He believed in the power of the human spirit; what is more important, he also believed in strength. He came closer than any romantic except Goethe to resolving the tragic duality of vision and boredom, purpose and entanglement in triviality. This was because he was less inclined to self-pity than any other romantic. Wagner was also strong, but the self-pity was there; it is present as an underlying emotion even in the eternal begging letters, as if he were saying, like a spoilt child: 'But I *shouldn't* be poor. How dare they . . .' The strength reaches a climax in *The Ring*. If we compare the *Rienzi* overture with Siegfried's 'Rhine Journey', we see how far he has come; this music seems to have some of the strength and purposefulness of life itself; it beats forward, retreats, then beats forward again. This strength is fundamentally what aroused the malice, for it is an implicit accusation of weakness and laziness.

When we turn to the music of Brahms, we have descended from these windy heights. According to the anti-Brahmins—and their host, unfortunately, seems to be increasing—we are in a stuffy drawing-room that smells of polish and geraniums. Indeed, it is strange that so many anti-Brahmins also find Wagner intolerable—B. H. Haggin, for example. Benjamin Britten claims that he plays through 'the whole of Brahms' at intervals to see whether Brahms is really as bad as he thought, and ends by discovering that he is actually much worse. The element of exaggeration here (it would take weeks to play *all* Brahms's music) indicates that a strong temperamental antipathy is at work. It may be no more than that Brahms is too heavy and Germanic: Britten is also on record as finding meaningless Beethoven's sonata op. 111, which Thomas Mann describes as 'the end of the piano sonata'. But I suspect a deeper reason. There is an un-grown-up element about Brahms; Cardus is right to speak of him as 'the intimate poet of mild-eyed romance'; one suspects that one of the reasons he did not get married was that he disliked the thought of bringing down his ideas of sex to reality; that he spent his life dreaming of the what might have been with Clara Schumann, and perhaps with the young girls who drifted in and out of his life like thistledown. With the change of one word, we might apply to Brahms what Ann Whitefield says to Tavy in *Man and Superman*: 'A broken heart is a very pleasant complaint for a man in Vienna if he has a comfortable income.' There is also something un-grown-up about Britten, but in a completely different way; at its best, his music is a glorification of innocence; but there are times when it can sound nauseatingly *faux-naïf.* So Britten is in no position to be tolerant and understanding of Brahms's type of arrested development.

And yet, as I have said, it seems to me that Brahms is fundamentally as 'authentic' as Wagner. There is certainly no evolutionary upsurging here. Brahms represents the other aspect of Victorianism—the sense that the universe, after all, is a pleasant place, that life means well by human beings, that the best a man can ask is to sit in front of his own fire in his slippers and sip a glass of good port. Essentially, Brahms is an intimate composer. I ceased to derive any great enjoyment from his symphonies and concertos years ago, although I can enjoy hearing them well played. (I must admit I retain an affection for the second and third.) But I find that I can continually derive new pleasure from the G major violin sonata (which Cardus beautifully describes as 'a twilight piece, silver greyness in everything'), from the Clarinet Quintet, from the 'Handel' Variations, the Four Serious Songs and the late piano works. I also find this gentle quality in the Alto Rhapsody and the Requiem.

On the other hand, Schumann did Brahms a considerable disservice by declaring that upon him had fallen the mantle of Beethoven, and the detestable Hanslick completed the bad work. When one listens to the opening of the First Piano Concerto it seems that we are in a Wagnerian world of thunder and lightning; but within minutes we are in the true Brahms world of twilight and melancholy with the second theme. And yet the first movement is far too long; its material could have been compressed into five minutes instead of a quarter of an hour. All that Brahms has gained by that tremendous opening—apparently originally intended for a symphony—and the exquisite second theme is lost in a waste of development. It is not even the sort of long-windedness that we can quite enjoy when it appears in Schubert or Bruckner or Mahler, that has a soothing and lulling effect under which one sinks into a world of hypnotic contemplation. It is too busy; it seems to be about to say something important, so that it continually arouses one's attention, and then there are more developments. Here, I suspect, Brahms feels that he should show his Beethoven quality, instead of wisely recollecting his affinity with Schumann. The same seems to me to apply to the Second Piano Concerto; it is precisely twice too long for what it has to say. That opening theme seems to have been designed for some slighter work, perhaps a violin sonata; there it would have been perfect, conveying the authentic Brahmsian melancholy.

Even Hanslick, surely one of the most loathsome figures of the late nineteenth century, admitted that Brahms often bored him; but he was never honest enough to say so in public.

To say that Brahms is an intimate composer who allowed himself to be bullied into pretending he was a second Beethoven would be no doubt to distort the truth; for Brahms is as authentically an orchestral composer as Mahler or Bruckner. But I think it would be closer to the truth to say that Brahms forced himself to adopt musical procedures that were not natural to him in order to assume his position as the great anti-Wagnerite. There are times when his handling of variations is masterly, as in the Fourth Symphony or the 'Handel' Variations, but this is not his natural mode of expression. In spirit, Brahms is not very far from Delius (although there is a world of difference in their modes of expression), and his natural medium would have been a free rhapsodic flow. (I must admit that I have always found the 'Haydn' Variations an irritating example of 'empty' music, with the exception of the Elgarian variation towards the end.)

But the very essence of Brahms, I feel, lies in his real, fundamental anti-Wagnerianism: not his 'classicism' which, I am inclined to believe, was of the same nature as Stravinsky's—a deliberate attempt to give himself a dimension he felt he did not possess—but his lack of the real 'all or nothing' spirit. But to express it in this way makes it sound negative, when it is actually very positive indeed. The universe is an enormous and cold place, and Darwin made it seem even more so to the late Victorians, who were all too aware of 'nature red in tooth and claw', of the 'death of God', of the monstrous indifference of the universe (that Hardy took to be active malice). And yet there was a powerful resistance to this feeling of emptiness, a current of real optimism, belief in human progress, in the fundamental rightness of things: 'God's in his heaven; All's right with the world.' This sentiment explains why Browning was regarded with such reverence by the late Victorians, when he seems to mean so little to our own generation. (Mr Eliot has led a Tennyson revival—even a Kipling revival; but no one has ever suggested a Browning revival.) We catch this feeling in Elgar, who might well be regarded as a kind of English Brahms without the top-heavy framework of classicism. The Victorian could believe in the rightness of things with an intensity and single-mindedness that was impossible after 1914. Darwinism and doubt are one face of Victorianism; its other face was symbolized by men like Brahms, Elgar, Edward Lear, Emerson, Anthony Trollope, Gilbert, and Sullivan. These men all convey a feeling that the world is ultimately a decent and solid place. No one criticizes Trollope for not being a Zola, any more than they criticize Dickens for graduating from the world of *Pickwick Papers* to that of *Our Mutual Friend*. There is as little point in criticizing Brahms for not being more like Wagner. At the bottom of his being he may have been troubled by doubts and melancholy, like Tennyson; yet his photograph belongs among that gallery of full-bearded late Victorian optimists and men of the world; we must listen to his music as we read Trollope—or Jane Austen, for that matter—accepting that his world had clear outlines and was fundamentally solid and sound. For Wagner, as for Nietzsche, man was in the process of becoming; his eye could not rest with any pleasure on the products of Victorianism, for they were another name for philistinism; his mind had to rove back into the past before it could find an object of contemplation that satisfied it. For Brahms, the present was more real than the past could ever be—satisfyingly real; and the future, when it came, would be like the present, but generally improved, one might hope. . . .

So these two great men seem to me to represent, musically, the two faces of Victorianism: its aspects of consolidation and of evolution. There are other men of this epoch whose music I enjoy as much as that of Brahms or Wagner: Bruckner, Mahler, Wolf, Fauré. But as soon as we think of these men in comparison with Brahms or Wagner we have to recognize how much more satisfyingly those two giants managed to symbolize the spirit of the age, and what an achievement is represented by their symbolic status.

Before leaving this subject of Brahms and Wagner, I should say something of the man whose name is linked permanently with theirs, in infamy. Eduard Hanslick was the sort of man who makes one hope that hell exists, and that the devil sends him a daily report of the current opinions on the men he attacked, and of posterity's verdict on himself. It is true that Hanslick has his modern defenders: Stewart Deas produced *In Defence of Hanslick* in 1940, and Henry Pleasants has edited an anthology of his writing with a preface that makes Hanslick sound almost likeable. But even if it were proved that Hanslick was a secret philanthropist and the founder of a home for tired composers, it would be impossible for posterity to forgive him for his part in driving Hugo Wolf insane. The Edinburgh reviewer who attacked Keats has gone down to literary history in infamy; but he only wrote one anonymous review. Hanslick spent a lifetime stabbing genius in the back.

I bring up the subject of Hanslick here because it is closely linked with what I have written on Wagner and Brahms, and not for the pleasure of throwing another stone at the grave of that stealthy literary executioner.

Hanslick's life should have been the subject of one of those bitterly satirical novels of Heinrich Mann. He was born in 1825, and intended to become a composer. Unlike so many of the great composers of the nineteenth century, he lacked the courage to burn his boats and plunge head first into music; instead, after four years of musical study, he went into law. At the age of nineteen he became unpaid music critic of a small periodical in Prague. Two years later he moved to Vienna, and laid the foundations of his reputation by writing a long and laudatory account of Wagner's *Tannhäuser*. Music criticism never paid much, but money was not what Hanslick was after. He wanted power. And for the next forty years Hanslick was musical dictator in Vienna. In his life of Hugo Wolf, Frank Walker notes: 'For more than a quarter of a century, Hanslick's word was law in Vienna. Those who stood up against him, or incurred his animosity in any way, were marked men for the rest of their lives. . . . Felix Mottl paid the penalty for his early misdeeds in 1897 [i.e., when Hanslick was seventy-two] when his chances of becoming director of the Vienna Opera were destroyed by the unrelenting opposition of Hanslick, who had still to be consulted on all important musical matters, although he was himself in partial retirement.' The image one gets is of Hanslick crouching over Viennese musical life like a large poisonous spider, bitter and permanently unforgiving.

Now, Hanslick had much in common with Brahms and Schumann, in the sense which I have described above. He was a happy family man who valued quiet and security, and his lifelong championship of their music indicates a gently romantic disposition, a very mild tendency to melancholy. *Tannhäuser* is the most conventional of Wagner's operas (except *Rienzi* and the early attempts). Besides, Hanslick was using it as a lever to insert himself into the musical life of Vienna. But Hanslick disliked *Lohengrin*, an opera which already had the 'all or nothing' quality; it is abundantly present in the prelude. Hanslick and Wagner met, and no doubt it was the clash of two conceits. As a result, Wagner caricatured Hanslick in *The Mastersingers*—Beckmesser was originally called Veit Hanslich. From that time on Hanslick was a rabid anti-Wagnerian. He never forgave. He later declared that he had never denied Wagner's greatness, but that he disliked the atmosphere of hysteria that surrounded his works. This only confirms that his criticism was based on personal feeling, and was not an attempt to assess the music on its own merits. He lacked ordinary honesty as a critic. After a concert that included one of Brahms's late chamber works, he admitted in a private letter that the only thing he had enjoyed had been some light-hearted Viennese waltz at the beginning of the programme—'barrel organ music'—and that he thought Brahms was becoming dull and long-winded. But in his review he dismissed the 'barrel organ music' in a patronizing note, and praised the Brahms work at length. His real taste in music was for light-hearted Viennese confections.

For Brahms, anti-Wagnerianism was a matter of temperament; he stood for the other aspect of Victorianism, and successfully embodied it in his music, as did Elgar. For Hanslick, it was also a matter of temperament; but Hanslick was uncreative, a musician *manqué*. Even a critic can be creative if he is true to his temperament. To some extent, Hanslick was. But he allowed his anti-romanticism to turn into a personal matter, with the consequence that he was a completely inauthentic embodiment of the qualities that make Brahms and Schumann great musicians. Even Brahms, who was a creator, found it impossible to be true to his temperament, and allowed himself to be pushed into competing with the Wagnerians on their own ground, in massive orchestral works that reveal that he is, by nature, a lyrical miniaturist. So there is no cause to be surprised that Hanslick became known as the arch-enemy of Wagner, Berlioz, Liszt, Bruckner, and Richard

Strauss rather than as a constructive critic, a midwife of the kind of music he wanted.

Brahms's anti-Wagnerianism is valid (although it should be added that Brahms was not personally opposed to Wagner's music; it was his followers who gave him that reputation). He was a minor composer who made the most of his gifts. Wagner is a major composer who, in many ways, dissipated his talent. In the ultimate sense, the 'evolutionary' composer will always be superior to the talented formalist. This is a truth that is too easily obscured. It is obvious enough if the evolutionist is a Beethoven and the formalist a Spohr or Hummel; but then, Beethoven is an exception in that he was in control of the self-destructiveness that is always involved with romanticism, and consequently realized most of his potential. But if we substitute for Beethoven and Spohr, say, Berlioz and Mendelssohn, or Wagner and Brahms, the issue is no longer so clear, for in both cases the minor composer developed his fullest potential while the major one turned half his strength against himself. It is a question of the difficult choice between a superbly built villa and a half-built palace. But where Brahms was concerned, a certain lack of appreciation for palaces was the precondition for his own less ambitious building projects. Where Hanslick was concerned, this excuse is not possible. It is a clear case of a man ranging himself against the forces of change and evolution out of pure *mauvaise foi*, personal pettiness, the refusal to face the self-condemnation that would be implied by a recognition of Wagner's greatness. It is to be regretted that there have always been such critics, and always will be. (We can at least attempt to make them less comfortable in their *mauvaise foi* by pointing out the precise nature of their motives.) Brahms's reply to Wagner is to be found in his music; Hanslick's is contained in a lifetime of bitterness and malice. Ultimately, Brahms's method is the only true method of 'criticism'.

The two composers of whom I now propose to speak—Bruckner and Mahler—are usually bracketed together. I don't know why, for they have absolutely nothing in common except that they both wrote ten symphonies.* On the same grounds one might as well bracket together Beethoven and Vaughan Williams, or Prokofiev and Sibelius.

*Bruckner, of course, wrote a 'Symphony No. O'.

Bruckner was a short, unattractive man, whose photographs make him look like the noted German murderer Fritz Haarmann. His father was a poor village schoolmaster in Upper Austria, only one degree above a peasant, and to the end of his life Anton Bruckner retained a certain peasant quality. His father died when he was sixteen, and Bruckner studied music for a short time, and then became himself a village schoolmaster. His development was extremely slow; in 1856, at the age of thirty-two, he became organist in the cathedral in Linz; twelve years later, he was installed as organ teacher in the Vienna Conservatoire. His career was not brilliant; he generally failed to obtain the jobs for which he applied. Little by little, he managed to rise in the world, until he ended as a member of the Imperial Chapel and something of a favourite with the royal family, who liked his rustic manners and his broad accent. Shy and unsure of himself, he never married, and seems to have been completely unattractive to women. He composed his first symphony ('no. 0') when he was almost forty. His ninth symphony, on which he was working on the day of his death (thirty-two years later) shows no really great advance on the first in thought or technique, although its violent scherzo anticipates some of the music of the twentieth century. He was a profoundly religious man, a Catholic, and some of his best music is to be found in his three Masses. In middle life his frustrating way of life caused a nervous breakdown, when he suffered from an obsessive need to count things —railings, paving-stones, leaves on a tree. A cold-water cure restored his health.

Bruckner's music is something that one either likes or does not. His symphonies are huge, sprawling affairs that move with the speed of a glacier. It might be said, without stretching the comparison too much, that they are musical counterparts of the poetry of Wordsworth—particularly his long works like The Excursion. Hanslick called them Wagnerian, but the modern listener would be baffled to discover any more resemblance to Wagner than to Brahms. To the modern listener the chief characteristic of Wagner's music is that it is exalted, ecstatic, an intensely personal and subjective music. Bruckner's music is objective; at its best, it gives a feeling of nature; it is as impersonal as a shower of rain.

It has often struck me as curious that so many of the great

nature-lovers, from Wordsworth to John Cowper Powys, were unattractive men who found social life difficult, and who derived no great pleasure from the activity of the intellect. Coleridge was not a real nature poet; he found ideas too exciting. Wordsworth was an awkward, self-centred man who was generally ignored at Cambridge by his contemporaries. It is significant that most of his best nature poetry contains expressions of his contempt for social life, the insincerity of city dwellers, etc. It leads one to suspect that his love of nature was not spontaneous, something inborn, but, to some extent at least, a form of compensatory activity. This is certainly not to say that it is in some way inauthentic; most human creative activity contains in it elements of reaction against some aspects of human life or society. A marriage is not necessarily unhappy because the husband was caught on the rebound, and Wordsworth's marriage with nature was, in its way, highly successful—far more so than Coleridge's. Still, it does not detract from one's enjoyment of Wordsworth's poetry to understand something about its origins; in fact, true enjoyment of a work of art depends upon full understanding of its origins. If the work cannot survive such understanding, then it cannot be truly great art.

Where Bruckner is concerned, it helps to understand that his personal life was completely unsuccessful. People were always treating him unkindly or even contemptuously; he was a humble little man who did not take much offence. His genius was real, but it was not enough to make him desirable to any of the many girls with whom he fell in love—even though his demands were not high. The briefest study of his life makes us aware that he was a singularly unlucky little man, something of a Charlie Chaplin figure, the kind of man on whom builders drop pots of paint from ladders. He always fell in love with girls under twenty—particularly as he got older—and sedulously attended all the balls and dances in Vienna. The nearest he ever came to marriage was when a clever chambermaid in a Berlin hotel managed to lure him into getting engaged to her—no doubt after he had clumsily seduced her; she had to be bought off by one of his friends. He was nearly seventy at the time. From the little we know of Bruckner, it seems not improbable that such unromantic encounters were his sole experience of sex.

If Bruckner had been another sort of man—more like Liszt,

for example (at whose funeral he played the organ)—he would not have written the kind of music that he left behind, and musical history would be a great deal poorer. For in a sense all Bruckner's music is devotional music; in its broad, onward sweep, it brings to mind the Passions of Bach. The symphonies are as much an act of worship as the Masses, and it is significant that he wanted the *Te Deum* to be used as the finale of his (unfinished) Ninth Symphony. It is difficult to make any other comment about Bruckner's music; it seems to be generally agreed that his finest music is to be found in the Mass in F (no. 3), the Fourth, Eighth, and Ninth Symphonies. But the quality of his music remains so uniform throughout that only a student of the scores would be able to guess whether a particular passage came from the First or the Ninth Symphony.

Mahler has little in common with Bruckner except the number and the length of his symphonies. He is in every way a more interesting figure, although this is not to pass judgement on the relative merits of his music and Bruckner's.

Mahler was a short man; he was also a Jew at a time when anti-Semitism was regarded as culturally smart. Since he was altogether more brilliant and sensitive than Bruckner, this double disability weighed heavily on him, and cost him a great deal in pain and spiritual energy. He might well have felt also that he was born unlucky. He was a member of a family of twelve, son of a coachman who became owner of a distillery. The family lived in continual poverty; the windows were stuffed with dish clouts to keep out the wind. He inherited his brilliance from his father—perhaps also his despotic temper—and his sensitivity from his mother, who was a cripple. His parents were ill-matched, and his father ill-treated his wife a great deal. Both parents died, almost simultaneously, when Mahler was a young man. Of their twelve children, one died in an accident, five of diphtheria, one committed suicide and one died of a brain tumour. It can be understood why Mahler seemed to feel that he had been selected by fate for tragedy. At the age of eleven he was sent to Prague to study music, was brutally treated for a year, and finally came home to study at the local Gymnasium. Later, as a student in Vienna, he became a close friend of two young musicians, Hugo Wolf and Hans Rott, both of whom later died insane.

Success came suddenly at twenty-five, after years of poverty, when he was appointed conductor of the theatre at Leipzig. He was a perfectionist and a tyrant; many of the artists hated him; yet they had to admit that his results were astonishing. His performances of Wagner's operas, of Beethoven's Ninth Symphony, of *Don Giovanni*, were classics. Still, he was hated, partly because he was a Jew, partly because of his despotic manners, and there was endless plotting against him that must have been a perpetual irritation. At the age of twenty-eight he went to the Budapest opera house, which was foundering, and soon had it flourishing again. Quarrels led to his resignation three years later, but Mahler immediately performed the same service for the Hamburg opera. Finally, in 1897, he obtained the most important appointment of his life, as conductor of the Vienna opera, where he remained for ten years, quarrelling and bullying, the best-hated musician in Vienna.

Alma Mahler suggests that he inherited his complete inflexibility of temperament from his paternal grandmother, a street hawker who was still going from door to door at the age of eighty. The trouble was that Mahler, for all his tremendous talent, had little capacity for human intercourse. His musicians resented him so much because he never made them feel that he was one of them; he always criticized them from above, as it were, and was incapable of conveying a feeling of warmth and spontaneity. He was forty-one when he met the girl who was to become his wife, Alma Schindler, and it is from her account that we can gain some idea of Mahler as a human being. She made the last nine years of his life happy. Even so, he never lost his profound mistrust of fate. This seemed justified when the year 1907 brought a number of blows. His eldest daughter—five years old—died, and his wife collapsed at the graveside, so that for a while Mahler believed he might lose her, too. A doctor discovered that Mahler was suffering from the same heart complaint that had killed his mother, and would have to give up working. The hatred at the Vienna opera was becoming stifling; his last concerts and opera were badly attended because of deliberate plotting; his farewell letter, pinned up on the notice-board, was torn into fragments by some enemy. The remaining years of his life were spent between America, where he conducted at the Metropolitan Opera House, and his home at

Toblach, where he went on to compose six more symphonies, bringing the total up to ten. (The last was unfinished, but has recently been completed from Mahler's manuscripts by Deryck Cooke.)

Where Bruckner's music is objective, calm, speaking of nature and God, Mahler's is turbulent, subjective, ranging in mood from a self-pity reminiscent of Tchaikovsky to an ecstasy that recalls *Tristan*. Mahler is a Viennese composer, fond of waltzes and ländler, so that this rather heavy music has a unique flavour: the gloom or ecstasy is continually being leavened with touches that sound like Johann Strauss or Lehár.

It might be said that in content Mahler's music has close resemblances to that of Brahms, but where Brahms's subjectivity and melancholy are disciplined into a classical mould, Mahler's spread with Wagnerian proliferation. For sheer 'silvergrey melancholy', nothing in Brahms surpasses the beautiful final movement of the Third Symphony. But any listener who is reasonably familiar with modern popular music will instantly note here another reason for Mahler's wide popularity; the main theme of this movement sounds like the first bars of the song called 'I'll Be Seeing You' (which Frank Sinatra used to sing with the Dorsey band). Mahler is full of these tunes that might well be adapted for popular songs, and that are particularly rich in sweet, melancholy melodies: there are lovely examples in the first movement of the Sixth Symphony (the love motive) and the Tenth. One does not sink into these melodies contemplatively, as with Bruckner, recalling the lines from *Faust*:

> O'er mountain caves with spirits hover
> Or float the moonlit meadows over . . .

This music induces a twilight mood, and does it even more effectively than Brahms or Delius; the world has temporarily established a truce; there is a luxurious peace, serenity, exhaustion. This is true romanticism, and this aspect was never more finely expressed in the whole of the nineteenth century. It had to wait for Mahler and Ernest Dowson.

Perhaps the finest expression of Mahler's peculiar genius is to be found in his Ninth Symphony, which is my own favourite among his works. This is, like most of his symphonies, a composite work; we do not feel the kind of musical logic which is to be found in Beethoven. In effect, the symphony consists of two movements, the first and the last; between these there is a ländler movement (Scherzo), interposed to offer light relief, and a curious Rondo Burleske, all counterpoint, mostly in march time, which is extraordinarily like Hindemith. (Compare the second movement of the *Music for Brass*.) The two outer movements contain some of Mahler's most characteristic music. The opening was bold for his day—dull, oddly uncertain noises, like a speaker clearing his throat, then a few melodic fragments that seem to drift in a void, but that gradually knit themselves together, to reach a powerful climax. This is the true music of *Sturm und Drang*, with its sudden ecstasies and its long periods of doubt and uncertainty. No one ever caught this more clearly than Mahler in the Andante of his Ninth Symphony. (The actual technique is not unlike that which Ravel employed in *La Valse*.) After all this storm and uncertainty, the final movement is an Adagio as beautiful as that of the Third Symphony—again, music of reconciliation. Yet it is not true reconciliation, like the calm of Beethoven's last quartets. It is not the true resolution of the battle fought in the first movement. It is a temporary breathing space only. Mahler is another romantic casualty, a man who never grew up because, to some extent, he did not want to. We love his best music—the choral movement of the Second Symphony, the Adagio of the Third, the opening movement of the Tenth, and the much underrated *Klagende Lied*, a very early work—because of its sheer beauty of sound; but it is difficult to swallow Mahler whole, to approve of his work as a total expression of the man. This would be as dangerous as the music of Delius proved to be to Peter Warlock.

It is true that Mahler had a difficult youth; but success came when he was twenty-five. Verdi's youth was even more difficult, and the blows he suffered—death of his wife and two children, the total failure of his *Giorno di Regno*—would have driven a weaker man to suicide. Yet Verdi could achieve the almost supernatural, Olympian gaiety of *Falstaff*, as extraordinary an achievement in its way as Beethoven's late quartets. Mahler would never have written his *Falstaff*, even if he had lived to be a hundred. He wallowed in defeat; he liked to believe that he had a certain power of foreseeing his future unhappiness—and the death of his favourite daughter, following the composition of the *Kindertotenlieder*, may well have confirmed him in this notion. Even after marriage, when he was writing his hymn to conjugal love, the Sixth Symphony, he could not resist introducing into the last movement three great blows on the drum, to symbolize the three blows of fate that would destroy him. (In her book on her husband Alma Mahler points out that this again seemed an example of prophetic insight.) One can be a lover of Mahler's music while rejecting his morbid self-pity, and the implicit Hardy-esque philosophy of the world's meaninglessness. It is unfortunate that Mahler is least convincing when he is trying to create his own version of the Finale of Beethoven's Ninth Symphony, the great affirmation—as in his 'Symphony of a Thousand'. To my ear this work, Mahler's Eighth, is his least successful symphony. Mahler can be superb when writing for voices—as in the Second—but his music is naturally subtle, nervous, delicate, so that as the voices burst out thunderously: 'Veni, Creator', we feel that he is in his wrong element. The shadow of Beethoven seems to produce the same unfortunate effect of overstrain as in Brahms.

For similar reasons, I have never been fond of *The Song of the Earth*, although there can be no doubt about the melodic richness of this work. There are things that we can accept from music that become a little too much if expressed in words. That heavy melancholy of the Adagio of the Tenth could be a passing mood; but in *The Song of the Earth* the passing mood is exalted into a philosophy of decay; the voices declare explicitly that 'dark is life, dark is death'. If Mahler had somehow managed to go just one stage beyond this, as his contemporary Rilke did, then *The Song of the Earth* could have been not only his greatest work, but one of the most significant works of the twentieth century. Rilke was as subject to melancholy and world-rejection as Mahler; but by sheer strength of spirit he transposes these into a new key, into something greater than resignation or reconciliation. We would not expect the Beethoven kind of affirmation—that is a matter for another temperament completely. But Rilke achieved his own dark strength, a death-mysticism that was not defeatism but a new synthesis; death became 'the dark side of life', but this also meant that life had somehow invaded death, carrying 'dishes of fruit for the dead to praise'. This was precisely the level that Mahler never achieved; it was too complex for him; it is fitting that his work fades into the final *Abscheid* of *The Song of the Earth*.

At a first glance it is difficult to explain Mahler's return to favour since the war. He was almost forgotten for several decades after his death, in spite of the efforts of his friend Bruno Walter. Music critics talked of him patronizingly; his symphonies were the last of the dinosaurs, but their great musical carcasses have rotted away, leaving little but enormous skeletons— so the critics claimed. And yet today his vogue is enormous; it is fashionable to speak respectfully of Mahler, no one is exactly sure why. He is admired by musical personalities as different as Britten and Shostakovitch, and it is not difficult to discern his influence in the work of both of them. (Parts of the last movement of the Eighth Symphony, particularly the children's voices, sound curiously 'Brittenish'.) As the forerunner of Schoenberg and Berg, he is admired by the 'modernists' who shudder at the mention of Sibelius, or even Bruckner. His influence is discernible throughout Schoenberg's early masterpiece the *Gurrelieder*, which is perhaps the finest product of his influence. (This work is generally passed over in embarrassment by Schoenbergians; at a recent revival in Edinburgh critics described it as watered-down Wagner, long-winded and melodically feeble. This is unfair. For anyone who can take Wagner or Mahler, this is a rewarding work, as well as showing more clearly than anything how Schoenberg developed from the style of *Verklärte Nacht* to *Pierrot Lunaire* and *Erwartung*.)

When one looks back on that remarkable half-century, from 1860 to 1910 (Mahler died in 1911), one cannot help remembering Yeats's remark that life is a long preparation for something that never happens. Romanticism was a great striving, like a mother straining to give birth. No one could soak himself in the music of the period and wish it was still with us; there is too much melancholy and death-worship about it. Yet it was a great period; greatness was in the air like the scent of spring. It was fitting that the ultimate expression of romanticism should be *Also Sprach Zarathustra*, with its implicit declaration that man was on the threshold of a new evolutionary leap. For if one listens closely to the voice of romanticism, this is precisely what it is saying. It announces something great, something important.

46

But since romanticism itself was the outcome of man's cry, 'Why am I not a god?' what else could it herald but a belief in a 'new deal' for human beings?

What it *should* have brought forth—if God wrote history along the lines of H. G. Wells's *Shape of Things to Come*—was a new optimism, a sense of power over the complexities of modern life. The reason we would not change our own century for the age of romanticism is that, for all our problems and urgencies, we have a deeper sense of reality than those men of the nineteenth century. The going is tougher, the air is colder; but it calls forth a certain toughness in us; there is something enfeebling in the vapours of the nineteenth century. And yet it remains fascinating, for all that striving came to so little: Berlioz, Wagner, Brahms, and Mahler, all that torment and effort; and when we ask to see their heirs, the spotlight switches on to Stravinsky, Schoenberg, Hindemith, Boulez—all looking a little blinded and more than a little embarrassed. Something went wrong. When we consider the musical development of Schoenberg, Stravinsky and Co., it seems logical enough; given the creative personalities of these men, we do not feel that they failed or compromised—as we might well feel of Shostakovitch if he had written nothing but symphonies. It is extremely difficult to put a finger on what went wrong, since any music critic can demonstrate that the major musical personalities of our century have shown great creative ingenuity in solving their problems. But if we again listen carefully to the voice of romanticism, and then to the voice of modern music, we can see instantly what is wrong. Even Mahler, who believed himself defeated before he started, felt that he was battling with life; this is the power of that Andante of the Ninth. Romantic music announces that the nature of man has changed conclusively, that man has found a new way of seeing himself, and that he *must* go forward without the old supports and comforts, and yet with the possibility of becoming a greater creature than any hero foreshadowed in ancient literature. One does not need to be a Shavian or a Bergsonian to agree that the art of the nineteenth century seems to announce this new man as persistently as the Old Testament announces the Messiah; one merely has to listen. The writers and musicians who succeeded these giants simply fell back; Joyce declared that art is not supposed to deal

47

with ideas; Stravinsky said that music does not 'say' anything, and tried to make his art as impersonal as a block of ice cream. Hindemith talked about music as an artifact; it is surprising he did not manufacture spare parts to replace those that became worn out by constant performance. They turned back to the art of earlier centuries and declared that *this* was their real tradition, ignoring the definitive change that came over man after the French Revolution. The concept of art as an extension of life disappeared; they were to be kept in separate compartments. Art had its own laws, like chess. For the romantic, art was *an organ for digesting life*, a weapon in the battle. In the twentieth century only existentialism continued the tradition; and regrettably there was no existentialist music. The music of Stravinsky and Hindemith was the reverse—a musical counterpart of logical positivism. Only Schoenberg continued the tradition to some extent; in this sense, his followers are right when they declare that he is the central musical tradition of the twentieth century. Yet even Schoenberg can be accused of the same kind of evasion as Stravinsky and Hindemith, for he allowed himself to believe that the real problem was how to develop the *musical language* of the romantics, ignoring its existential content. The content of his music remains close to that of Mahler: sadness and defeat.

To musical historians of the future it may well be that this fifty-year relapse will be seen as an historical necessity, *reculer pour mieux sauter*. In any case, the 'leap' is still to come.

I shall return to this problem of modern music in the third chapter.

2

MOZART AND BEETHOVEN
—A RETROSPECT

I HAVE deliberately placed this chapter here, rather than at the beginning of the book, because what I have to say about Mozart and Beethoven is best understood in the light of my comments on the 'evolutionist' reaction that we label romanticism. There is very little to be said about the actual music of either Mozart or Beethoven that has not already been brilliantly said by someone else: in the case of Mozart, by Einstein or W. J. Turner or Girdlestone; in the case of Beethoven, by Romain Rolland, R. H. Schauffler, or (perhaps the best of all) J. W. N. Sullivan.

But all these books are for people who already appreciate Mozart and Beethoven. There are thousands of people, even intelligent, literate people, who can perfectly understand why Lucky Jim referred to 'an orchestra playing some effusion of filthy Mozart'. I can remember feeling rather the same on sitting through the complete *Don Giovanni* for the first time, feeling that the quality of the music in the arias was not exciting enough to compensate for the boredom of the long recitatives. Luckily, I was already familiar with parts of the music, from having seen the complete *Man and Superman* performed several times at the Princes Theatre, where *Don Giovanni* was used as *entr'acte* music as well as during the long 'Don Juan in Hell' scene (which, incidentally, still seems to me the greatest dramatic writing since *Hamlet*); so that when I finally acquired the Busch version of *Don Giovanni* on LP, it was easy to acquire an appetite for the music. It has been my favourite Mozart opera ever since, with *The Magic Flute* running it close.

CHORDS AND DISCORDS

My problem—and I know it to be true for thousands of other listeners—is that I am inclined to agree with the American composer Carl Ruggles, who said: 'Music that does not surge is not great music.' I would qualify that; I do not think that 'surge' is a good word here. And yet I feel that great music, like great literature, should be more than a skilful exercise, should possess a quality of imagination that makes itself immediately felt. I am inclined to believe that Bach can only be truly appreciated by someone who is able to play him, and can compare, let us say, a harpsichord sonata by Bach with one by Scarlatti or Vivaldi, and really understand the originality of mind that made Bach the greater composer. This requires a considerable amount of knowledge and study; it means, in effect, making the imaginative effort to become a contemporary of Bach. As to the people who say that they know nothing about music but infinitely prefer Bach to any romantic composer, I am inclined to believe that the explanation here is to do with individual temperament. I do not wish to be at all dogmatic about this, and I advance the opinion with some diffidence. But I *have* noticed, for example, that a rather emotional girl of my acquaintance, who is always torturing herself in unsuccessful love affairs, prefers Bach to any romantic composer because she seems afraid to abandon herself to emotion. She is like a person who has been burnt, who finds even lukewarm water too hot to bear. I, on the contrary, find that it requires a considerable discipline to induce the state of mental intensity in which I can produce writing that satisfies me, and *all* music is a welcome aid. Bach will do if there is nothing else available; but ten minutes of thunderous Bach organ music only whets my appetite for Beethoven or Mahler or Verdi.

The Victorians had a naïve way of assuming that whatever was new was necessarily better than what was old. Carlyle and Ruskin were, in some respects, necessarily better than Descartes or Spinoza, and Palestrina was better than Gregorian chant, and Haydn was better than Palestrina, and Beethoven was better than Haydn, etc. The modern age has been inclined to reverse this way of thinking—T. S. Eliot is as much responsible as anyone— so that we play Monteverdi's *Orfeo* or John Blow's *Venus and Adonis* as if they had strange depths of significance that are almost beyond our decadent modern understanding. This latter attitude is as absurd as the other. Art is not science, where all fresh development is necessarily a triumph over ignorance; but neither is it like religion, where later forms may be only decadent forms of the earlier. T. E. Hulme made a useful, if rather too general, distinction between two forms of art, the geometrical and the vital. Geometrical art usually expresses the religious attitude; it is geometrical and impersonal because it attempts to express an intensity beyond the merely human, and can only do so, as it were, symbolically and indirectly. It says: 'Not human', and it means: 'Beyond the human.' Hulme adds contemptuously that since man became the centre of the universe, humanism has come to mean lack of intensity, the merely human; what a whining old drunk might mean when he says: 'We're only human, after all.' Here Hulme was wrong; he could not foresee the existentialist revolution that stemmed from Nietzsche. But what Hulme failed to recognize fully was that 'humanist man' has fundamentally more dignity than religious man—if he faces up to the implications of his attitude. Religious man saw himself as a mere creature. This is the real distinction between Gregorian chant and Wagner, or between Byzantine art and Van Gogh.

Bach is still 'religious man'; yet the change had already taken place, even if he was never fully conscious of it. Compared to Ambrosian or Gregorian chant, the *St Matthew Passion* is romantic music; it is essentially dramatic; it does not rely on the geometrical—the formal—to express its moments of greatest intensity, but tries to *rise* to them, just as Handel rose to the Hallelujah chorus, or Wagner to the Magic Fire music. We can easily recognize the truth of Constant Lambert's remark that composers like Bach and Purcell were not really aiming at effects different from Beethoven or Wagner in their most dramatic moments; they were not deliberately underplaying the emotions, as Hemingway deliberately underplays them, to produce an effect of whole volumes left unsaid; it was simply that they did not possess the language, the techniques, to express them more powerfully. If they had done, no doubt they would have.

This is the reason that I do not feel more guilt at not getting the same pleasure out of Schütz, Monteverdi, and Bach as out of Mozart, Beethoven, and Mahler. I am no antiquarian; I do not enjoy old things simply because they are old. The modern Bach enthusiasts, encouraged by Stravinsky, assure me that to appreciate Bach I must attune myself to a new musical language, just as really to appreciate Dante I must read him in Italian. I take the liberty of doubting this. I believe that the musical language of Bach is not fundamentally different from that of Beethoven; his aims were not really alien to those of the romantic composers. It was only that he was making the awkward transition from religious art to humanist art. His extraordinary genius was poised between two stools (it would be untrue to say it had actually fallen between the two). As a humanist, I can make the act of sympathy to appreciate Gregorian chant; but in certain respects Bach is a little too near home.

To a lesser extent this also applies to Haydn and to Handel. I find the introductory music to *The Creation* some of the most interesting in Haydn—that strange, brooding, modern-sounding music that is meant to describe primeval chaos—because it confirms my belief that Haydn did not sound so formal and classical because he wanted to, but simply because classicism was the only convenient mould into which to pour his genius; and his genius was not great enough to break the old forms and create new ones, except in the Chaos music of *The Creation*. As to Handel, I early acquired a taste for his music through the advocacy of Samuel Butler, and soon came to recognize its essential spirit as romantic. Handel himself was a romantic personality in the truest sense. I do not mean that he was flamboyant, like Liszt; but he was as much a romantic individualist as Berlioz or Wagner; strong-willed, intransigeant, impatient of fools, contemptuous of compromise. There are people who enjoy Handel for the antique flavour, and insist that performances of his work should aim at sounding as much as possible like the original performances, conveniently forgetting that Handel himself would have taken fullest advantage of the sounds of a modern symphony orchestra, if he had had one available. If I have to choose between a recording of the *Messiah* based on the original Dublin performance, with a small chorus and a few strings and a harpsichord, and Sir Thomas Beecham aiming at maximum effect and noise, I seize the Beecham version without hesitation. And when I buy the Swarowsky version of *Julius Caesar* with most of the recitatives cut, I do not complain about the philistinism of the record companies, but feel thankful that Vox felt it necessary to pack it on to four sides and saved me forty minutes of boredom.

These confessions will pain many music lovers, so let me

52

hasten to add that I am not stating that I have a total blind spot for Bach and Monteverdi, or even Schütz. I find many musical longueurs in the Mass in B minor, or Monteverdi's *Vespro della Beata Vergine*, or Haydn's 'St Cecilia' Mass, but I would rather sit through them than through Hindemith's *Mathis der Maler* (the opera) or Pfitzner's *Palestrina*, both of which belong to my 'preferred' period, in spite of the many fine moments in both these works. And yet when some musical friend asks me if I would mind removing Bruckner's F minor Mass from the turntable and playing Purcell's *Dido and Aeneas* instead, I wonder whether this is a genuine musical preference, or some extra-musical nostalgia for a past era. For how can we possibly appreciate Purcell as his contemporaries did? Too much has happened in music since then, and it is as difficult completely to accept his musical idiom as it would be for us to go to a children's pantomime and allow it to conjure up the magic of childhood. We can, indeed, accept the pantomime in a different spirit, and still derive a certain enjoyment from it; but the children who are watching it are in a completely different world. It makes one understand Blake's lines:

How do you know but every bird that cuts the airy way
Is an immense world of delight, closed by your senses five?

I am willing to believe that Benjamin Britten can hear many things in *Dido and Aeneas* that I cannot hear, since he can see it through a composer's eyes; but I find it most difficult to imagine the music of Purcell ever assaulting my sensibility and touching my imagination as directly as Berlioz or Wagner.

Now when I come to Mozart, I find myself at once in a musical landscape that is somehow familiar to me. But it is not the musical idiom itself that makes me feel more at home with Mozart; there is a great deal of Mozart that would be indistinguishable from Haydn except by an expert. It is—and I apologize for the trite sound of this remark—that Mozart's peculiar genius gives his best work an unmistakable sparkle. There is already present in his work some of that 'surge', that vitality straining against its bonds, that becomes the familiar mark of romantic music. There are pages of the great G minor Quintet, of the Nineteenth and Twentieth String Quartets, of the Clarinet Quintet, of the

Twenty-first Sonata for piano and violin, that make me think of rockets bursting against a black sky—a romantic, a glittering spectacle, yet also clean, precise, delicate. Surely no one would dispute that this is the quality of all the greatest music of Mozart. The form has not changed greatly from that of Haydn; but there is as much difference between Mozart and Haydn as between a beautiful girl of sixteen and a beautiful and stately woman of fifty. There is no other key word to Mozart except genius— the sense of bursting vitality that is not to be matched again in music until Wagner, not even by Beethoven. Incidentally, this quality has been caught perfectly by the poet Mörike (better known to music lovers through Wolf) in his short novel *Mozart's Journey to Prague,** which describes how Mozart, on his way to Prague to produce *Don Giovanni*, scrapes up a chance acquaintance with an aristocratic family who revere his genius, and who entertain him—and are entertained by him—for two days. It is difficult to imagine prose conveying the quality of Mozart's music, but Mörike succeeds, and the result is a book so delightful that all Mozart lovers will read it once a year. It comes close to making us feel a contemporary of Mozart, and allowing us to listen to his music as his contemporaries must have heard it.

While on the subject of works about Mozart, a curiosity well worth the trouble of hearing is Rimsky-Korsakov's short opera *Mozart and Salieri*, which exploits the story that Salieri murdered Mozart by poison. It is a dialogue between the two composers, and when Mozart plays a short piano piece that has just floated into his head (a delightful piece of imitation Mozart that would impose on most Mozart lovers), Salieri is so twisted up with envy that he slips poison into Mozart's drink. They then have a conversation about crime, during which Mozart assures him that genius and crime are incompatible; Mozart feels ill and goes home, leaving Salieri alone—to reflect that, since he is a criminal, he cannot be a genius. Surprisingly enough, Rimsky-Korsakov manages to catch a great deal of the Mozartian quality in the opera. Music lovers who are inclined to think of him as a man who composed music that was all colour and no content will

*Fortunately at present available both in England and America: in England in a Calder paperback, and in America in *Nineteenth-Century German Tales*, edited by Angel Flores (Doubleday Anchor Books).

be pleasantly surprised by this opera, and may go on to discover that the operas of Rimsky contain some of his most beautiful music.

The essence of Mozart is, of course, to be found in the 'big six', the operas *Idomeneo, The Seraglio, The Marriage of Figaro, Don Giovanni, Così fan Tutte* and *The Magic Flute*. The first is Mozart's only successful *opera seria*; (a later one, *La Clemenza di Tito*, is hastily written and of poor quality).* There is a fashion to look down on *Idomeneo*, to place it lower than the others. I find it impossible to subscribe to this view. As soon as one gets to know the work well, it exerts as much attraction as *Don Giovanni* or *The Magic Flute*. It is interesting to compare this *Idomeneo, King of Crete* with Handel's *Sosarme, King of Media*, performed half a century earlier (in 1732). Opera has come as far in fifty years as it was to advance in the next ninety—up to *The Ring*. That tense, brooding overture is already close to the Weber of *Der Freischutz*, and not at all far from *La Vestale* of Spontini, that magnificent and much-neglected opera that sent Berlioz into ecstasies, and that was performed a quarter of a century after *Idomeneo*. Indeed, *Idomeneo* stands with *La Vestale*, Cherubini's *Medea*, and Gluck's *Iphigenia in Tauris* as one of the greatest monuments of *opera seria* in musical history. Our age seems to have lost its taste for these tremendous works (although a recent revival of *Medea* was successful enough), but this is no reason for pretending that they are not great music in their own right, quite apart from their historical importance.

The Seraglio is spoiled to some extent by its spoken dialogue (just as its brother opera *Zaide*, which has a similar plot, is spoiled by the irritating sound of recitation to the music). Someone should perform for Mozart the same service that Ernest Guiraud performed for *Carmen*, and set this spoken dialogue as sung recitative. The other operas of the 'big six' make their impact because of the continual flow of music, even though the recitative may be occasionally somewhat dull.

This recitative is a difficult problem. It would be no solution to cut it short and bring the arias closer together, yet undoubtedly longish patches of dialogue, sung tunelessly to a plinking harpsichord, are rather tiresome. The only remedy that

---

*Although, having since had the opportunity for a closer study of this opera (in the Gustav Lund recording), it seems to me to be not so far below *Idomeneo*.

seems reasonable is to sing the recitatives in English, so that the audience gets some sense out of them. At the end of the nineteenth century most operas performed in England were sung in English; since then there has developed a snobbery about it, for obvious reasons. People who understand the language, or have studied the libretto, prefer the opera in its original language. Opera libretti are often so feeble that to hear an opera in a foreign language is to be protected from its inanity. Where an opera has plenty of tunes, then it does no harm to sing it in a language that the audience cannot understand—although I personally would still prefer it in English. But I feel that there is a strong case for singing Mozart recitatives in English, even if the main arias and ensembles are sung in German or Italian. (After all, no one really cares about the words of 'O Isis und Osiris' or the Queen of the Night's aria; one simply enjoys the magnificent noise.)

Don Giovanni is my own favourite among the operas, probably because it is Mozart's most human opera. *Idomeneo* is too monumental; *Così fan Tutte*, for all its flowing musical line, is only one stage better than Gilbert and Sullivan (which for me is no disparagement); in *Figaro*, the hard edge of Beaumarchais' satire shows throughout, even though Mozart has softened it; *The Magic Flute* is inhuman in quite a different way from *Idomeneo*. But there is evidence in the music of *Don Giovanni* that Mozart threw himself with delight into the seduction fantasies of that Falstaffian reprobate Da Ponte. We know that he was a good husband who adored his wife; but listening to the *Don*, one could almost suspect that he found sex as exhilarating as H. G. Wells. I am aware that my familiarity with *Man and Superman* and Shaw's treatment of the Don Juan legend add a dimension to the music that it may not possess; one somehow supposes that Mozart's Don Juan is as witty and as basically serious as Shaw's. If this is misunderstanding, then it is not a misunderstanding I wish to remove; it adds to my pleasure.

The only other Mozart opera that has as much magic as *Don Giovanni* is *The Magic Flute*. I will own that it was a remark of Hesse's Steppenwolf that first set me listening to it with attention, and that on first hearing it I was somewhat confused and disappointed. It is a curious hotch-potch, and as Brockway and Weinstock have pointed out, its main musical numbers are

such an assorted bunch that it is hard to believe that some of
them come from the same opera. But a good stage performance
gives one the necessary perspective (I saw an excellent one in
Washington, for which my friend Day Thorpe was to a large
extent responsible), and the altogether weird quality of the
work makes its impact. What no one would suspect on a first
casual gramophone hearing (following it with a libretto) is that
this opera is the real predecessor of *The Ring*. The idea of
Tamino's ordeals, to prove himself worthy of initiation into the
sacred rites, is a magnificent one, and it is evident that it moved
Mozart deeply. For this reason, *The Magic Flute* is fundamentally
a superb hymn to life. This, I am convinced, is the quality that
Hesse discerned in it. What is more, it seems to be almost a
clairvoyant commentary by Mozart on his own life and death.
Mozart seems to typify Romain Rolland's remark that artists
are 'the masters of the world, the great defeated'; yet his
answer is in Tamino. In a way, it is fundamentally stronger than
The Ring, for *The Ring* seems to express the view that the hero's
triumph must come after his death. The courage of *The Magic
Flute* is the real evolutionary article; somehow, it expresses man's
most fundamental experience of life and the world; it is strangely,
disturbingly moving, like some of Blake's prophetic poems,
although it is difficult to express exactly why.

Talking of the music of Mozart—and Beethoven—brings us
near to the absolutely fundamental problem of music, the almost
inexpressible problem, for which ordinary language is barely
adequate. Why do we love the music of Mozart? Because it
somehow expresses faith in life. But that means very little. In
another sense, all nature expresses faith in life. For me, nothing
expresses faith in life as intensely as a tree; it is a mystical
symbol of the divine. But we are—necessarily—tied down to the
present, to the human, to problems connected with survival; so
most of the time we look at nature through thick, dusty glass.
Nothing is so untrue as that 'beauty is in the eye of the beholder'.
Beauty is *out there*. This is like saying that beauty lies in the
dusty window pane because cleaning it makes the garden more
visible. The beauty is really there, and if we could disconnect
ourselves from our pushing humanity for a moment, I think we
would dance and sing like madmen at what we should see. Well,
the greatest music has the power to get through the glass in

spite of the dust, to tell us something of the absolute value of life, quite apart from our boring personal preoccupations. It would be wrong to say that the content of Mozart's music is mystical, for all music is mystical in that sense, like nature. But for those who can hear it says something completely primitive about the nature of life, something that cannot be translated into words. Aldous Huxley found himself up against the same problem when writing about his mescalin revelation in *Doors of Perception*. We find it hard to imagine the world of objects being infinitely significant and ourselves unable to translate its significance into words, except perhaps into some strange word like 'is-ness'. Language has got attuned to the world as seen through dusty glass, so there is no way to express meanings that are *more* simple than the ones we are accustomed to.

Mozart's music is too simple to 'mean' anything in the ordinary sense. Wagner's music means something in a sense we can all understand—ecstasy, the unimportance of the everyday obstacles that take up most of our energy, power, affirmation. It swings a sledgehammer at the dusty glass. Mozart's music is far more primal; it has very little of personality in it, compared to Wagner. If we could hear it with the 'doors of perception cleansed', it would produce much the same inexpressible revelation as Van Gogh's chair that 'quivered with existence'.

I am trying to express why I love the music of Mozart—and, I feel, not making a very good job of it. Mozart himself was not a great man. He had a noble soul, but the heart of a child. Besides, he was rather spoilt. His intellect was not of unusual quality, although his intuitions were so nimble that he could easily have developed into a first-rate thinker. If it had not been for *The Magic Flute*, I doubt whether I could even have made a beginning on explaining why I have such an appetite for his music. But *The Magic Flute* expresses something basic about man's relation to life, and in some respects its absurdity and frivolity express it better than the seriousness of the Choral Symphony or *The Ring*. As we live it day by day, life is more like *The Magic Flute* than like Beethoven's Ninth. It only becomes a Beethoven Ninth occasionally, for a Scott of the Antarctic or Edmund Hillary climbing the last lap up Everest. For the rest of us, its frivolity disarms us, prevents us from making any real effort. And Tamino's courage under these circumstances is closer to the kind of courage that human beings need in order to achieve greatness, or any kind of decently fulfilled lives. Anyone can be courageous when the trumpet sounds and the hair stirs with excitement; it requires something far more godlike to create inner values in Regent Street on a Thursday afternoon. This is something Mozart knew by instinct.

Beethoven is in every way easier to write about. To begin with, he is a 'personality'. This is a pity; it means that his admirers are tempted to simplify him and make everything fit in with a preconception. Robert Haven Schauffler's *Beethoven: The Man Who Freed Music* is in many ways an excellent book—he has considerable understanding of the music—but it suffers from that disadvantage: the writer turns Beethoven into a fictional character. The young Beethoven is called 'Spangy' (because he had a dark skin like a Spaniard), and he is described in terms that would be better applied to the hero in one of Ayn Rand's romantic novels. If he throws a dish of lung soup in a waiter's face, this is merely an expression of his untamed genius. If he sets out deliberately to swindle his publishers, this is because his contemporaries failed to show their appreciation in monetary terms. If he could write cynically of his most loyal friends and declare that he merely 'used' them, this was an expression of his superman morality. The main thing was that he fought his long battle against the gods with courage, and came close to winning. His life seems to be the ideal moral fable. Romain Rolland and (more recently) David Burnett James have treated it in this way.*

This over-simplification disturbs me; I am inclined to think it would be a good idea if someone wrote a book proving that most of Beethoven's troubles were his own fault; that he was suspicious, neurotic, bad-tempered, and in many ways stupid. This would not be the whole truth, but it would be no less untrue than that other Beethoven.

I must admit that too much of Beethoven's music gives me a sense of *personal* self-assertion. It brings to mind the well-known story of how Beethoven and Goethe were walking together when a royal party approached; Goethe stood politely aside, while

Beethoven the Creator, by Romain Rolland (1928). *Beethoven and Human Destiny*, by Burnett James (1960). See also *Goethe and Beethoven*, by Romain Rolland.

Beethoven rammed his hat on his head, and strode through the midst of them scowling at the ground. Like so many other stories about Beethoven's bad manners, this makes a painful impression on me. The extenuating circumstances are easy enough to advance. Mozart had been a lackey of princes; Beethoven was determined to assert that he, too, was a prince in his own right. He got angry if anyone suggested that all the great music had been written in the past, knowing how easily he could surpass Haydn. But I still find a little too much of this bad-tempered self-assertion about him. He reminds me of a man driving the car with the hand-brake on, but stubbornly refusing to stop, even though there is a strong smell of burning rubber. There is something self-destructive about his assertiveness and bad temper, and it seems to me to indicate that, under the surface, he was not as sure of himself as he liked to appear.

This makes no real difference to the greatness of his music. It is a quite different kind of greatness from Mozart's. Lightness of touch is certainly not Beethoven's forte. His music is a triumph of personality rather than of life. Mozart seems to belong to a paradise world of innocence; Beethoven has drunk deeply of the knowledge of good and evil, and in many cases his demon gets the better of his angel. He is the sort of man whom his contemporaries probably hoped would prove to be a passing fashion. Cherubini and Spontini were two such: wilful men, tyrants, completely convinced of their own greatness, egotistical, bullying. (It is said that Cherubini even overawed Beethoven.) Music seems to produce such types in fair abundance; Wagner and Mahler were another two. In the case of Cherubini and Spontini, the hopes of their enemies were well founded; today they are almost as forgotten as Salieri or Spohr (the latter another of the 'great musicians' of his era; many thought him greater than Beethoven). Beethoven, like Wagner and Mahler, has managed to pass the test of posterity. But reading Thayer's life of Beethoven one can sympathize with the enemies who hoped that he would turn out to be a vast windbag. In many ways he was a most objectionable man.

For those who love his music without qualification this is a part of his fascination. I do not enjoy his music without qualification, although I enjoy a large amount of it very much indeed, from the early Septet and quartets to the last quartet, op. 135.

What interests me about Beethoven is his inner battle, the battle between the good and evil angels. It seems to me that Wagner and Mahler were very much at the mercy of their evil angels; they did a great many people a great deal of damage at different periods, often out of sheer spite and ill nature. To a large extent, they knew this. But one cannot carry the evil angel into great art, for his essence is spite and pettiness. He is the ideal muse for writing a pamphlet attacking Meyerbeer as a Jew, and proving Nietzsche to be another of the chosen race; but the muse of great art is magnanimous, open, trusting, forgetful of resentments, a lover of the human race. The evil angel thinks too much about other people in the worst sense; great art springs out of self-forgetfulness, and therefore forgetfulness of the impression one is making on other people. Wagner and Mahler found that they could achieve this forget-fulness only in one way: by negating the everyday personality, turning to ecstasy and death. They were not healthy men, as Mozart was; there is a strong flavour of the Christian ascetic's obsession with sin about them. Their great art had to be an art of self-rejection, world rejection, life rejection, since for them self, the world, life, were all tainted by the dark angel with his 'aching lust, to rid the world of penitence'. (Lionel Johnson, who wrote these lines, had to be another world rejector, who drank himself to death with a calculated suicidal mania.)

Now Beethoven is by no means one of the company of world rejectors, and the reason is that he found other ways to circum-vent the dark angel. He was capable of inducing in himself a real love for nature and humanity—it had to be humanity in the abstract, of course. He could wrestle with the brutal part of himself, recognize that in the eyes of his fellow men he was 'morose, crabbed, and misanthropical', and so, to some extent, purge himself of his worst qualities. Chuang Tze said: 'He who follows the part of himself that is great will be a great man; he who follows the part of himself that is little will be a little man.' This is the problem for all men of genius. Following the part of oneself that is great does not merely involve trying to follow one's better impulses; it also means a constant struggle to bring a sense of values, of evolutionary purpose, to clear conscious-ness. One's laziness, stupidity, and lack of self-knowledge are more powerful enemies than one's tendency to give way to spite or pettiness.

But at least Beethoven knew something about stifling the part of himself that was little when he wanted to compose. The stifling is not always successful; sometimes the music seems to be all personal self-assertion, a jarring, thumping quality, which is no doubt what made Britten say that he found the Piano Sonata, op. 111, grotesque and incomprehensible. One is aware of the struggle going on in Beethoven, and this is the reason that those late quartets seem so impressive. They are not easy works, and I would not blame anyone who said that four out of the five are exactly twice too long. Yet one feels that, after a tremendous battle, Beethoven has emerged somehow a greater man—exhausted, but calmer. Perhaps if Beethoven had been a less mistrustful personality, the struggle might have cost him less energy; Mozart also had his spiritual struggles; but they were easier than Beethoven's because he trusted the world and life fundamentally, and had no chip on his shoulder. Mozart was spoiled and petted from an early age, while Beethoven was supporting his family at the age of twelve; it should have been Mozart who was the spoilt one of the two. But it is not so; it is Beethoven who often strikes us as a bad-tempered child who is capable of cutting off his nose to spite his face.

Beethoven heralds the age of romanticism; his gesture of shaking his fist at the thunder on his deathbed is as symbolic as Manfred shaking his fist at God. And, as with most of the romantics, the keynote of his life is self-division. The romantics were fond of talking about the 'battle against God'; but it strikes one forcibly that for many of them the battle was really against their own weaknesses. Mozart is quite simply great. When he does bad work, as in *La Clemenza di Tito*, it is bad in a simple way; he has obviously failed to bring his genius to bear on it. One cannot pass any such easy judgement on Beethoven. He makes one think of the title of Aldington's book on D. H. Lawrence: *Portrait of a Genius But* . . . To assess his greatness needs a careful job of adding and subtracting. This is why every book on him, with the exception of Thayer's enormous Life, is misleading. There is surely no harm in recognizing that many of Beethoven's struggles were his own fault, the outcome of his weakness. He was no superman; in a basic sense, Mozart was closer to the superman type than Beethoven. He was fundamentally un-neurotic; he believed the universe meant well by him. He had his difficulties; but he did not create any of them himself. He saw the dark spots on the universe, but he was never tempted to take a paint-brush and add a few of his own. Our century would produce a healthier art if it took Mozart for its model instead of Beethoven.

3

MODERN MUSIC—
THE PROBLEM

THE ESSENCE of the 'Modernist' controversy was stated in the 1880s by Max Nordau in his book *Degeneration*; since then it has turned up in various forms, sometimes modestly, as in Haggin's chapter on modern music in his *Musical Companion*, sometimes thoroughly aggressively, as in Henry Pleasants's *Death of a Music*. As Mr Pleasants's book is the most recent, I may as well take it as the starting-point.

Modern music, says Mr Pleasants, has edged itself into a cul-de-sac; it has become intellectualized to an extent where it is meaningless to the general listener. And it may well be that the musical historian of the future will see jazz as the vital musical tradition of the twentieth century. Why do we snobbishly insist that a symphony *must* be a more important form of music than a Broadway musical, when the musical may be artistically vital and the symphony arid and formal? Is it not time that we faced the decadence of our serious music, and stopped looking down on jazz and popular music?

It is difficult not to feel at least some partial agreement with Mr Pleasants. The 'modernists' argue that all important art-works are ahead of their time, and that Schoenberg, Webern, and Boulez will be one day as acceptable in the concert hall as Bach is today. They may point out that contemporary critics accused Eliot of a kind of deliberate practical joke in offering *The Waste Land* as poetry, while nowadays any college student can appreciate its emotional force. But, as Mr Pleasants points out, *Wozzeck*, *Pierrot Lunaire*, and *The Rite of Spring* sound as

64

strange today as they did fifty years ago; they have not been assimilated in the same way.

And yet it seems to me that this kind of arguing fails, to some extent, to grasp the essential root of the matter. We cannot argue as if popularity in the concert hall were the only criterion of value. Artistic experience is related in a curious way to the personality of the spectator. One might say that it affords an escape from personality, a broadening of the personality. Men can mature only by allowing themselves natural expression; the emotions have to be taught to flow. The inner being has to be kept in motion. In the same way, a woman might feel that she must have a child if her personality is to find its natural expression. But there is an obvious difference. In becoming a mother, a woman has allowed a certain part of her personality its fullest expression; having a dozen children will not necessarily enlarge it further. But the fulfilment brought about by certain artistic experiences has no clear limitation. A youth may discover that the music of Wagner brings about an inner release, an expansion of his personality; but that is not to say that he will not find still greater release in Schoenberg or Bartók.

We do not yet know enough about the psychology of personality to know whether it could go on developing indefinitely, or whether it has a certain limit of expansion analogous to the blooming of a flower. The artistic career of such men as Yeats and Gide seems to indicate that there are no true limits. But since it is impossible to know how far a personality is capable of development, it is equally impossible to make rules about whether various forms of art are valid or not. It may be true that *Pierrot Lunaire* remains an intellectual rather than a musical experience. But then, it is possible to imagine a person for whom its strange sounds create an experience that he could find nowhere else in music.

In short, the point that is generally overlooked in arguments about modern music is the question of the psychology of the kind of people who enjoy it. Both the attackers and defenders write as if music had an absolute value, to which Schoenberg either conforms or does not conform. This is like assuming that everyone who professes to be a Roman Catholic has carefully thought out his beliefs, and weighed them against the claims of Buddhism and Mohammedanism. In fact we know that, ideally speaking,

65

religion and philosophy ought to be concerned only with 'truth'. And yet we only have to hear a convinced Catholic arguing with a convinced Communist to know that the emotional needs of the personality play an important part in a man's conception of 'truth'. The true philosopher is not discouraged by this; he attempts to allow for his emotional prejudices. But the philosopher has the advantage of being able to appeal to the laws of logic. The logic of art is an altogether more difficult matter, since art is essentially an appeal to the personality rather than to the reason.

It must therefore be conceded that for certain people the rarified atmosphere of 'modern music' is pleasant to breathe. To some extent, then, modern music is justified. But it might be contended that previous revolutions in music—from modal polyphony to diatonic harmony, from classicism to romanticism —were natural evolutions of public taste. Wagner may at first have sounded odd to the admirers of Bellini, but it did not take long for the general public to find the new music assimilable. Is it ever likely that the general public will follow the admirers of Schoenberg, or come to accept Boulez's *Marteau Sans Mâitre* at a concert, sandwiched between the Beethoven Fifth Symphony and Debussy's *La Mer*?

Conceding that the answer is 'probably not', might it yet be contended that serial music *is* the central musical tradition of the twentieth century, whether the public accepts it or not? After all, no one denies that the theory of relativity is a natural development in physics, even though the general public does not understand it.

Again, this seems to be missing the point. Music is not eventually judged by *how* it says things, but by *what* it says. Beethoven seemed a difficult composer to the general public of his day, and his late quartets are still as 'difficult' for the average listener as any Schoenberg; but the manifest importance of what he had to say carried the day. The proof that the public responds to *what* is being said can be found in Alban Berg, whose only two 'popular' works are *Wozzeck* and the Violin Concerto, both clearly driven by a powerful emotion. The Chamber Concerto or the Altenberg Songs say nothing of comparable importance, and are seldom heard.

The emphasis in all the discussions seems to have got mis-placed. Composers who have defended their right to compose 'difficult' music include Schoenberg, Copland, Roger Sessions, and Hindemith. If any of these men were obviously of the stature of Beethoven, there would be no argument; the works themselves would carry the day.

Where Schoenberg is concerned, the unpopularity is very clearly a matter of content as well as of form. The artists of the early nineteenth century tended to be 'popular' in that they spoke of unifying emotions, of the brotherhood of man. The late nine-teenth century—the era of 'decadence'—cultivated a kind of artistic solipsism, and the idea of individualism was sometimes carried to an absurd point of selfishness, as in Lautreamont, who seemed to believe that a man would be justified in murder-ing a baby if it gave him pleasure. Far from feeling universal brotherhood, the 'decadent' poet tended to make no secret of his contempt for his reader, the 'hypocrite lecteur'. So it was hardly surprising if most readers responded with coolness to the work of these artists.

Now Schoenberg, Berg, and Webern most emphatically belong to this tradition. Berg set Baudelaire poems in *Der Wein*; Schoenberg and Webern both set Stefan George. The strange, solipsist world of decadence is always present in Schoenberg's music. In the *Gurreleider*, *Verklärte Nacht*, *Pelléas and Mélisande*, the First Chamber Symphony, and the First String Quartet, it is open and undisguised. It is still obviously present in the choice of text of the George songs (op. 15), *Pierrot Lunaire*, *Erwartung*, *Die Glückliche Hand*, and *Herzge-wächse*. An unkind listener might still detect it in the over-dramatized self-pity of the *Survivor from Warsaw* (which has always seemed to me Schoenberg's one total artistic flop). Schoenberg's admirers claim that *Moses and Aaron* reveals a greater Schoenberg, preoccupied with the universal issues of man and God; but again, one observes that the centre of the opera is the dance around the golden calf, and Schoenberg's text dwells on the lust and violence with an obvious satisfaction that recalls Oscar Wilde. (People eat raw meat, a youth is murdered, four naked virgins are sacrificed, then men strip women and possess them on the altar; Schoenberg spares no

67

details in describing the orgy.) Moreover, when Schoenberg returned in later life to writing 'tonal' works—the Second Chamber Symphony and the Suite for string orchestra (1936)— they sound as if they had been written thirty years earlier. (The Second Chamber Symphony was, in fact, begun in 1906.) The idiom is still that of *Verklärte Nacht*. Finally, we have the curious fact that Schoenberg never expressed any kind of dissatisfaction with his earlier music. Most critics have seen in this only evidence of his iron consistency, his recognition that his development had proceeded according to a rigorous musical logic. But when one considers his lifelong failure to escape the decadent romanticism of his youth, it seems equally plausible that his development after 1908 was a technical development only, concealing an inability to develop in a more fundamental sense. The curious rigidity of Schoenberg's personality, his lack of humour and the unwavering hatred with which he regarded anyone who was even lukewarm towards his music, tends to reinforce this probability.

The comparison with James Joyce affords some interesting parallels. Both began by writing in a naïve and romantic idiom; both showed a curious innocence in their total self-preoccupation. Both suffered a number of early snubs, and developed a formidable intellectualism to cover the over-sensitivity. Joyce also refused to 'disown' his early work—the poems *Chamber Music* (1907) reveal an unexpected strain of Irish sentimentality —and the later *Pomes Penyeach* show that Joyce was writing exactly the same kind of poetry twenty years later, although the achievement of *Ulysses* came between the two volumes. Acquaintances who knew Joyce in his later years have all remarked on a certain naïve element in his personality: the childish sense of humour, the constant dwelling on the past, which seemed to indicate that, in a certain way, he never grew up. His stature as an intellectual was considerable, since he had forced it on himself by sheer will-power; but his stature as a human being never equalled it. His portrait of himself as Shem the Penman in *Finnegans Wake* shows that he still saw himself in exactly the same light as thirty years earlier, when he wrote *Stephen Hero*; pride and self-pity are still the leading traits of his character. One might also observe that the sexual perversion and violence that erupt in *Ulysses* and *Finnegans Wake* bring to mind the central scene of *Moses and Aaron;* the same perverted romanticism is apparent.

All this is not intended to minimize the achievement of either Joyce or Schoenberg. The achievement remains; but it must be recognized that it was largely an achievement of will, not the true development of the whole human being that we find, for example, in Beethoven. One must recognize this in order to see the music of Schoenberg in perspective. It is something that one would not realize from reading books about Schoenberg, or listening to the kind of discussion of him that is presented on the Third Programme: for example, a recent* discussion of *Pierrot Lunaire* between Hans Keller and Egon Wellesz that seemed to be based on the assumption that Schoenberg is the only interesting composer of the twentieth century.

The parallel with Joyce raises a further question. Joyce's influence in literature has been equal to Schoenberg's in music; and yet, in a certain sense, his work is a dead end. No one can continue it, and one might perhaps be forgiven for suggesting that Joyce himself never really continued the work he began with *Ulysses. Finnegans Wake* is an elaborate game rather than a living work of literature. Joyce's influence was not fundamental and seminal; no one could say, as Dostoevsky said of Gogol's *Overcoat,* that a whole literature came out of it. Joyce's technical influence is present in Döblin's *Alexanderplatz, Berlin,* in Wolfe's novels, even in the Graham Greene of the 1930s; but only in the most superficial sense.

In the perspective of another half-century, Schoenberg may well be seen in the same light. His language has obviously exercised an enormous influence; but how profound is this influence? Has it, like Gogol's *Overcoat* or Schiller's *Robbers,* really created a new kind of sensibility, a new 'world outlook' that will continue to bear fruit?

For a new language to exercise a genuinely profound influence, it must be an integral part of a new sensibility, a break with old patterns of feeling as well as of expression. The language of Wordsworth and Coleridge was such a breakaway from the sensibility of the age of Pope: hence its seminal influence on the nineteenth century. But, as we have already pointed out, Schoenberg's 'feeling' is a continuation of the

*December 1963.

'feeling' of Wagner and Mahler; he might be regarded as the last fruits of their line of Teutonic romanticism, rather as Delius could be described as the ultimate expression of the French school of musical impressionism. Delius has exercised no influence comparable with Schoenberg's because his technical procedures had less to offer; but it may well be that, in many other ways, he is Schoenberg's musical equivalent.

The only way in which the listener can judge this is, of course, by ear. And the difficulty of Schoenberg's musical language may make it difficult to reach any conclusion. Berg's musical language is easier to come to terms with. It presents initial difficulties in the more formal works, but the listener can have no difficulty in recognizing the relationship between the Violin Concerto or the D minor interlude of *Wozzeck* and the world of Mahler's Ninth Symphony. And yet Schoenberg's language is not so inaccessible, as soon as one has an inkling of what he is 'saying'. Getting to know Schoenberg's music is like getting to know a person whose haughty and abrupt manner conceals shyness and a desire to be liked. The listener is advised to begin with the *Verklärte Nacht*, the two Chamber Symphonies and the 1936 Suite for string orchestra; after these, the transition to the Violin Concerto and Piano Concerto should prove both interesting and pleasant. The language of the Violin Concerto may seem strange at first, but the opening cadences make it clear that this is a romantic concerto wearing a false moustache. There is none of the harsh feeling of torn silk that one gets from Stravinsky's Violin Concerto. In fact, Schoenberg's concerto is in many ways reminiscent of Berg's, allowing that Berg's feeling is tragic, while Schoenberg's is only dreamily romantic, somewhat after the manner of *Verklärte Nacht*. The Piano Concerto is equally easy to get to know. One critic described it as 'Brahmsian', and in fact much of the orchestration has a curiously Brahmsian sound. A great deal of the concerto sounds as if someone had accidentally played a tape of a Brahms concerto backwards.

Part of Schoenberg's difficulty in finding wider appreciation is undoubtedly due to the excessive claims made for him by admirers who seem determined that admiration for him shall be confined to a small clique. Hence we have Hans Keller writing (on a Schoenberg sleeve note): 'The sole trouble about Schoenberg is that he is the first composer of supreme greatness

who is more talked about than played. This is our age's fault,
not his, and if he is the least played and most talked about,
that may only go to show that he is the greatest of them all.'
The uninitiated listener is thus prepared for tremendous mes-
sages of Olympian profundity; and if Schoenberg is the 'greatest
of all' composers of 'supreme greatness', then this profundity
must, at the very least, be equal to that of the late Beethoven
quartets. These absurdly excessive claims only tend to conceal
from the listener the fundamentally simple romanticism of
Schoenberg's music; they seem, in fact, designed to increase its
inaccessibility.

Schoenberg has been accused of many things including deliberate faking—musical confidence trickery. But the worst that
can fairly be alleged against him is that the complexity of his
musical language is not true complexity—the complexity that
is the attempt to communicate a complex emotion. (Eliot once
made the same point against Milton, citing Henry James as an
example of 'true complexity'.) Moreover, it would be unfair
to say that Schoenberg tries to pretend to be profounder than
he is. Irritation at the cliché-ridden nature of one's language is
a legitimate reason for trying to change it. The linguistic
complexity of Mallarmé, Valéry, Joyce, and Dylan Thomas is
of this kind. No one can blame an artist for making what he has
to say as interesting as possible. It is true that the greatest
artists have never had need to resort to linguistic fireworks for
their own sake, and that extreme preoccupation with technique
is usually a sign of a certain dilettantism. But it might be said
in Schoenberg's favour that he is a German, and the Germans
have a tradition of making heavy weather of self-expression.
No one claims that Kant or Hegel were fakes because they did
not express themselves as clearly as Hume or Descartes.

The other composers who are usually mentioned in attacks on
'modern music' (I continue to write 'modern music' in inverted
commas, meaning 'difficult modern music') are Stravinsky,
Hindemith, and Webern. Thirty years ago Bartók was usually
mentioned as well, but time has shown that his music has a far
wider appeal than that of the others.

Webern is the easiest to justify. He is a musical contemplative
who never set out to be popular. He practised music with the

same mystical devotion that Flaubert and James practised writing. The most essential Webern works are very short, and for small numbers of instruments; it is typical that many should regard the Piano Variations, op. 27, as his masterpiece. One cannot conceive of Webern writing an opera; even the songs (many to Stefan George poems) strike one as 'impure' Webern.

He sits above music like a hermit on a mountain-top; or perhaps a better simile would be a great chess player looking down on a chess board. At long intervals he reaches down and makes a single move. Webern reminds us of a line of Yeats:

> Like a long-legged fly
> His mind walks upon silence.

It is pointless to include a musician like Webern in an attack on modern music, because he seems to have almost no interest in communication: he plays music like a game of patience.

Hindemith is a totally different matter, and the objections raised against him by Constant Lambert in 1933 still hold good today. It is slightly difficult to understand why Hindemith should be regarded as one of the three colossi of modern music (the other two being Schoenberg and Stravinsky) if men like Poulenc, Milhaud, and Honegger are to be regarded (rightly, in my opinion) as minor composers. The sheer quantity of his musical output is impressive; but so is Milhaud's; he owes much of his reputation to his teaching, but so does Milhaud. One can only assume that his fashionable creed of 'classicism' and his Germanic seriousness recommend him to people who are irritated by Milhaud's Gallic frivolity.

W. J. Turner has an interesting passage about Bach that applies, in many essentials, to Hindemith. 'Bach had arrived at the point of being able to sit down at any minute of any day and compose what had all the superficial appearance of being a masterpiece. It is possible that even Bach himself did not know which was a masterpiece and which was not, and it is abundantly clear to me that in all his large-size works, there are huge chunks of stuff to which inspiration is the last word that one could apply.' Haggin, who quotes this, goes on to remark that he agrees with it, and that he has also come to find only certain passages 'moving'.

The word 'moving' causes one to pause for reflection. Modern Bach enthusiasts often claim that what they like about Bach is that he is *not* moving—that he was aiming for something quite different, a kind of mathematical perfection. And it is as well to remember at this point what Constant Lambert said of this idea that emotional and romantic music is a 'late and decadent excrescence'. 'Music, far from being abstract, is . . . naturally emotional. . . . The romantic and emotional nature of music is latent in its origins.'* And elsewhere he points out that 'classical music has little sense of horror about it, not because classical composers despised such an appeal to the nerves, but because they were unable to achieve it.'† Bach may strike us as unemotional if we have been listening to Wagner; it is doubtful if he saw himself in this light.

Now Hindemith appears to be suffering from the mistaken notion that Lambert exposed in *Music Ho!*—that there was a time when music was a kind of abstract exercise, meant to appeal to the mind alone. This is the kind of music that he writes. Listening to Hindemith is often like listening to Bach in the sense that there are often long periods in which very little seems to be happening. The consequence is that when Hindemith wishes to be moving and impressive—as in the climactic passage of his opera *The Harmony of the World*, where the music has to suggest music of the spheres—he has forgotten how, and the result is totally unexpressive.

There seems to be a kind of fallacy in Hindemith's music. It may be that Lambert is right when he suggests that the whole idea of *Gebrauchsmusik* (utility music for everyday purposes) is a misunderstanding of the nature of music, since 'there is no regular demand for musical material as there is for writing material or boxes of matches; there is only a demand for something which creates its own demand—a good piece of music. . . .' One can see that, in Hindemith's early days, the unexpressive quality of his music must have contrasted piquantly with the violence or satire of his chosen subjects, as in *Murder, Hope of Women*, *Das Nusch-Nuschi* (which has a chorus sung by monkeys), and *Cardillac*, based on a Hoffmann story about a jeweller who murders his customers because he cannot bear to part

Music Ho!, Penguin edition, p. 83.
†ibid., p. 40.

with his work. It was this Hindemith who exercised a dubious influence on the young Kurt Weill—dubious because the Hindemithian passages of *Mahagonny* are the drearist in the score— and who was regarded as the *enfant terrible* of his generation. But in the 'respectable' later Hindemith there are only occasional flashes of beauty or power to sweeten the pill. *Gebrauchsmusik* has been translated 'bread and butter music', but Hindemith's later music better deserves to be called 'bread and water music'! As with Schoenberg, one feels that his music must be understood as an attempt to escape a romantic heritage; but Hindemith's method of escape is altogether less interesting than Schoenberg's. In his best works, Schoenberg scrambles his language, but does not betray the emotion he wants to convey. Hindemith deliberately turned his back on his romantic heritage for many years, and wrote what Haggin describes as 'harmonically sour and emotionally dry works'. Later he allowed a certain romantic element back into his music, but it only served to underline the mechanicalness of long passages of textbook variations. Works like the 1940 Symphony in E flat and the 'Harmony of the World' Symphony begin with purposeful-sounding fanfares that promise an interesting musical journey; but within minutes the traveller is in the old musical desert, with miles of flat, bare country on either side.

Part of the trouble is Hindemith's unwillingness to write anything that sounds as if it has a definite key. But unlike the music of Schoenberg and Berg, which has a harsh, mountainous quality, Hindemith's music moves along so uneventfully for much of the time that the ear feels that it *ought* to have a key. The consequence is that the ear often feels a kind of embarrassment, as if in the presence of some disability, like a stutter or a tendency to sing slightly off-key.

The truth is that, whether Hindemith likes it or not, he is by temperament a romantic composer, and romantic music must have a feeling of a key centre. The most effective moments in some of his best works—the opera *Mathis der Maler* (not the symphony, which tends to aridity), the 1939 Violin Concerto, the 1937 *Symphonic Dances*, the ballet *Nobilissima Visione*, the *Concert Music* for brass and piano, op. 49—have a strong feeling of tonality. (This need of romantic music for a key centre can be seen even more clearly in Kurt Weill's *Mahagonny*; at its

best—the scene in the 'Do-what-you-like' bar, the chorus
'Rasch Jungens, hé!'—it is romantic, tonal, and has a sense of
musical economy and drive; when it is being *avant garde* in the
manner of Hindemith, as in the long passage following the
Benares song, it loses direction and drifts.)

Like Schoenberg and Bartók, Hindemith has achieved one of
the few individual styles of the twentieth century; any piece of
his music identifies itself in a matter of seconds; but it is the
dubious individuality of the club bore, whose voice sends everyone scurrying for magazines to hide behind. It is a pity that the
man who could achieve the bizarre effects of *Cardillac* and the
sense of weight and sincerity of *Mathis der Maler* should have
chosen to be identified with *Gebrauchsmusik* written according
to a Bachian formula, and should have become best known to
concert audiences for the comparatively trivial *Metamorphoses
on a Theme of Weber*.

Stravinsky is more difficult to discuss than Schoenberg and
Hindemith because his character seems to be more intricate.
Moreover, there has been so much learned discussion of his
stature and place in modern music that it is difficult to keep the
source of one's intuitions about him untainted. The dissenting
opinion on him was expressed typically by Brockway and
Weinstock in *Men of Music;* they feel that he ceased to exist as
a serious composer about 1930, and has since shown only
spasmodic signs of life.

In all essentials, it might be said that Stravinsky followed the
familiar course that we traced in Schoenberg and Joyce: early
romanticism, the sudden alarm in mid-career and the feeling of
the need for brakes, followed by a deliberately cultivated intellectualism. The intellectualism at least served its purpose of
impressing the intellectual critics, so that Stravinsky, like
Schoenberg, now tends to be discussed on a theoretical level
that is miles above the reality of his music, and that has little
relation to its content.

It is easy to understand why Stravinsky should have felt the
need for some new direction in his music. The great musicians
of the latter part of the nineteenth century are grim warnings.
Brahms, Wagner, Mahler, Bruckner, Saint-Saëns, Tchaikovsky,
all display the same failure to develop beyond a certain point;

mid-period Wagner sounds like later Wagner; Bruckner's first symphony sounds much like his ninth. This does not diminish their greatness; most of us would not be without a single symphony of Bruckner or Mahler. But this kind of thing could not go on for ever; people had begun to lose interest in Richard Strauss forty years before his death because it looked as if he would go on indefinitely composing sequels to *Rosenkavalier* and *Ariadne*. Stravinsky's master, Rimsky-Korsakov, was a case in point. Except for a certain additional ripeness in the orchestration, no one would guess that more than forty years separate *The Golden Cockerel* (1908) from *Sadko* (1867).

Stravinsky's artistic intellect, and his will, were a great deal stronger than Rimsky-Korsakov's. But even these qualities cannot make musical inspiration spin out indefinitely. What seems to be lacking in Stravinsky is a heavyweight artistic *personality*. No one doubts that he possesses a genuine musical personality; even T. S. Eliot, who is not given to passing judgements on music, has written: 'Mr Stravinsky is a real musician.' The question is whether this personality has shown a development commensurate with his musical 'development' from *The Firebird* to *Threni*, or whether Stravinsky has forced himself to experiment in order not to repeat himself. In the music of certain composers—Mozart, Beethoven, and Bartók in our own century—one feels that changes in the musical idiom are a by-product of a development of the composers' whole spiritual being.* Does Stravinsky's music show this kind of development?

If Schoenberg's development is paralleled by that of Joyce, Stravinsky's artistic personality has affinities with that of Eliot. Both began as heirs of a 'decadent' tradition, both made an early reputation as artistic rebels, both announced their conversion to classicism and traditionalism and developed 'detached' personalities, both later made religion their artistic centre of gravity. But the parallel fails to hold in one important respect. Eliot accepted the consequences of his subjective attitude, declared, in effect, that his inner life was no one's business, except in so far as he chose to reveal it in his poetry, and consequently ceased to write poetry. Stravinsky also had a try at the haughtily detached attitude (at one point he told his critics:

*Although, as regards Bartók, I shall qualify this judgement in the next chapter.

'There is nothing to discuss or criticize'); but it was clear that this was an assumed personality; he is naturally self-explanatory, even garrulous, as becomes clear from his volumes of *Conversations* with Robert Craft. His musical output has likewise remained enormous, like that of Hindemith; but much of it produces the same sense of lack of inner compulsion.

There can be no doubt that, if judged on the level of a musical innovator, Stravinsky must be regarded as a great composer. Like Schoenberg, he has been determined always to be an interesting composer; there is plenty of material for discussion in his work. But the question still remains: is it valid development, or simply a kind of game, like Joyce's development after *Ulysses*? An examination of his career throws some light on the problem.

If Stravinsky had died in 1912, he would have been regarded as a minor follower of Rimsky-Korsakov, who took Rimsky's style further in certain respects, much as Strauss 'developed' Wagner's style. *The Firebird* and *Petrouchka* are pleasant works, slightly more interesting than Rimsky's *Legend of the Invisible City of Kitezh* or *Coq d'Or* suites simply because Stravinsky has also learned something from Debussy, and his palette contains some transparent water colours as well as the garish pigments of *Schéhérazade*.

When an artistic personality feels that it has reached a limit in a certain direction, its tendency is to explode, to produce something that has nothing in common with what has gone before. This kind of thing never occurred in Mozart or Beethoven simply because they developed organically, never feeling that they had reached a limit. (Beethoven's Hammerklavier Sonata is perhaps the only analogous example.) We feel that with *The Rite of Spring* Stravinsky is momentarily disowning his Russian nationalism and all that it implies—particularly the music of Scriabin, who was then regarded as the last word in musical sophistication and mysticism. The *Rite* has no musical 'argument', even though it proceeds in a series of episodes; it stands at an opposite extreme from a work like Sibelius's Fourth Symphony, that develops slowly, statement by statement. The *Rite* is a musical explosion, a shout of defiance. It is also, of course, an orchestral show-piece, like Strauss's *Don Juan* or *Till Eulenspiegels lustige Streiche*. But my own experience is that it will not bear repeated listening; once one knows it, one knows it, and there is no point in listening to new performances, even by someone as dynamic as Leonard Bernstein. Generally speaking, show-pieces are of limited musical interest; no one is likely to maintain a lifelong affection for Beethoven's 'Battle' Symphony or Tchaikovsky's *1812* Overture, any more than for such eminent descendants of the *Rite* as Prokofiev's *Scythian Suite* or Bartók's *Miraculous Mandarin*. At the most, one buys the latest stereophonic recording to astonish and deafen one's friends. Historically speaking, the *Rite* may be the most important piece of music of this century; but from the perspective of half a century later, we can see that the critic who said that it was the twentieth-century equivalent of Beethoven's Ninth Symphony was talking nonsense.

There followed what must have been for Stravinsky a period of artistic anxiety. The warm nationalistic manner of *The Firebird* was not susceptible of development; but if anything, *The Rite of Spring* was even more of a dead end. Fortunately for Stravinsky, it was also, for the time being, the end of his association with the Diaghileff ballet, so that for a few years he could afford to stop worrying about the public who looked to him for new thrills. The next few years, 1913 to 1918, produced only a few minor works—a few songs, short piano works, pieces for string quartet, and the completion of an opera begun in the *Firebird* period, *The Nightingale*. There was only one major work, *Les Noces*, written in 1917, and it shows Stravinsky attempting to develop the rhythmic implications of *The Rite of Spring*. Many regard it as a masterpiece; its first five minutes certainly arrest the attention with their rhythmic vitality and the oriental sound of the vocal line (which, in this respect, bears some resemblance to Ravel's Two Hebrew Melodies written three years earlier). But continued acquaintance reveals the same defect as in the *Rite*; the lack of melody is tiresome; the ear grows tired of barbaric rhythms, which have the same effect of blunting the sensibility that one finds in some of Wagner's noisier passages. The same thing applies to the 'burlesque tale' *Reynard*, although here a certain lightness of touch gives the work the quality of an agreeable romp.

The Soldier's Tale (1918) again shows Stravinsky preoccupied with helping out the music by buttressing it with words. The attempt would have been more successful if it had not been for

78

the puerile nature of the text by C. F. Ramuz. The quality of the music shows that Stravinsky is not entirely at home when he cannot rely on his rhythmic effects (the music having been written for seven instruments). Nevertheless, *The Soldier's Tale* succeeds in holding the attention for forty minutes, and in this respect may be regarded as his most successful work since *The Firebird*.

The twenties were Stravinsky's phase of 'time travelling' (to use Constant Lambert's description). The 1923 Piano Concerto became associated with the catch phrase 'Back to Bach', and is the first of a number of 'harmonically sour and emotionally dry works'. It would appear that Stravinsky had come fully to realize that the actions and reactions of his early years were essentially rootless, and had decided that 'tradition' should give him the dimension that he otherwise lacked—the ability to develop logically. Tradition, to begin with, meant various eighteenth-century procedures. And what is equally clear is that Stravinsky himself was not enough of a personality, that is, a living and suffering human being, to develop in the existential manner of a Mozart or Beethoven. His colleague Nijinsky sensed this instinctively, and wrote of him: 'He seeks riches and glory. . . . Stravinsky is a good composer, but he does not know about life. His compositions have no purpose. . . .' He goes on to tell how Stravinsky and his wife declined to look after Nijinsky's child while the dancer toured America, and implies, what Madame Nijinsky states flatly, that Stravinsky was a cold fish. Certainly one feels about all the music written after *Petrouchka* that it is 'cold fish' music, that it was never written as a spontaneous outpouring of something that had to be expressed. This un-satisfactoriness is easiest to pin down in the works based upon other composers: *Pulcinella* (based on Pergolesi), *The Fairy's Kiss* (Tchaikovsky), and *Norwegian Moods* (Grieg). Somehow the 'Stravinsky-izing' of the music has the effect of devitalizing it, removing its flavour, like putting salmon into tins; it is like putting it through some processing machine.

The thirties and early forties were, on the whole, a bad time for Stravinsky. He produced a number of remarkable works that compare favourably with *Les Noces* in rhythmic force: the *Symphony of Psalms*, the Concerto for two pianos, the *Danses Concertantes* and the *Symphony in Three Movements* (1945), as well as some works that have all the characteristics of the processing machine, and that seem as colourless and unsatisfactory as the 'classical' works that Hindemith was producing at the same period. In 1948 he began work on what Roman Vlad has described as the culminating work of Stravinsky's neo-classical period, the opera *The Rake's Progress*. As with *The Soldier's Tale*, this work holds the interest—the libretto is a great deal better than the one by Ramuz, in spite of a few absurdities, such as the bread-making machine, and the marriage to the bearded lady—but the music is frequently even less inspired than in *The Soldier's Tale*; there are long 'Mozartian' recitatives that are accompanied by a tuneless plinking on the harpsichord. This would be excusable if they were separated by arias of Mozartian melodic invention; but there is no other work of Stravinsky in which it is so clear that he has no melodic gift of any kind.

Once again Stravinsky found himself at the end of his musical tether. By this time both Schoenberg and Webern were safely dead. Up till this point Stravinsky's name had been mentioned with sneers by the 'serialists', and to have shown any interest in Schoenberg would have seemed a capitulation. But twelve-tone music now provided another avenue of development—the only possible one, in fact. Stravinsky therefore began to experiment with twelve-note procedures. One of the first of these works was a setting of Dylan Thomas's 'Do not go gentle into that good night'. It is intended as a dirge for Thomas, and the instrumentation—string quartet and four trombones—is deliberately lugubrious; but the music itself is completely undirge-like; it rises and falls arbitrarily, and again manages to give the impression of being machine-made. It was something of a mistake on Stravinsky's part to set the text of such a well-known poem, since anyone can grasp the emotion of the poem, and decide whether the music expresses its feeling. He here shows none of the delicate feeling for words that Britten often displays in his setting of poems.

Possibly warned by this experience, Stravinsky returned to the setting of a Latin text in his next major work, the *Canticum Sacrum*, a procedure that had produced one of his most successful operas, *Oedipus Rex*. In its way, *Canticum Sacrum* is as effective as *Oedipus*; the frantic trumpets at the beginning contrast strangely with the 'churchy' associations of the organ and choir (a hint that Britten borrowed for the *War Requiem*). Roman Vlad describes it as 'the most comprehensive . . . synthesis of elements it is possible to imagine at this particular stage in the evolution of European music', and speaks of its various influences: Gregorian chant, Webern, Byzantine modes, polytonality and atonality. One can imagine the late Constant Lambert wrinkling his nose and muttering, 'Pastiche again.' The same basic objection applies to the *Canticum Sacrum* as to the Dylan Thomas poem. In Schoenberg's twelve-note music, one is aware of the underlying romantic emotion; in Stravinsky's, it is difficult to perceive any underlying emotion. There are moments when it becomes moving or exciting—usually moments of sudden contrast, when the old rhythmic Stravinsky breaks through—but for the most part it sounds like ruler-and-compass music.

Since the *Canticum*, Stravinsky has produced two more twelve-note works: *Threni* and *The Flood*. *Threni* is a great deal longer than the *Canticum*, but on the whole the same remarks apply to it. (Once again, it is apparent that Britten has noted certain effects for his *War Requiem*.) According to some critics, it can be regarded as the culmination of Stravinsky's life work, a lofty and inaccessible masterpiece that will not be generally understood for many years. At this stage, it is too early to decide; one can only say that if it is true, then it is the first time in his life that Stravinsky has been lofty and inaccessible; most of his works set out very obviously to make an immediate impact.

Judgement must also be reserved on *The Flood*, a short opera commissioned by television. It is perhaps the worst text that Stravinsky has set since *The Soldier's Tale*. One wonders what to make of passages like this:

> Mother, we beg you all together,
> Come into the ship for fear of the weather.
> The flood is flowing in full fast,
> For fear of drowning we are aghast.

Admittedly, the text is supposed to be a medieval morality play, even so, was Stravinsky unaware of its comic naïvety? Or was this perhaps a part of the intention? If so, the twelve-note music, which sounds mostly as abrupt and disconnected as

Webern, is completely inappropriate and likely to ruin any joke. It is almost as if Stravinsky wanted to test the faith of his admirers by deliberately making himself a sitting target for unbelievers.

When writing about a composer's shortcomings, it is difficult not to sound completely destructive. It seems to me that Stravinsky's development has not been entirely authentic, and that Constant Lambert was right when he said that Stravinsky's chief desire was to remain fashionable and controversial. There is, it seems to me, distinctly an element of insincerity, of the desire to be thought a great composer rather than to become, as far as possible, a complete human being. This insincerity may not be entirely conscious; it is clear from the irregular line of his development that Stravinsky is an exceptionally suggestible person. (And from reading the *Conversations with Robert Craft*, one suspects that Mr Craft may be the Svengali behind some of his most recent metamorphoses.) But it undoubtedly makes it impossible to consider seriously the claims that he is, in the final sense, a 'great composer'.

And yet all this is only to say that Stravinsky will probably be placed one day in the gallery of minor composers, which includes his master Rimsky-Korsakov, and that probably includes Schoenberg himself. This is not to say that his music has not its own authentic value; only that, for the present, this value is enormously overrated.

The problem stated at the beginning of this chapter now presents itself in a new light. The followers of Schoenberg, Hindemith, and Stravinsky can see only that these artists were wholly sincere; they can also point out that they were accomplished musicians, not mere rebels. (Schoenberg and Hindemith both composed classic textbooks on musical composition, and Stravinsky has also written on the 'Poetics of Music'.) Their opponents, on the other hand, are aware mainly of the preposterous mystique that has come to surround these figures, and which is due mainly to intellectual snobbery. Schoenberg's principles of composition are justified because, in many cases, they have produced impressive music; the same goes for

Webern and Berg. But it is preposterous to pretend that therefore serial music has a general and universal validity, and that non-serial composers are betraying their frivolity. Joyce wrote the manuscript of *Finnegans Wake* in different-coloured inks on different-coloured sheets of paper; this does not mean that this method should become *de rigueur* for all serious writers. The most that can be said is that serial music demands a fairly serious approach to composing, and therefore may help to sort the sheep from the goats. But it does not guarantee anything.

The worst aspect of all this is the influence it has had on young composers, who have swallowed their serialism as eagerly as writers of thirty years ago gulped down their Joyce, Eliot, and Proust, and who, in some cases, feel that real originality demands that they go 'beyond Schoenberg' (since, they argue, Schoenberg displayed conservatism in retaining any kind of 'scale'). There was recently published a volume of interviews with British composers, ranging from John Ireland to Peter Racine Fricker and Alexander Goehr, which reveals the kind of total split that exists in the musical world. Thus the interviewer (Murray Schafer) can open his interview with Goehr (born 1932) with the staggering remark: 'In comparison with your European contemporaries you might be called a "reactionary". Your music owes more to Schoenberg than to Webern. . . .' (Goehr sensibly replies that the merit of a composition does not depend on whether it is experimental or not, and that experimentalism has been greatly overstressed.) The result is that the symposium has the curious effect of a volume on philosophy written by a mixture of militant atheists and bigoted Roman Catholics.

The younger composers are hardly to be blamed for this. The need for discipline of some sort is generally felt by all healthy minds, and if their elders assure them dogmatically that Schoenberg may be the greatest composer of all, it is not surprising if they come to accept that serialism is the only serious way of composing. The result is that experimental music becomes an offshoot of the mainstream of music, rather like jazz, and its adherents announce that their method is the only true way of salvation.

All this is not the result of the musical theorizing of Schoenberg, Stravinsky, and Hindemith, but of the systematic over-

83

rating of these interesting minor composers.* (The constant use of the word 'greatness' in connection with Britten is another example.) The result of this overrating is that the argument tends to proceed to extremes, and Henry Pleasants can speak indignantly of 'the twelve-tone aberrations of Boulez and Nono' (neither of whom are serialists), and then go on to suggest that twentieth-century American music, including jazz and the musical, is fundamentally more valuable than European 'serious' music of the same period; while on the other hand a composer like Sibelius is ignored in several reputable volumes on twentieth-century music, and is no longer played on the B.B.C. Third Programme.†

There is, of course, a fundamental fallacy in Mr Pleasants's way of arguing. It is not in the least difficult to show that Beethoven inevitably gave way to Wagner, who in turn gave way to Bruckner and Mahler, who set the scene for twentieth-century music, and that therefore twentieth-century music finds itself in a cul-de-sac from which there is no escape, no possible route for creative development. One is reminded of how literary critics of the forties argued in the same way about the novel and poetry, and ended by pointing to the dearth of important writers since Joyce and Eliot to prove that their diagnosis was correct. The literary revival of the fifties, in America as well as Europe, proved that the real problem was lack of writers with something to say. The same is true of music. Tradition is important; it can enable a minor composer to produce a major work. Conversely, a lack of tradition (or the inheritance of a moribund tradition) produces the 'race for originality' that may prevent a serious composer from finding his feet. (This seems to me to be true of Tippett.) But ultimately the great composer creates what tradition he needs, or manufactures it from odds and ends of other ages. If the music of an age is disappointing, it is for lack of musicians with something important to say rather than because the musical tradition has become enfeebled. History may be to blame, but only individuals with the courage to be subjective can remedy it.

*At the time of writing these words I discover in an obituary of Hindemith the comment that his *Harmony of the World* was a failure, 'and with it failed Hindemith's claim to the sort of greatness achieved in his time only by Schoenberg and Stravinsky'.

†This comment was made in 1964. Since then, in the Sibelius centenary year, the B.B.C. has made up handsomely by playing all Sibelius, even the fine and unrecorded *Kullervo*, his earliest success.

4

THE TRAGEDY
OF BARTÓK

O F T H E major composers of the twentieth century, Bartók is certainly the most difficult to
assess. The reason sounds paradoxical: his
music is too easy to understand. When he died in America in
1945, after years of hardship and illness, the tide suddenly
turned in favour of his music; new recordings piled up, and
within ten years he seems to have occupied the position that
had been enjoyed in the mid-thirties by Sibelius. (This would
probably have delighted Bartók, particularly if he could have
known of the reaction against Sibelius; the Finnish composer
seems to have been one of his antipathies.) Critics were not
slow to talk about the 'tragedy' of his last years and the indifference of the public, with the result that the public hastened to
hear his music and found it enjoyable.

Indeed, it is difficult to understand why his music took so
long to gain appreciation. A few works are 'difficult'—some of
the quartets, the Sonata for solo violin. But most of the others
present no difficulty, once one has grasped the Bartók idiom;
and a few, like the *Dance Suite* and *Divertimento*, are as immediately appealing as the Brahms *Hungarian Dances*. The
works that most critics seem agreed to regard as his best—the
Sonata for two pianos and percussion, the *Music for Strings,
Percussion and Celesta*, the Violin Concerto—are as colourful
and almost as easily assimilable as Dvořák, or at least as his
friend and contemporary Kodály.

Wherein, then, lies the difficulty of assessing Bartók's music?
The problem lies in the word 'assessing'. Certain composers

85

are 'intimate', and easy to get to know for this reason; no doubt this is why many people begin to appreciate music with Chopin or Schumann. Others are less intimate, but their musical personalities emerge clearly enough, as with Beethoven or Wagner. Others may seem so impersonal that it needs a fairly long acquaintance for the listener to be able to *feel* the connection between the music and what the composer wanted to 'say'.

Now where Bartók is concerned the problem is to achieve any kind of insight into the composer's creative processes. One may be impressed by the sound and brilliance of, say, the Violin Concerto, but when it is all over one is uncertain what to feel about it all. No doubt most major violin concertos have this kind of effect on first hearing; and yet even with the concertos of Berg, Hindemith, or Stravinsky, one can get a vague inkling of the basic aim of the musical personality behind the concerto on a first hearing. Somehow, Bartók says everything and yet leaves one wondering whether anything has been said. The effect is most strange. At no point is the musical language 'difficult' in the sense that Schoenberg or Webern can be difficult; and yet when one tries to sum it up afterwards, it seems a foreign language.

Bartók's work tells us little about the man. Like Beethoven's, it divides conveniently into three periods. The early period is experimental, and sometimes the music seems to have been conceived for effect rather than for expressiveness. The middle-period Bartók is an intellectual; the music is complex and difficult. The Bartók of the last ten years has a new simplicity; the work becomes directly and immediately expressive. This is the period of the Violin Concerto, the popular Third Piano Concerto, the Concerto for Orchestra and the unfinished Viola Concerto. Certainly, on the surface, there is evolution enough here, every sign of a serious and interesting composer whose mind never ceased to develop. It has often been pointed out that the six quartets illustrate this development; they were written over a lifetime, and have been described as the most important body of chamber music since Beethoven. The first sounds almost conventional, and shows the influence of German romanticism; the second contains a kind of concentrated essence of folk music; the third is 'polyrhythmic' and seems designed to test the ingenuity of violinists; the fourth, still difficult, is more obviously romantic in feeling; the fifth, one of the largest and most ambitious, is even more lyrical in feeling; the sixth seems relatively simple in texture, and yet is somehow elusive—and the critic may interpret this elusiveness as a sign that Bartók had achieved the kind of sublimation of Beethoven's late quartets.

And yet even in the first five quartets Bartók remains elusive. One might assume that he possessed something of Yeats's power to develop continuously, and that this is revealed in his tireless revision of his means of self-expression—but *what* was he trying to express? One feels in late Beethoven, as in late Mozart, that certain changes in technique reflect a change of temperament, a deepening, a serenity which, in Mozart's case, gives the music a kind of weight without changing its basic quality of gaiety. It is almost as subtle a change as the kind that came over Caruso's voice between 1905 and 1920, a mellowing, an increased assurance. But it is not this quality that distinguishes Bartók's Sixth Quartet from the second or third. Certainly no one would argue that the Concerto for Orchestra (1944) reveals a 'deeper' Bartók than the *Music for Strings, Percussion and Celesta* (1936). The technical changes are obvious enough; but what changes do they signify in Bartók's creative spirit?

Many years ago Ernest Newman expressed the wish that every composer should publish a volume of prose or poetry every three years, so that the intentions of the music would become more apparent. Listening to Bartók's music, one can understand what he meant. But if the composer has no inclination to express himself in prose, one can often learn a great deal by reading books about him, particularly reminiscences by those who knew him well. Eric Fenby's book on Delius reveals things that the most intimate acquaintance with the music would never reveal. And in the case of Bartók this method yields some interesting results.

Bartók struck most of the people who met him as a curiously inexpressive person, remote and aloof. As a small boy he had a skin disease that covered him with sores for six years; during this time he was so ashamed of his appearance that he felt at ease only in his mother's society. The disease ultimately disappeared; instead of becoming less introverted, Bartók spent

87

his nights worrying in case it came back—which apparently it did.

Already the story strikes a Proustian note; it is clear from the beginning that Bartók is one of those with a basic mistrust of life, and a desire to retreat into some inner world of darkness. And this seems to be the recurring pattern of his life—gloomy mistrust and certainty of failure, followed by disaster.

Bartók's father, director of an agricultural college, died when he was seven (in 1888); his mother continued to support her son by school-teaching. Bartók was something of a musical prodigy, displaying an accurate sense of rhythm at the age of three. After several moves, the family (now including a sister) settled in Pozsony, and Bartók studied under Laszlo Erkel, son of the Hungarian national composer Ferencz Erkel (whose operas deserve to be better known in England). Bartók also met Dohnányi, who advised him to study in Budapest; Bartók moved there when he was eighteen (declining a scholarship at the Vienna Conservatoire—presumably his mother was still helping to support him). At first, it looked as if success might come easily. His Richard Straussian *Kossuth Symphony* was performed with great success in 1904, and Bartók took his bow in Hungarian national costume. At this stage he probably thought of becoming a Hungarian Smetana. But a year later, his *Rhapsody* for piano and orchestra was rejected for the Rubinstein prize—the first of a series of failures and misunderstandings that continued to his death.

In Africa, in 1906, Bartók heard some Arab folk music that electrified him; back in Hungary, he investigated Hungarian folk music, and decided that it had a tension and austerity that distinguished it from the cheap modern imitation. From that time Bartók began collecting folk music with his friend Kodály. But as far as his own music was concerned there were many setbacks. Neither critics nor public liked his style, and works like the *Allegro Barbaro* for piano provoked a storm. The *Allegro Barbaro* (1911) is one of the first of the typically Bartókian percussive works; the style is driving, harsh, and violent. Kodály once suggested that this harshness may have been the result of Bartók's rage at the failure to understand his 'gentler' works. The Bartókian percussive style is distinctly his own, although it bears some slight resemblance to the Stravinsky percussive style (the earliest example of which, the King Kaschei dance in *Firebird*, is roughly contemporary with the *Allegro Barbaro*). Its origin is probably the same—an attempt to turn away from his earlier romanticism, to shed his old personality. It was at just about this time that Schoenberg made his leap from the romantic style of the *Verklärte Nacht* to the strange sounds of *Pierrot Lunaire* and *Five Pieces for Orchestra*.

Bartók had been given a piano professorship in 1907, and in 1909, at the age of twenty-eight, he married a sixteen-year-old girl, a pupil. The story of his marriage is typical of Bartók's withdrawn and aloof personality; he spent most of the day with his pupil, then at supper told his mother: 'She will stay; we are married.' And when Dohnányi sent him a note of congratulation he was resentful of this intrusion into his privacy. Fourteen years later Bartók was to abandon his wife for yet another young pupil, who became his second wife Ditta.

There were still many disappointments; his opera *Bluebeard's Castle*, which owes much to Debussy's *Pelléas et Mélisande*, was rejected in 1912, but a ballet, *The Wooden Prince*, was a success in 1917, and *Bluebeard's Castle* followed it. Now it might have seemed that Bartók was at last on the straight road to international recognition. But unfortunately his collaborator, Béla Balazs, was a communist, and when the communist régime fell in 1919, Balazs had to flee the country, and Bartók was blacklisted as a fellow traveller. His ballet *The Miraculous Mandarin* seems to have been deliberately conceived *épater les bourgeois*; the plot is bloody and violent, concerning a mandarin who is murdered by pimps, but consents to die only after he has satisfied his desire with the prostitute; the music is clearly influenced by *The Rite of Spring* (1913) and possibly by Prokofiev's *Scythian Suite* (1914); it is as deafening and spectacular as anything in the orchestral repertoire. But one never feels, as with Prokofiev, that the music is an expression of vitality and noisy energy; it has a certain atmosphere of morbid concentration. And when one compares it with some of the noisier tone-poems of Bartók's early hero Strauss, one feels immediately that Bartók lacks a certain quality of extraversion, expansiveness. The concentration of his music is due to complete self-centredness.

Between 1920 and 1940 he made many concert tours as a

pianist, and gained a reputation as an *avante-garde* composer; he also did a great deal of work on Hungarian folk music with Kodály. During this time he did little work of his own; the few important works are the two piano concertos, the *Cantata Profana*, the *Dance Suite* (1923) and the *Music for Strings, Percussion and Celesta*. Political upheavals worried him; he hated the Nazis so much that he withdrew German texts from all editions of his music. In 1940, after the death of his mother, which affected him deeply, he emigrated to America with his second wife.

The story of his last five years is told in an interesting book, *The Naked Face of Genius*, by Agatha Fassett, who became Ditta Bartók's best friend. Even taking into account the possibility that Miss Fassett may have been a somewhat irritating and naïve person, it still seems that Bartók's manners were generally those of a spoiled child. There are times when his bursts of self-pity bring to mind the hero of Osborne's *Look Back in Anger*. I have had occasion to remark elsewhere that it seems generally true that artists who have to fight their way up 'from the bottom' develop a streak of optimism, while those who have had easy beginnings seem predisposed to defeatism and life-mistrust. Bartók bears this out. Agatha Fassett's first meeting with him seems to have set the tone for their subsequent relationship. Bartók was in ecstasies over a huge round coconut, never having seen one of such a size. (It was actually still in its husk, but Bartók's wife decided not to tell him this—a typical example of her tendency to treat him as a child.) Miss Fassett admitted that she *had* once seen such a coconut, painted as the head of a Red Indian. She was startled at Bartók's instant reaction of disgust and withdrawal; he had sentimental ideas about the Red Indians (although it is still difficult to see why he should have taken offence at her remark).

From Miss Fassett's account, Bartók emerges as conceited, spoilt, and totally self-centred. In every other sentence occur phrases like 'he said coldly', 'he said bitterly', 'he said with quiet anger', etc. The self-pity and tendency to wallow in despair also become apparent; Bartók seems to have shared the chief characteristic of the Old Woman in the Vinegar Bottle in the fairy-tale. His trunks had failed to arrive in America—containing most of his collection of Rumanian folk songs. Bartók refused to be consoled about these, and would not institute enquiries, prefer-

90

ring to believe that nothing could be done. But when the trunks eventually arrived, Miss Fassett records, Bartók emerged from his clouds of pessimism only for a moment; then he declared that they might as well never have arrived, since he had nowhere to store them.

Miss Fassett's account is too long to summarize here; but it is difficult to feel much sympathy for Bartók. Even allowing that he was upset about being uprooted from Hungary, he still seems to have enjoyed seeing things in their worst light. When Miss Fassett found a comfortable and quiet apartment for the Bartóks, and spent weeks helping to furnish it, Bartók did not even bother to say thank you; all he could do was to complain that she had washed a Hungarian tapestry and so prevented him from telling where it came from by its smell. When the Bartóks spent months with Miss Fassett in her summer home, Bartók treated her as a kind of tiresome intruder, and grumbled about the noise of the electricity generator. Again and again his onslaughts on his hostess bring to mind Osborne's psychoneurotic hero. Ditta Bartók seems to have picked up some of her husband's nervous tension, and it is clear from later passages in the book that she became distinctly paranoid at times. They seem to have got Miss Fassett into a state in which she felt constantly apologetic even about wanting to help them. At the same time, she obviously admires Bartók to the point of worship, and she reports his bad-tempered snarls as though they were another authentic expression of 'the naked face of genius'.

It is clear that Miss Fassett regards Bartók as some kind of a mystic. Although he apparently found human beings intolerable and could hardly bear to be civil to them, he rhapsodized about animals, particularly horses and cows, and would talk mystically about dung beetles or maggots in a corpse. It is very difficult to gather from Miss Fassett's book how genuine all this was, and how far it was merely another expression of his homesickness for the countryside of Hungary. It is obvious that Bartók's feeling for his country is deep and intense; but Miss Fassett's account makes it so clear that he loved to wallow in his emotions that one is inclined to feel the same doubt about them all. Homesickness is a valid emotion—even if not suitable to philosophers; but Bartók's again has a morbid intensity that reminds one of a spoiled child. He resents life for not making everything smooth and easy, and turns the resentment on those nearest at hand, while at the same time plunging deeper into his pessimism as if he could somehow spite his fate. The whole exhibition, with which one is at first inclined to sympathize, finally becomes irritating. If Bartók was really a nature mystic, then he should surely have been less bad-tempered and fretful than he was. William Blake and Jakob Boehme met with a great deal less recognition and appreciation than Bartók, but both managed to stay cheerful.

All this is not, of course, to say that Bartók might not be a great composer. Most of the great writers of our century have been highly neurotic—Proust, Joyce, and D. H. Lawrence come to mind. But it surely means that *if* he was a great composer, then his greatness was of a completely different kind from Beethoven's. Beethoven himself was a highly disagreeable man, and no doubt some contemporary Agatha Fassett could have written a scathing book about his bad manners, ingratitude, etc. But although the faults of Beethoven are undeniably regrettable —whatever sentimentalists say, he would have been a greater man without them—most of them can be understood in the light of the strains under which he lived, his deafness, ugliness, social uncouthness, loneliness. And there is a total lack of self-pity about Beethoven. When his playing made his friends weep Beethoven remarked: 'The fools . . . They are not artists. Artists are made of fire: they do not weep.' This difference is quite fundamental, the most fundamental difference there can be between two human beings.

It is possible that a certain superficial similarity of style has led some critics to compare Beethoven and Bartók. Bartók's style has sometimes been described as 'hard', 'muscular', to describe its lack of romanticism; Beethoven also struck his contemporaries as hard and unromantic. It might be said loosely that both their styles are 'assertive'. But having said this, it becomes clear that Beethoven's assertiveness is only a part of his personality, its exterior, as it were. The first impression his music gives is of hardness and strength; but one soon begins to discover the other Beethovens; there is Beethoven the lyricist, Beethoven the rhapsodist, Beethoven the pastoralist, the predecessor of Bruckner's symphonies; finally, there is Beethoven the mystic. In Bartók there is no equivalent of the sudden melodies that bubble up as pure life-affirmation, as natural as the song of a bird, and above all, no equivalent of the Beethoven of the *Heilige Dankgesang*. Bartók never seems to let himself go. The Sixth Quartet occasionally brings to mind the Beethoven of the last quartets, particularly in the serene final movement; but the comparison reveals how unexpressive Bartók is by comparison. He not only never wears his heart on his sleeve; he seems to have deposited it in some bank vault. The surface of his music is always technically impressive, as the surface of Joyce's *Ulysses* is always technically impressive; but Bartók the human being never emerges.

I have cited Joyce as a comparison elsewhere, in speaking of Schoenberg. From the point of view of the existential critic, one of the most interesting things about Joyce is the way that he turned himself into a major writer by sheer discipline. The early Joyce wore his heart on his sleeve and sang sentimental Irish songs; the Dublin literary set found his conceit and gaucheness unacceptable; so Joyce went into exile, muttering, 'I'll show them.' He *did* show them; what is more, he showed all artists for evermore what can be done by concentrating all the will-power on creating a great book. But what is most interesting to the existential critic is not the extraordinary achievement of *Ulysses*, or even *Finnegans Wake*, but the fact that the emotional world of the early *Stephen Hero* is identical with the emotional world of Shem the Penman. One of the most moving passages of the *Wake* is Shem's expression of his credo (as Mercius, p. 193); but in substance, it says no more than Stephen Dedalus said at the end of the *Portrait of the Artist as a Young Man*. Buck Mulligan was right when he told Haines in *Ulysses* that Stephen would never capture the Attic note, the joy of creation ('Wandering Rocks', section 16). Joyce is trapped for ever in his intensely subjective world; he can never create out of self-forgetfulness, as a Tolstoy or Goethe; to write well, he must write of himself, relate everything to himself.

The same would seem to be true of Bartók. Of the works generally known to the public (that is, available on record), only the early piano *Rhapsody* and the First Quartet reveal an 'open' personality. Both these works tend to get dismissed by Bartók's admirers as juvenilia. But the quartet at least is one of his most appealing works; it has a feeling of youthful energy and optimism

that he never recaptured. It dates from his twenty-seventh
year, three years after his first disappointment at the rejection of
the piano *Rhapsody*; but the barriers do not yet seem to have
gone up, and the music has a lyrical flow, and little of the later
percussive mannerism, except towards the end. For the next ten
years, Bartók tried on various 'masks'. As always when a
romantic personality deliberately represses its romanticism,
there is an undercurrent of violence. In *Bluebeard's Castle* we are
in the ambiguous half-world of Maeterlinck and Debussy
(Balázs's treatment was based on a Maeterlinck play), but lit
with a sickly red light. In *The Miraculous Mandarin* the sickly
dream has changed into nightmare. In the ballet *The Wooden
Prince* (Bartók's first success—again in collaboration with
Balázs) the story itself, in spite of some curious morbid touches,
has an undercurrent of radiance and optimism. It concerns a
prince who falls in love with a princess; she rejects him, but is
immediately attracted by a wooden image of him, which is
brought to life by a fairy (here the morbid element appears).
But when the prince falls asleep the forest comes to life at the
fairy's order and pours renewed life into the prince. Now the
princess pursues him while he flees; she humiliates herself before
him, and he finally takes her in his arms. Bartók clothes this
legend of man's servitude to appearances in music that is reminiscent of the Stravinsky of *The Firebird* and *Petroushka*. But it is
clear that he is more at home with the early part of the ballet,
describing the prince's symbolic frustration (which has something of a Kafka-esque dream about it), than in describing the
happiness of the lovers at the end. It is also clear that Bartók will
never capture the 'Attic note, the joy of creation'. In connection
with this ballet, Serge Moreux speaks penetratingly of 'compensatory psychic activity, which should not . . . surprise us in
a man at once tormented and driven on by a fundamental inner
dualism'.

Although Bartók's output falls off in quantity between 1920
and 1935, this period contains some of the works that are usually
described as his masterpieces: the fine Second Sonata for violin
and piano, the *Cantata Profana* (based on a fairy-tale about nine
sons of a woodman who are changed into stags), the *Music for
Strings, Percussion and Celesta*. The first two Piano Concertos
are also among Bartók's most characteristic work. And yet

although the Bartókian style is now fully developed, these works are more puzzling than anything that has come earlier. In certain respects they bring to mind Stravinsky's later music using serial techniques; it is obviously music, and technically accomplished music; but what is it saying? (Sometimes the sound is somewhat Stravinskian, in the son's monologue in the *Cantata Profana*, for example.) One of the chief characteristics of Bartók's music, from *Bluebeard* to the Concerto for Orchestra, is the alternation of curiously muted passages with noisily assertive ones. In the 'muted' passages it seems to be Bartók's determination to keep the music in a minor key, to keep it ambiguous, as if he is determined not to be trapped into making any definite statement. Then, as if by way of proving that he can be as definite as anyone when he likes, he flings down startling percussive passages. (This technique can be noted particularly in the Sonata for two pianos and percussion.) And yet there is a feeling of sleight of hand, as if a clever politician is apparently giving a straight answer to a straight question and yet succeeding in saying nothing at all. The assertiveness is there in the manner, but what is it asserting?

This tendency is related to another characteristic, which is also shared at times by Hindemith. Hindemith may start a work (like the 'Harmony of the World' Symphony) with an exciting statement, but within five minutes we are merely listening to the Hindemith voice droning on, weaving patterns of sound that are no doubt of interest to the music student, but which seem curiously uneventful to the listener. Bartók can also start with these arresting statements, as in the Violin Concerto or the third movement of the Sonata for two pianos, but within a few minutes the ambiguous Bartók is back; the music is recognizably Bartók—that is to say, it follows technical procedures that we recognize as his—and yet somehow the content is elusive.

Some years ago a rather bad recording of the *Cantata Profana* was issued (on the American Period label) with Prokofiev's cantata *Your Health* (written in honour of Stalin's sixtieth birthday) on the other side, and the contrast underlines this feeling of Bartók's inexpressiveness. Prokofiev's *Zdravitsa*, op. 85, is one of his popular works, to be classified with *Alexander Nevsky* and the Seventh Symphony; it has one beautiful melody which is extended for a quarter of an hour. And yet it has the feeling of 'openness' about it; it expresses what it has to express with no feeling of interposing barriers between listener and composer. Bartók's work would be judged by most standards as in every way more important than Prokofiev's—and so it is. Prokofiev might be accused here of fake simplicity and naïveté. Even so, it is impossible not to feel that Prokofiev is speaking in his own person, with his own voice, as uninhibitedly as Mozart, while Bartók is concealed behind some great mask of technique, like the actors of ancient times behind their *personae*.

The problem of which one is constantly aware on reading Agatha Fassett's book is: Was Bartók a real mystic or a pseudo-mystic? This is closely related to the whole question of Bartók's 'mask'. Miss Fassett was willing to be impressed when he talked of the 'warm friendly smell of sleeping horses and cows', about his feelings for the poor peasants, the sufferings of animals, etc. But for much of the time his fads seem a mere handle with which to beat Miss Fassett. For example, when Miss Fassett had found him an apartment and helped to furnish it, Bartók admitted grudgingly that it was 'truly miraculous' how she had managed to furnish it for so little, and in such a short time, then added immediately, 'Yet the very ease with which you've done it strikes me as somehow immoral.' He then goes into a sentimental harangue about poor Hungarian peasants who are forced to make their own furniture piece by piece. It never seemed to strike him that this had no relevance whatever to Miss Fassett's achievement. If there was possibly a dark side of anything to look upon, then Bartók sniffed around until he had found it.

In the same way, Bartók professed to be a great lover of animals, and was furious with Miss Fassett when the ironing-board collapsed and crushed a kitten; he took the other kittens back to New York with him. When eventually these fell ill and died Miss Fassett presented Bartók with another kitten, but he declined to take any interest in it. Ditta commented of the new kitten: 'It hurts me to see how good he is, and how hard he has to work for a little love. He feels so uncertain and always a bit afraid. . . .' This kitten was later given away, and immediately fled from its new owners, probably dying in the midst of New York. The animal-lover Bartók was not willing to keep on handing out affection to strange cats. This suggests that Bartók's love was not something that flowed from him naturally, but an inverted form of self-love, an offshoot of pride and egoism.

It seems possible, then, that Bartók's talk about the life in a pat of cow-dung was simply another complex emotion built up from homesickness, desire to impress, and dislike of urban life. (Another sign of Bartók's romanticism was this anti-modernism, as emotional and vague as Morris's medievalism.)

These questions take us to the heart of the problem of artistic creation. The basic impulse behind all art is the artist's need to broaden his personality. It is as if the artist had a kind of internal bulldozer, broadening the foundations of his mind, and the rubble that is cleared out is the work of art, a by-product of an internal process. This may not have been true of Homer or the old ballad singers, who felt the same impulse to create that a good carpenter or wood carver feels to work with his hands. But it is certainly true of most romantic and post-romantic art. The romantic, as Nietzsche pointed out, is peculiarly susceptible to self-disgust that may reach a point where a Van Gogh attempts to cut off his own ear or an Andreyev shoots himself through the hand. This means that *the romantic aims at expressing himself in such a way that, if possible, his own voice shall be strange to him.* Hence Rimbaud experimented with new uses of language; then, when even this failed to free him from self-disgust, deliberately donned a new and self-destructive personality from which the poet had been excluded. The same motive lies behind Joyce's linguistic innovations and behind Schoenberg's creation of the twelve-tone technique.

Bartók turned to the past for his 'strangeness'. Agatha Fassett quotes him as saying that as a child he had 'an awareness of being confined within certain uncomfortable boundaries'—his own personality. He also described his first experience of Arab music. 'I went into a dark and dingy inn and, happy to lean back and rest, I almost fell asleep in that musty heavy-smelling atmosphere. But all at once I found myself fully awake, startled and whipped into wild attention, as there came to my ears the singing of a group of old men. I could barely see through the smoky mist at the other end of the room. Listening to their songs and their unknown Arab words, I was overcome by something of such significance for me that I knew instantly this would have to be followed up and investigated to the utmost, even if it should take my entire lifetime.' Here was a language that, if he could only learn it, would give him an entirely different voice. So far (this was in 1906) his music had been influenced by Strauss, Erkel, and Liszt; this music could give his language a flavour of originality. One of the characteristics of Hungarian peasant music that impressed him most was its terseness and freedom from ornament. (Most folk poetry also has this pre-romantic terseness; compare, for example, the Scottish ballad *Helen of Kirconnel* with Wordsworth's long-winded and enfeebled version of it.) It seemed an excellent language for expressing a new anti-romanticism. This element became the chief ingredient of Bartók's style, and it is the Bartókian counterpart of the twelve-tone system. The result is that Bartók's music is easily recognizable from a few bars; and since his language is closer to ordinary tonality than Schoenberg's or Stravinsky's, much of his music is immediately striking, uniquely flavoured, and well deserves its place in the concert repertories. It is when one comes to assessing Bartók's stature as a composer that the difficulties arise. A unique language is all very well, but a major composer must also have something to say in it. It is true that music can never say things in the same way as prose; still, it can express the composer's developing vision of the world, and the chemical changes in his own personality. Stravinsky's declaration that music cannot express anything is mere evasiveness, an attempt to disarm criticism of works of his own that fail to 'say anything'. Beethoven's music is a commentary on his development as a human being. Any attempt to apply this standard to Bartók's works—even to the quartets—meets with bafflement.

The fundamental question raised by Bartók's music is the one that has recurred elsewhere in this volume: how far is it necessary for a great composer to be a great man? The self-evident answer would seem to be that a great composer *must* be a great man in some sense, since a composer is a human being, or an aspect of one. In that case, in what sense does the great artist have to be a great man? It can be argued that the greatness need become apparent only when he is creating; but if that is so, what connection does it have with the rest of his personality?

There is one answer that covers the whole problem. Greatness is a form of life-affirmation, when life is understood to mean 'spirit' rather than everyday activity. When William Blake wrote:

> The Angel that presided o'er my birth
> Said, 'Little creature, formed of joy and mirth,
> Go love without the help of anything on earth',

he was expressing an ultimate form of human greatness. Everyday consciousness tends to be confined to a single state, or small number of states, and consequently the mind is inclined to believe that it 'knows the world' when it actually knows only one aspect of it. The result is boredom and life-failure. Art has the power, possessed by alcohol and certain drugs, to remove some of the mind's filters so that the world is seen to be a more varied and interesting place than one had supposed. Blake was only expressing this in an extreme form when he suggested that mysticism is seeing 'a world in a grain of sand'. With sufficient control over consciousness, a grain of sand could provide material for a lifetime of contemplation. But human beings live in a kind of mental strait jacket without ever being aware of it; they are forced to look perpetually in one direction, like a paralysed man facing a window. Great artists achieve a little freedom by a lifetime of discipline, and with the use of the scaffolding of language (whether it is the language of music, painting or speech).

Unfortunately, all human beings are 'spoilt'. To some extent adversity stimulates them, but a point always comes when they refuse to make any more effort. It is like a tired child who demands to be carried. Beethoven had hard beginnings, so that he was closer to Blake's ideal of loving 'without the help of anything on earth'; that is, feeling a basic delight simply in being alive, whether life chooses to carry one or not. His fundamental demands on life were low, and his vitality was consequently high, because it was easy to receive more than he expected. Bartók was far more spoilt from the beginning. He spent his whole life being spoilt by women, demanding total attention, total affection, and getting it. Like most egotists, he felt little sense of his responsibility towards other people; his own pleasure seemed the most important thing in the world. (His desertion of his first wife when a younger and prettier girl turned up would seem to support this view.) Considering the early closeness of his relationship with his mother—which retained its Proustian intensity all his life—he was lucky that he never became homosexual; but he seems to have developed characteristics of one of the most unpleasant types of homosexual: self-centredness and a tendency to become absorbed in trivialities. In an important way Bartók never became adult. It is notable that when Agatha Fassett describes his somewhat infrequent good moods she always remarks on his childlike quality, the impulsive smile (kept as a reward for his women-folk), the tendency to do or say whatever came into his head. Bartók was a very long way from loving without the help of anything on earth; everything had to be just so, or he sulked. One feels that, like a child, he was constantly looking for people to blame for his misfortunes. He had, after all, every reason to be fairly cheerful. He had made many earlier trips to the United States, so it was not entirely a strange country. He had a job waiting for him at Columbia, even though it seemed at first that this would last only for six months. (Actually he still held the appointment at his death.) His music might not be widely appreciated, but much of it was on record, and there were fairly frequent opportunities to play it over the radio or at concerts. Even so, he had no sense of judgement of how much an audience could take; and when a well-meaning friend gently reproached him for performing whole Bartók concerts, he thought that this proved that he was a neglected and misunderstood genius. He had many musical friends willing to help spread his reputation and perform his music. Altogether, in spite of minor discomforts and inconveniences, he had every reason to feel grateful to his adopted country, and to anticipate even greater benefits (his reputation was rising steeply at the time of his death). Instead, he seems to have sunk into a state of irritable apathy that ended by making even his devoted wife paranoiac. It is difficult not to feel that his illness was, to some extent, psychological; he reminds one of those African savages who are reputed to be able to sit down and die simply by stopping all life impulses.

Since his death there has arisen the legend of the 'Bartók tragedy'. The Americans are accused of inviting this man of genius to their country, as they had earlier invited Schoenberg, and then allowing him virtually to starve to death. The facts hardly support this. Bartók was a singularly unfriendly person;

his aloof and irritable personality hardly invited help. In fact he received generous help and support. He was not an old man when he came to America—only forty-nine. There was not even a question of making a new start, since he was well known as a concert pianist. Instead, he chose to behave as if the malicious fates had wrecked his life, and the whole world was in on the conspiracy. The real tragedy of Bartók occurred in his childhood, when his mother spoiled him into thinking he was the centre of the universe.

5

TWO MYSTICS—
SCRIABIN AND BLOCH

THE TWO men whose names appear above are at the moment as unfashionable as they could be. Most of Scriabin's major works are not even available on record in England, while the work that is sometimes regarded as Bloch's masterpiece—the Piano Quintet—is not, as far as I know, available in any record catalogue in the world.

The case of Scriabin is a strange one. Fifty years ago a thoroughly respectable English music critic, Eaglefield Hull, wrote a book in which he took it for granted that Scriabin was, without qualification, one of the greatest names in musical history; today, any critic who even hinted as much would display a boldness approaching insanity.

Alexander Scriabin, the most controversial musical personality of the early twentieth century, was born on Christmas Day 1871. His mother soon died of consumption, and he was brought up by an aunt who spoiled him. He was small, pale, delicate, and good-looking; from the beginning he showed signs of being a musical prodigy. It seemed that Scriabin was to be a darling of destiny. His extraordinary intelligence brought him abundant admiration. He was sent to a military school, but he thoroughly enjoyed it. Influential relatives secured his exemption from drill; his unusual personality made him well liked by his fellow cadets in spite of his effeminacy. At the age of twelve he decided to make a career of music; as usual, he got his own way, and was sent to the Moscow Conservatoire, where one of his fellow pupils was Rachmaninov. He was an irritating and somewhat spoilt pupil, who could play the most difficult music at sight, but who could not be bothered with the exercises set by his professors. When he was refused a request to work shorter hours (which Rachmaninov had been granted) he left the Conservatoire in a pet. When his right hand became paralysed it looked as if his hope of becoming a pianist might be at an end; but he managed to restore it to use by constant exercise, and eventually became one of the best-known pianists in Europe. Everything came easily. He loved the music of Chopin, and his early piano works were little more than imitations of Chopin. However, they won the praise of serious critics, and in his early twenties his name became known to a small but discerning public. He had several love affairs and a few disappointments in love, then married a young pianist at the age of twenty-six. They produced two children, and for about a year had a rather hard time of it, although Scriabin found work as a professor at the Conservatoire. He disliked the drudgery; he wanted to do creative work. He was a small, dandyish-looking man who wore extravagant fancy waistcoats and a small, pointed beard. He was as interested in philosophy and religion as in music; he read Nietzsche, Dostoevsky, and Soloviev—a remarkable Russian mystic—and dreamed of somehow unifying philosophy, literature, and music. A piano concerto was still somewhat Chopinesque, while a first symphony was rather Wagnerian. One of his first really individual works was the large-scale Third Piano Sonata, ending with a magnificent climax.

He decided to travel, and was helped by a rich pupil, who offered him an annuity for as long as he needed it. Another admirer, Belaiev, also contributed a great deal of money during the next few years. Scriabin was able to live on the shores of Lake Geneva, at Vesenaz, and work on his strange ideas, and on music that was supposed to express them. The first of these works was the Third Symphony or *Divine Poem*. Like much of his earlier piano music, this is a music of tension and sensuality; it derives from *Tristan and Isolde*, but it lacks Wagner's melodic impulse. Scriabin came to believe he was a Messiah, and even preached a sermon to the waves of Lake Geneva from a boat. The beautiful young sister of his pupil Boris Schloezer, Tatiana, came to stay with them and became an ardent disciple. Soon she became Scriabin's mistress. Scriabin decided to leave his devoted wife and lived with Tatiana, even though his wife had sacrificed

103

her career for him, borne him children, and devoted herself entirely to his music and his welfare. He told her that his destiny required solitude, and went off to Paris. Tatiana quickly followed him. With incredible loyalty, his wife continued to devote herself to his music; she became a professor of the piano at the Conservatoire and gave many concerts of his music.

A concert tour in America was at first successful, then turned to failure when Tatiana arrived; the puritanical Americans were shocked by the relationship. Back in Russia, Scriabin had become one of the most controversial figures of his time. He believed that the human race was close to some great apocalypse when spirit would finally overcome matter, and man would become a god. This was to be achieved through a union of music, religion, and all the other arts. Scriabin would write a great 'mystery', to be performed somewhere in a temple; he would start a kind of religious colony for true believers. His music became increasingly tumultuous and tempestuous. His Fourth Symphony, the *Poem of Ecstasy*, was even more sensual than the *Divine Poem*. It shows some of the limitations of Scriabin's musical ideas. He has only one note: ecstasy; the work tries to be a long-drawn-out sexual orgasm; but to the casual hearer, that is to say, the hearer who is not willing to contribute his own nervous ecstasy to the music, it sounds like a slightly more sensual Delius, with little melody to speak of. It is the furthest extreme of pure romantic music, as far as one can imagine from Haydn and Mozart. And it is hard to see how any development is possible.

Scriabin produced one more symphony, *Prometheus: a Poem of Fire*, which is not very different from the *Poem of Ecstasy*, except that it tries to be even more ecstatic. Scriabin was aware that his music could go no farther, and wanted the music accompanied by a 'colour organ', colours thrown on to a screen, blending into one another like shapes in a mist. What he really wanted, of course, was some kind of religious orgy in which the audience could participate, possibly with drugs and sexual rites. All this gave him a strange reputation, which excited the young intellectuals of the years before the First World War. Petersburg was a city of dreams, preoccupied with debauchery and mysticism; Scriabin was regarded as a kind of artistic Rasputin. Many suspected him of witchcraft; it was said that Tatiana had given birth to a monster. Everyone assumed that he spent his life

possessing his female disciples one after another. In fact his life
seems to have been relatively blameless; he continued to live
with Tatiana, having now taken a house in Moscow (where he
lived until his death, when it became the Scriabin museum). He
still dreamed of his Mystery, but his inspiration was drying up.
Whether it had dried up permanently, or whether he might have
gone on to produce other kinds of music—perhaps operas or
sacred music—can only be guessed at; he died of blood poison-
ing, due to a boil on the lip, in 1915, at the age of forty-four.

Nowadays, Scriabin is represented in the record catalogues
(in America, at least) by the last three symphonies, the Piano
Concerto (an early and uncharacteristic work), and by a great
deal of piano music. In this latter field he is unsurpassed, and his
future fame will rest securely on it. Much of the early music is
Chopinesque, and yet its quality is quite unlike Chopin. I personally prefer Scriabin. Chopin's piano music has delicacy and
precision; one can understand why the author of *A Musical
Pilgrim's Progress* came to love it so much. But it is no deroga-
tion to say that its mood is usually of gentle melancholy, sometimes of self-pity, and that one is always aware that it is the
music of a sick and over-sensitive man. One must feel a kinship
between Chopin's personality and one's own really to love his
music; it is intensely personal and individual. There is a great
deal of Chopin that I enjoy; all the same, a little Chopin goes a
long way with me. Scriabin, on the other hand, has a glint of
madness in his eye. The music may sound superficially like
Chopin; but it is really quite different. It is not personal, and it
has no self-pity. (Why should it have? Scriabin was an exceptionally lucky man.) Its delicacy is impersonal, like a Japanese
painting. Rimsky-Korsakov sneered about its unhealthy eroti-
cism, and called the composer mad. He was not entirely wrong.
It is a music of sex and sensuality, but it strives to pass beyond
these into contemplation of man and the universe. Scriabin was
fond of talking about good and evil, the creative agony, lust for
life. 'The tortured universe awaits a miracle', he wrote. This is
conveyed more powerfully in the piano music than in the symphonies—the composer's metaphysical preoccupation. As he
grew older the piano music became steadily more individual,
until in the Ninth and Tenth Sonatas he is really writing orchestral music transcribed for the piano—or perhaps it would be

equally true to say that his piano music is a more successful realization of the ideas of his orchestral music. Scriabin has an astonishing talent for making the piano behave like an orchestra, in relatively small works like the *Étude* in C sharp minor, op. 42, no. 5, as well as in full-scale sonatas. He has an almost perfect interpreter in Horowitz, who has recorded much of his music, including the magnificent Third Sonata.*

Much can be said against Scriabin. He was a small man and therefore aggressive and egoistic, a dandy, something of a libertine, selfish, irritating. One writer has referred to his later orchestral works as musical masturbation, and this is not entirely unfair. If the great test of a creative musician is how long he can go on developing, then Scriabin fails. It is difficult to see how he could have gone on developing beyond the *Poem of Fire*, except by plunging deeper into musical sensationalism and decadence. Although he talked of the Mystery for the last five years of his life, he seems to have done nothing about composing it. In some ways he brings to mind the Marquis de Sade, placing more and more importance on sensual indulgence until sensuality becomes distorted and overloaded, and he reaches the absurdities of the *120 Days of Sodom*. Scriabin was, to some extent, on the wrong track; when he had pulled out all the stops he looked for more stops to pull out instead of recognizing the need for a new discipline. For all this, he was one of the most interesting minds of his time; he had a kind of boldness that had been absent from European music since Wagner, and from European literature since Schiller. The reason that he is exciting, in spite of the obvious crankiness of some of his views, is that he was somehow in the mainstream of evolutionary thought. His great Mystery (which was to be presented by two thousand white-robed performers) would mark 'the end of this stage of human consciousness', and place man on the road to a new freedom. He saw instinctively that, in a profound sense, man does not yet exist; he is still almost entirely animal—material whose aims and purposes are almost wholly biological. Yet he has a scrap of another kind of motive, a motive that transcends any need for mere survival or dominance (although cynics like to suggest that

*In England there is available an excellent recording of the 24 Preludes, op. 11 (a relatively early work), by Julius Isserlis, on DEL 12022; this gives an excellent idea of Scriabin's range and the fertility of his pianistic invention.

all man's spiritual and intellectual urges are only another form of the need for dominance). Wells once said that he did not wish to go on living unless his life could become completely geared to that need for more consciousness. It seems possible that the human race is producing a creature who needs this new kind of freedom as urgently as he needs air, and cannot bear life without it (I have elsewhere called such men 'outsiders'). Scriabin, for all his egoism and selfishness, was one of them.

The case of Ernst Bloch is also a curious one. Son of a Swiss clock-maker, he composed his first symphony at the age of twenty-two (in 1902). Unable to gain a hearing in Paris, he returned to Switzerland and entered his father's business, continuing to compose at night. An opera, *Macbeth*, was performed in 1910, and gained Bloch the friendship of one of the greatest music critics of our time, Romain Rolland. In 1916 Bloch went to America and lived there for the rest of his life, relatively comfortably off, fairly well patronized by American orchestras and foundations, and yet no longer one of the fashionable composers. He died in 1959, and it might be said with little exaggeration that his name was forgotten by that time. Certainly he was one of the 'unmentionables' with the intellectual music critics.

This is strange. I have discovered that if I play a composition of Bloch to someone who has never heard of him—say the *Three Jewish Poems* or the Violin Concerto—he usually produces an effect of revelation; the auditor will say: 'Who on earth is that?' and then, 'But why isn't he better known?' This music has a power and authority that is as undeniable, although of a completely different kind, as that of the early Sibelius.

There are two reasons. First, Bloch began as a 'modernist' with an immense and difficult First String Quartet, and his Second String Quartet was found so impressive by Ernest Newman that he compared it to the late Beethoven quartets. If Bloch had continued as a modernist, he would undoubtedly have become as fashionable as Schoenberg or Stravinsky, particularly as he possessed a gift for powerful emotional expression that is more reminiscent of Berg. It may be that America had the same effect on Bloch that it later had on Kurt Weill—of causing him to aim at popularity, at easy communication, and so knocking the backbone out of his inspiration. At all events—and this is the second reason—Bloch not only 'popularized'; he sometimes wrote music that sounds as if it was commissioned by Hollywood for an epic called 'How the West Was Won'.

This is the paradox about Bloch. Take an intelligent music lover for whom Bloch is only a name (and there are thousands) and play him the last movement of *America, an Epic Rhapsody*, and he will wrinkle his nose and hazard a guess that it is by Ferde Grofé, or perhaps even Jerome Kern trying to sound grandiose. (It solemnly uses tunes like 'Swanee River' and 'Pop Goes the Weazel', with the full symphonic treatment, and must be one of the most agonizing things ever perpetrated by a first-rate composer.) Play him the First String Quartet or the Piano Quintet, and he will probably have no hesitation in saying that here is a composer who certainly ranks with Bartók and Schoenberg.

In defence of Bloch, it should be pointed out that works like *America* and the *Israel* Symphony were written long before the talkies were invented, and so can be acquitted of trying to sound like film music (or of unconsciously assimilating its influence). After all, the flowing melody from Vaughan Williams's *Wasps* overture is frequently used in cowboy films, which does not prevent it from being an extremely beautiful melody in its own right. Still, it must be conceded that Bloch is a most puzzling mixture, and extremely difficult to place.

Primarily, he is a Jewish romantic. Much of his music has an exotic, oriental flavour reminiscent of Rimsky-Korsakov. The *Israel* Symphony and *Three Jewish Poems* are at least as good as *Schéhérazade*. But the mention of the *Israel* Symphony brings to mind another objection. Bloch frequently sets words in his symphonic music, and the result is thoroughly unhappy. He seems to have natural bad taste, of the disconcerting kind that Schoenberg revealed in his *Survivor from Warsaw* and *Ode to Napoleon*. The words used in the *Israel* Symphony might be bearable if Bloch had set Hebrew words with religious associations; instead, he has written his own 'poem', with lines like 'O I implore thee, O my Elohim, Thou art my refuge'. The lines are not actually bad, but they are trite, and their evocative power is so far below that of the music that they cannot help being a 'come down'. In the same way, *America* ends with a preposterous hymn, 'America! America! Thy name is in my heart', which he expects the audience to join in. There is an element of almost unbelievable psychological miscalculation here, of the same kind that is shown in his use of 'Pop Goes the Weazel' (which for most of us has more or less comic associations) in the middle of the 'symphonic rhapsody'. (The American record company that issued *America*—Vanguard—have shown the same kind of miscalculation by ending with a tape recording of the composer's voice, which sounds like a parody; the whole second side of this record sounds as if it were made at a Gerard Hoffnung concert.)

Undoubtedly, this is the kind of thing that stopped Bloch from being taken seriously after about 1920. His music continued to be widely played; there was even a Bloch society. But the name Bloch no longer had the same modernist associations as Schoenberg or Stravinsky. This is somewhat unfair, for Bloch did even more than Berg to make modern music acceptable to a wide public. He seems to be at his best in chamber music—the five quartets, the Piano Quintet, the fine Piano Sonata, the suite for violin and piano *Baal Shem*—and most of his chamber music combines intellectual intensity with passion. Many of the larger works deserve to be better known to concert audiences. The *Three Jewish Poems* sound as exotic as *Schéhérazade*, but have more musical content. The Violin Concerto stands with those of Berg, Schoenberg, Bartók, Shostakovich, and Hartmann as one of the finest of this century; again, much of the flavour is exotic and Jewish. Two of the best-known orchestral works are the 'cello 'rhapsodies', *Schelomo* and *Voice in the Wilderness*. Both are impressive on a first hearing. My own experience is that, after several hearings, they strike one as strongly emotional, but, unlike the quartets, are low in intellectual content; they stand somewhere midway between the quartets and a work like *America*. (Significantly, the original title of *Voice in the Wilderness* was 'Visions and Prophecies'.)

One of the most interesting things about much of Bloch's orchestral music is that it sounds so English. It is amusing to ask some musical friend to guess the composer of *Voice in the Wilderness* or parts of *America* or the *Israel* Symphony. At times Vaughan Williams is an obvious guess, no doubt because both composers have an interest in 'mysticism'. But elsewhere one might guess Delius, Holst, or even Bax. This applies particularly to the music of Bloch's middle period, from his arrival in America until about 1930. (He was earlier under the influence of the German romantics—Bruckner, Strauss, Mahler, and others.)

In his 'third period', which dates approximately from 1930, Bloch attempted to leave behind some of the emotionalism of the earlier works—perhaps affected by adverse criticism—and produced some less programmatic music. But it would not be accurate to speak of Bloch's 'classical period'. His best-known classical work, the first *Concerto Grosso* (written as an exercise for his students, rather in the manner of Handel) was written in 1925, while the Violin Concerto (1938) and Piano Concerto (1948), both highly romantic works, fall in the middle of the 'classical' period.

The two *Concerti Grossi* are deservedly among Bloch's most popular works. Writing in the style of a past era seemed to free his musical inspiration, so there is no feeling of a musical exercise here, as in Stravinsky's *Pulcinella* or Britten's 'Purcell' Variations; the music is sometimes clashing and discordant, always exciting. The second *Concerto Grosso* is less emotional than the first, but equally delightful in its way. The opening is extraordinarily Elgarian, and again this impression of English music persists throughout. A third Concerto Grosso, to be written in a more modern style, became the *Sinfonia Breve*, which I personally find the least interesting of the three. The first two are superbly recorded by Howard Hanson, and the disk makes the best of all introductions to the music of Bloch; it is difficult to imagine anyone, modernist or classicist, disliking it.

There are two other major works of Bloch that are obtainable on record: the *Sacred Service*, and the *Concerto symphonique* for piano and orchestra. The first is deservedly well known, but to some extent the same objection applies to it as to *America* and the *Israel* Symphony; the passionately romantic music is ideally suited for parts of the Jewish service; but as soon as a voice with an American accent begins to preach against the musical background, the effect is somewhat spoilt (particularly as the preacher prays for the day 'when superstition shall no longer enslave the mind'). However, it undoubtedly contains some of Bloch's finest music. This, unfortunately, is not true of the *Concerto symphonique*, which does not live up to such an imposing title. The music is very pleasant indeed; the work does not deserve to be regarded as one of Bloch's failures. But it is no masterpiece; the musical thinking seems loose; its feeling seems closer than ever to Delius.

Another fine work that should be mentioned is the 1918 Suite for Viola and Piano, written two years after the First String Quartet and sharing some of its qualities; this has also been excellently recorded on a Supraphon disk.

In the last analysis, Bloch is not a great composer. Yet he is one of the finest composers of the twentieth century, and has produced more individual and immediately appealing music than anyone except Sibelius. His current neglect is another of those absurd fashions that will seem so incomprehensible to our grand-children.

6

THE NATURE AND
SPIRIT OF JAZZ

LET ME begin these remarks on the nature of jazz with a few comments on my own history of 'jazz appreciation'. Unlike most jazz lovers, I cannot say I first enjoyed jazz as a child. As a child, I was somewhat snobbish about jazz—in fact, it annoyed me. I saw the film *Stormy Weather* at the age of nine, but it had on me no such impact as *Fantasia* had only a few years later. And I can remember being affronted for twenty-four hours after hearing a song called 'Why don't cher do right?' on the radio; it seemed needlessly nasty and vulgar to sing 'Git outa here, and git me some money too'; I felt as E. M. Forster felt about *Ulysses*: that it was 'a determined attempt to cover the universe with mud'.

When I was twenty a Soho friend talked to me about a trumpeter called 'Big Spider Beck' who had drunk himself to death in his twenties, and this struck me as a typical jazz legend. I asked the friend to play me some of his records, but they meant nothing to me. Then, in Thomas Merton's *Seven Storey Mountain* (which fascinated me, since at the time I day-dreamed about becoming a monk), I came across a reference to 'lying on the floor and listening to the melodies of the long-dead Beiderbecke'. The phrase 'long-dead Beiderbecke' did what Bix's trumpet had been unable to do: placed me in a state of receptive nostalgia. So whenever afterwards I visited my friend with the old 78s, I got him to play me 'Royal Garden Blues', 'Jazz Me Blues', and the rest *ad nauseam*. But when he tried to persuade me to graduate to Armstrong, I firmly refused. Armstrong struck me as coarse and exhibitionistic—even the Hot Fives. And yet I firmly believe that it was the phrase 'the long-dead Beiderbecke' that I was enjoying rather than the records; for a long time I couldn't even distinguish Bix's trumpet; it was the general tone and flavour of the music that appealed to me rather than any feeling of Beiderbecke's artistry.

When I finally came into possession of a gramophone and enough money to buy records, I bought myself a couple of LPs of Bix, and one of the Original Dixieland jazz band. I didn't enjoy the latter as music—I still don't—but it was amusing to play my friends 'the first jazz record ever made'. I bought a second-hand disk of the Goodman 1938 Carnegie Hall concert, but loathed it so much I gave it away. And an attempt by another friend, Dick Heckstall Smith (himself a fine tenor-sax player), to introduce me to the work of Charlie Parker was also a failure. I had often heard 'Bop' on the radio in the days when it first became fashionable over here (about 1948, I suppose), and found it meaningless.

In 1957, after moving to a cottage in Cornwall, I spent much time systematically exploring music through the gramophone record. One day, out of curiosity, I bought Eddie Condon's *Book of Jazz* and the *Decca Book of Jazz*. Once I could approach the subject intellectually, so to speak, it interested me more; I began ordering jazz records by the dozen, and one day procured two of the London set of Parker. Having read about the Parker legend, and paid hard cash for the records, I was in a more receptive frame of mind. I became a jazz enthusiast overnight, and would play Bessie Smith and Dizzy Gillespie, Bunk Johnson and John Coltrane in quick succession. I still had something of a prejudice against 'mainstream'—Goodman, Lunceford, Henderson, Bob Crosby—but even this disappeared in my enthusiasm for Bunny Berigan.

My interest is still there, although it has grown somewhat static. I 'got to know' jazz in the way that some people promise themselves to read Walter Scott or Lord Lytton one day. But even when I bought jazz records every other day my interest in other kinds of music was unabated, and gradually, for lack of time as much as any other reason, I have ceased to take an active interest in jazz.

To some extent this is clearly because jazz is never likely to appeal to me as a medium for self-expression, even vicariously.

CHORDS AND DISCORDS

In 1957 I bought myself a trumpet, resolved to learn to play it as Bix learned—by trying to play to records. Now six years later, I still play as badly as after my first week of practice. Also—and I hope this does not sound like intellectual snobbery—I think perhaps I am not inarticulate enough really to identify myself with the spirit of jazz. I have talked to many jazz men, including Coleman Hawkins, Roy Eldridge, Thad Jones, and Cannonball Adderley, and discovered most of them to be interesting and likeable human beings; but have found it impossible to connect these men, as human beings, with the excitement that I often derived from their playing. Now to some extent this is also true of writers; meeting an author one admires is usually a disappointment; but I have generally been able to recognize a link between an author's books and his personality. I suspect that jazz men are on a different wavelength. It is a disturbing thought that I would probably have found Bix Beiderbecke or Bunny Berigan as personally unsatisfying—in that sense of 'non-communicating'—as other jazz men; but I have no doubt it is true.

From what I have said above, I think the reader can probably infer some of my views on the nature of jazz. When I read, say, Leonard Feather on the subject of jazz improvisation or its musical structure, I find his remarks almost meaningless. Surely all that it is necessary to say about jazz, musically speaking, is that it is based on a regular beat, not very different from march time, or even the kind of beat one often finds in Bach or Vivaldi (as many modern experimenters have shown), but with the addition of syncopation—the accenting of normally unaccented beats and vice versa, the slurring of the last note of one bar into the beginning of the next.

But to say this is rather like saying that the essence of communism is to be found in *Das Kapital*. Clearly it is not. Communism, like jazz, is a mood, a state of mind, a mythology. To define jazz precisely, one must define its state of mind.

The first thing that strikes a newcomer to jazz is that its mythology is so involved with self-destruction. There is Bix Beiderbecke killing himself on corn alcohol; Bessie Smith on gin; Charlie Parker on drugs. The whole legend is bound up with early death, like the myth of romantic poetry. Jazz history

114

is extraordinarily dramatic. It starts with Buddy Bolden blowing his trumpet through the railings of the park to call the people from the rival bandstand. And the person of Bolden contains all the elements of the myth. He rises from the unknown mass of the negro poor to become the idol of New Orleans; his trumpet is so powerful it can be heard several blocks away. (The myth of power enters here; it is like a gorilla beating its chest and screaming for a mate.) He is proclaimed 'King of the Zulus'; he is seldom seen around without several adoring women clinging to his arms and begging for the privilege of holding his coat—and his trumpet. He leads a fast life and a gay one, then collapses into madness, so that although he lives on well into the great jazz era, he never knows what he started. Finally, there is the mystery of the 'Bolden cylinder', the record of his playing that all jazz fans hope will turn up one day, and that, when it does turn up, will be worth more than the few records of Jean de Rezske that at present repose in a Paris bank vault.*

There is no need to ask why this kind of story exercises so much fascination. It is pure romanticism. In the early nineteenth century bored and well-brought-up young girls imagined themselves transported to sinister Gothic castles where the evil count planned to drug and ravish them. In the mid-twentieth century bored teen-agers identified themselves with James Dean, becoming overnight one of the highest paid actors in Hollywood, living fast (bongo drums, racing cars, and beautiful starlets) and dying violently. The success myth itself is one of the great romantic myths of the twentieth century—it accounts for much of the hysteria that has surrounded popular entertainers, from Frank Sinatra to Elvis Presley and the Beatles. But death gives it a new dimension of morbid nostalgia. The root of it all is still boredom, unfulfilment. The uninhibited stage personality of Presley or the Beatles is simply another expression of triumphant animal vitality, like Bolden's screaming trumpet. (It lacked purity of tone, said Armstrong, but possessed tremendous power.)

Fifty years ago the taste for jazz was looked down on by people who preferred 'serious music'; today jazz enthusiasts can

*Albert Macarthy once told me that he thought he came close to tracing the Bolden cylinder; he tracked it to a house in New Orleans, but was told that a large number of old cylinders had been thrown into the dustbin the week before.

look down in the same way on the fans of Presley or the Shadows; in comparison, their subject is 'highbrow'. To begin with,
it is something of an act of faith to listen to Ma Rainey or the
New Orleans Rhythm Kings in these days of high fidelity, not to
mention the even stronger objection that most old blues records
—Ma Rainey, Trixie Smith, Lovey Austin—sound incredibly
dull to ears grown accustomed to rock 'n roll and the twist. But
apart from that, jazz began to take itself seriously after the
Christian-Gillespie sessions at Mintons; and the records of the
Miles Davis 1948–9 band or the Bud Powell-Fats Navarro
group of 1950 are almost as much an acquired taste as the music
of Schoenberg. The old jazz 'greats'—Bessie Smith, King Oliver,
Leon Rappolo, Pine Top Smith—are like mountain-tops wrapped
in their myths of tragedy, and no one questions whether they
were really as great as they are supposed to be. But with Charlie
Parker, Charlie Christian, Fats Navarro, Clifford Brown, one
can also point to a considerable degree of technical achievement.

All this inclines the jazz enthusiast to forget something that
stares the more detached observer in the face: that the kind of
excitement that greeted the Original Dixieland jazz band in 1918
or the King Oliver band in 1923 was in every way the same kind
of phenomenon as the excitement that makes a modern teen-age
audience scream as their latest idol sings. Jazz has drifted away
from its origins, has been inclined to take itself perhaps too
seriously in recent years. But in a certain sense it could be
argued that the Beatles or the Shadows are closer to the essence
of jazz than Ornette Coleman or John Coltrane; for jazz is a
myth of vitality, not simply an exploring of new rhythmic
territory.*

In saying this I am not attempting to depreciate jazz, and
certainly not to claim more serious consideration for 'the top
ten'; I am only trying to point out that although the enjoyment
of jazz undoubtedly requires a certain perceptiveness, a certain
developed taste, it is still a very long way from what is absurdly
called 'serious music'. The enjoyment of a Bartók quartet, a song

*Purists will argue that (a) the kind of music the Beatles play is not jazz, and
(b) it lacks true inventiveness. But is it clear to any unprejudiced listener that the
Beatles are only one step away from the kind of music Sister Rosetta Tharpe was
playing before the Second World War, and that they are very close indeed to the
kind of music that Howlin' Wolf was recording less than five years ago. It is true
that there is a certain monotony about the music of the modern teen-age idols,
but surely not more so than with the O.D.J., the N.O.R.K., or Bix's Wolverines?

by Wolf, a sonata by Beethoven, may be increased by knowing something about the life of the composer and about music in general; but the musical intellect plays a far greater part in it. The enjoyment of jazz depends to a greater extent on awareness of the jazz myth.

I have not yet defined precisely what I mean by the jazz myth. It is not simply animal vitality, or success, or misery and tragedy. It is something far more complex. In a sense, it is only a twentieth-century version of the myth of 'La Bohème'—the kind of thing that has been captured, on a rather cheap level, by Somerset Maugham in *The Moon and Sixpence* or by Irving Stone in *Lust for Life*. Art has the power to raise us above the exhausting complexity of everyday life. But much great art requires a long apprenticeship, as well as a certain detachment. A beggar on the Embankment is not likely to be led into forgetting his miseries by hearing Monteverdi's *Orphée*, or even Beethoven's Fifth Symphony. But an art that can stay 'popular', close to the complexities of everyday life, and yet make its audience feel detached from these complexities, has a power that is altogether more raw. It demands no down-payment of culture or study. This is the power of jazz. The lover of Beethoven feels that his music successfully transcends the sufferings of human existence, that such music was distilled out of torment by a man whose spirit could not be broken. Jazz does exactly the same thing on a lower level. Most lovers of jazz have never experienced anything like the long-drawn-out misery and degradation from which the American negro created his music. And yet here it is, like the music of Beethoven, yet another proof that the human spirit cannot be broken, that it can create delight and love of life out of the most unpromising conditions.

This is the heart of the jazz myth. This is why the jazz enthusiast, trying to convert an unbeliever, emphasizes the violence and tragedy, the murder of Pine Top Smith and Chano Pozo, the frustration of Beiderbecke and Parker, the final agony of Bessie Smith. The 'unbeliever' might well point out that the jazz success stories far outweigh its tragedies. From Buddy Bolden to Clifford Brown and Stan Hasselgard, jazz can count about two dozen tragedies—and this by including minor figures like Robert Pete Johnson and Chano Pozo. But for every dead Bix there's a living Louis Armstrong and Duke Ellington; for every Charlie

Parker, a living Dizzie Gillespie and Miles Davis. The successful and long-lived jazz men probably outweigh the tragedies by
four to one. And in a profession that sprang up in the brothels,
continued in prohibition speakeasies, and even today depends
largely on short engagements and one-night stands, this is not
unreasonable. But tragedy is part of the jazz legend, and must
be taken into account in any attempt to understand the nature of
jazz.

Most modern books on jazz end by asking: What now? Most
of them admit that they can hardly see the possibility of a new
jazz era. But one often feels that the question is based on a complete misunderstanding of the nature of jazz.

I have indicated earlier* that I cannot agree with Henry
Pleasants that jazz is the true music of the twentieth century,
while Schoenberg and the rest are a decadent left-over from the
nineteenth century. One of my reasons is stated above: 'serious
music' must engage the musical intelligence; jazz is seldom
capable of doing this to any great extent. Its impact is immediate; but beyond that there is very little. The same objection
applies to the modern musical comedy, which Mr Pleasants, in
company with Mr Ivan March,† also believes to be 'the music of
the future'. At its worst it is puerile; but even at its best—say
in *The Threepenny Opera* or *West Side Story*—it tends to be
derivative, and will not bear repeated hearings even to the extent
that good jazz will.

It must be recognized that jazz is a confined musical idiom;
attempts to develop it tend to turn it into something that is not
jazz. Bix Beiderbecke wanted to develop jazz, and he told Mezz-
row that he was interested in Delius and Holst. His 'experiments' can be heard in two piano recordings, and it is obvious
that they could not have gone much farther. Beiderbecke was
not a musical intelligence of a high order; he was simply a
tremendously gifted trumpet player with a kind of personal
directness and honesty that appears in his playing; for us, the
greater part of his charm is that he catches the atmosphere of the
twenties more than any other jazz man of the time. But his
attempts to develop jazz were obviously pushing it in the direc-

*Chapter 3, 'Modern Music'.
†Editor of *The Stereo Record Guide*, etc.

118

tion of a sophisticated cocktail music—impressionistic 'mood' music that would make an ideal background for upper-class couples taking dinner instead of for Chicago bootleggers out on a spree; in the fifties and sixties John Lewis, Dave Brubeck, and Don Shirley have all developed this part of Bix's legacy.

Jazz has always had two currents: the personal and the extraverted; and the two have frequently mixed. The O.D.J., the N.O.R.K., the Oliver Creole jazz band, Jelly Roll Morton's early groups, all belong to the extravert tradition that was carried on in the thirties by Goodman, Lunceford, Henderson, and Basie (and, to a lesser extent, Ellington). Ma Rainey is the source of the other tradition, that continues through Bessie Smith, Billie Holiday, Leadbelly, Pete Johnson, and Blind Lemon Jefferson. The bop revolt was an attempt to turn the stream of jazz back into the personal; it was a kind of desire to avoid meeting the customers half-way. It might be said that it was an intellectualized music; it was certainly more complex than anything that had gone before. At its best, in some of the solos of Parker and Bud Powell, it succeeds in sounding a personal note that had been missing since Bessie Smith—although Billie Holiday remains the exception. But it is interesting to note that both Powell and Parker simplify their idiom when it is most personal, as in 'Parker's Mood' or 'I Cover the Waterfront'. This is also observable to an even greater extent in Gillespie and Miles Davis: one of Gillespie's most moving solos is his 'Thinking of You', which might have been made by Bobby Hackett or Buck Clayton. The inference seems to be that Bop is not a natural language. It was developed in response to a need —the need to be subjective, to turn away from the audience (the dark glasses and the playing with one's back to the audience, which Davis still practises, were another sign of this). It was also developed as a language for a kind of exhibitionism— although the word is not here used in a pejorative sense. Gillespie admitted that part of the intention of the bop language was to keep bad players from 'jamming' with them at Mintons. As well as expressing his feelings, the executant could also express his seriousness on another level, by sheer brilliance; the break with the older type of jazz, and its attitude towards the audience, was made even clearer.

Bop has produced its classics—many of the recordings of the

Parker-Davis combination, of Powell and Navarro, of Parker and of Gillespie and Roy Eldridge—but the question that strikes the listener is whether this music is an individual and organic expression of its mood, or whether it is an uncomfortable hybrid that one must judge by intention rather than by achievement. In certain ways it reminds us of twelve-tone music; not that they sound alike, but that both are clearly a reaction, a kind of 'anti-mask' (to use Yeats's phrase), the complex response of over-sensitive men to a world that they are afraid would reject the natural expression of their emotions. Parker's most brilliant solos do not convey any direct emotion—not to this listener, at least; one recognizes that they are a complex expression of a personal intensity, that their complexity is a mask of impersonality. The true Parker emerges in a technically poor solo like that in 'Lover Man' (which Parker made on the verge of a nervous breakdown, and after drinking a pint of whisky); the voice here is honest and compelling, and proves that the complexity was not necessary to impress the listener.

Gillespie, of course, is a different case. Emotionally, he seems to have little in common with Parker. He belongs to the other jazz tradition—the extravert, the entertainer. He can play an excellent 'straight trumpet', as in some of his big band recordings such as 'Stormy Weather' or 'Jealousy'; or an exhibitionist bop trumpet, as in the big band recordings of the late forties with Chano Pozo. In recent years, he seems to have determined to go 'farther out' than most jazz men in sheer technical virtuosity, and has had whole concertos written for him that seem as dry and lifelessly complex as anything by Hindemith. The result of all this is to make one wonder whether Gillespie ever really had anything to 'say', or whether he would not be a better artist if he expressed his good nature and high spirits less pretentiously, like Cannonball Adderley.

The truth would seem to be, then, that jazz took something of a false direction in bop. Bop aroused legitimate enthusiasm because it seemed to announce jazz's coming of age, a new level of seriousness. But the reactionary Hugues Panassié saw penetratingly that it was a dead end. Jazz is essentially a rhythmic expression of exuberance or of melancholy; and sometimes of both at the same time, which gives it its peculiar flavour. But it lacks the foundation to become anything more complex. It can legitimately be argued that a fine improvisation is as truly a musical creation as any 'serious' composition. But the technical apparatus of the serious composer is designed to allow him to build large musical structures if he feels so inclined, and to concentrate his musical thinking. If Sonny Rollins or Jimmy Giuffre improvises with the Modern Jazz Quartet, the result may be interesting and agreeable, but one feels instinctively that, in spite of all attempts at complexity, it can never be more than musically light-weight. And when Rollins and Gillespie get together on 'Sonny Side Up', one feels that this music has lost all contact with the kind of jazz played by King Oliver and Jelly Roll Morton and Fats Waller, or sung by Bessie Smith or Billie Holiday. It is no longer expressive; it has moved closer to the Bach fugue. But jazz began as a romantic idiom, and this return to classicism seems as artificial as Stravinsky's. Even so Stravinsky was better at hiding in a cloud of theory. Jazz is an altogether simpler form of self-expression, and it shows clearly when an artist simply 'wants to be clever'.

This, then, seems to me to be the situation in jazz in 1964. For twenty years now a great deal of jazz has been taking itself far too seriously. The older school of jazz—that regarded it purely as entertainment—is felt to be *passé*; Louis Armstrong, with his cheerful exhibitionism, is looked upon as a kind of traitor by many jazz fans, the man who cashed in on 'playing Uncle Tom'. The totally different attitude of the two schools can be seen by comparing the public performances of Count Basie and the Modern Jazz Quartet. Basie merely sets out to give the customers brilliantly played, high-powered jazz; but, recognizing that even this may be too austere for some of the audience, the programme is given variety with dancers, singers and comedians who specialize in 'blue jokes'.* Audience participation is as warm as at a pantomime. The M.J.Q., on the other hand, go through the performance as if they were celebrating mass; they enter quietly with grave faces, acknowledge the audience with a nod, then get down to the serious business of creating strange and delicate traceries of sound. They are 'serious artists', they seem to imply in every careful movement. But the quality of the

*I am thinking now of a performance of Basie that I saw in Washington in 1961.

121

music makes these pretensions somewhat absurd; it is very pleasant, with its gentle tinkling of the vibraharp; as background music in a restaurant, it would aid the digestion; but it creates a perpetual sense of anticlimax in the Bayreuth atmosphere of a dimly lighted theatre.

All this is not to say that these semi-intellectual developments —Brubeck, Rollins, Gillespie, Coleman, Tristano, the M.J.Q.— are not of considerable interest; jazz would certainly be poorer without them. But they represent a kind of dead end. Good jazz has always been the intense expression of personalities—Bessie Smith, Bix Beiderbecke, Charlie Parker. In our own time it can be found in the singing of Howlin' Wolf, John Lee Hooker, Lightnin' Hopkins. It may express itself through a band if the band leader possesses a touch of genius, as with Jelly Roll Morton, Duke Ellington, King Oliver. Experimentalism may produce interesting jazz, as with some of Kenton's early experiments, or the Davis–Mulligan band, the Brubeck octet, or some of Mingus's groups. But these experiments are not likely to cause any development of the mainstream of jazz, any more than Sterne's method of writing a novel is likely to lead to a new school of anti-novel. When a new jazz genius arrives, another Parker or Armstrong or Ellington, he will no doubt create his own individual type of jazz; but this will not lead to any general 'development'. The notion that jazz can develop is a myth, based partly upon the false analogy of jazz and serious music. Jazz is not a 'new music', running parallel with 'serious music'; it is a small offshoot of serious music. The changes that have taken place in music since the seventeenth century have been changes of sensibility; music wanted to express new things. Jazz is a particular type of sensibility, and it has remained unchanged in fifty years of jazz development. Certain social changes have produced an illusion of development. At first sight it might seem that the change from the negro jazz of the twenties to the white jazz of the thirties, then to the new negro jazz of the forties and fifties, is analogous to the change from Bellini and Donizetti to Wagner and Mahler, and then on to Schoenberg and modern experimentalism. But these changes are, in fact, superficial. The Louis Armstrong of the sixties is still playing the kind of jazz he played in the thirties; the Duke Ellington of the sixties still composes much the same kind of music as thirty years ago. The most important change that has taken place is that jazz has become a cult, and the jazz player—particularly the negro—need no longer feel that he is working against the current. Early jazz was a kind of life-affirmation against a background of misery and poverty. There is no reason why jazz men like John Lewis, Miles Davis, Dave Brubeck, Gerry Mulligan, should feel the slightest sympathy for this type of jazz feeling. Consequently, they create a sophisticated kind of jazz that has almost no connection with the jazz played by the Hot Seven or Morton's Red Hot Peppers. But this is not an evolution, or change of sensibility; it is the simple outcome of a social change, like moving from a cottage into a semi-detached villa.

Seen in historical retrospect, jazz will almost certainly appear to be a phase in the development of the American negro, and will be connected with the first three decades of this century in the way that we connect the operettas of Offenbach with the Paris of the 1860s, or those of Gilbert and Sullivan with London in the 1880s. It is doubtful whether most of the things that have been done since 1930 will be counted as of great importance. Since the early forties jazz has had two faces: experimentalism, and a nostalgic backward-looking at the twenties. Today, 'traditionalism' (which means in practice a rather vapid re-creating of the jazz sounds of forty years ago) is far more popular than 'modern jazz'. This in itself seems to prove that jazz is a period, an historical phase and the sensibility connected with it, rather than a new development in pure music.

The main objection to be made against jazz is its narrowness, its limitedness. Duke Ellington has been playing for forty years now, and has issued numberless records. Jazz would not have suffered if Ellington had retired twenty years ago, and if all but fifty of his records were destroyed. Louis Armstrong has been in jazz even longer; but he played his best jazz in the last five years of the twenties. Again, it would be no great loss to jazz if all his other recordings were destroyed—although this is not, of course, to maintain that he has not issued many records since that compare with the best of the Hot Five and Hot Seven. Jazz enthusiasts often say that it was a tragedy that so and so died so young—Bix Beiderbecke, Bunny Berigan, Fats Navarro, Clifford Brown; yet considering the careers of most of the 'great' jazz men, one can hardly agree with them. It is, indeed, a pity that Beiderbecke did not live on into the age of great soloists, so that we might have a few records of his playing with tolerable bands and taking long solos. But even so, no one can say that he died too young to fulfil his promise. What we have is a satisfying body of work, as self-complete in its way as that of Ellington or Armstrong. It is unlikely that he would have shown any interesting developments. No jazz man so far has displayed any development analogous to the development of many 'serious' composers; in fact, I can think of no case in jazz where it would have seriously mattered if the composer had died after ten years of making records. (With many of them the period could be reduced to five.) This means that jazz is a limited field—like, say, that of the operetta or zarzuela, or the modern Broadway musical. It is an interesting minor branch of music, and deserves to be studied as such by serious musicians.* Whether it has any future, apart from popular music, is open to doubt. The sensible attitude would be to be grateful for its past.

*Some years ago I heard a musical quiz programme on the radio, with a number of well-known musical personalities, many of whom could identify a piano sonata by its three opening notes, or a composer by one bar from the middle of a symphony. The only question that baffled the whole team was the identification of a recording of Django Reinhart and Stephan Grapelli playing a classical pastiche. Obviously, these experts did not regard jazz as a branch of music, but as a separate subject of which they could not be expected to know anything.

7

DELIUS

THE CENTENARY of Delius' birth in 1963 seems to have proved what many of us have suspected for a long time: that since the death of Sir Thomas Beecham interest in Delius has dwindled almost to the vanishing-point. Few reputable critics even took the trouble to attempt a 'revaluation', a notable exception being Mr Deryk Cooke on the B.B.C. Third Programme, who produced a perceptive defence. To some extent the reason for this lack of interest is unpleasantly obvious: it is the same cultural snobbery, the curious narrowness of sympathy, that led the editor of the Pelican *Modern European Music* to omit all reference to Sibelius, and that leads so many leading music critics to talk as if Schoenberg, Stravinsky, and Webern are the only interesting composers of the twentieth century. We can afford to ignore this kind of snobbery; in fifty years' time it will appear as quaint and dated as the Victorian enthusiasm for the oratorios of Stainer and Parry.

I have only one criticism to make of Mr Cooke: he prefers to meet these critics on their own ground, and attempts to defend Delius by pointing out that he has far more sense of form than his opponents will allow, was in many ways throughly *avant-garde*, etc. Now, all this is neither here nor there. It reminds us of the attitude of the defenders of Joyce's *Ulysses* in the twenties, ignoring the protests of critics who thought the book a libel on human nature and talking learnedly about the mythological method and the Thomistic theory of beauty. (Mr Stuart Gilbert later admitted that they felt this was the best way of bullying their critics into silence.) Delius would have been the first to insist that all this kind of wrangling is evasion. His music stands or falls by its content, not by extraneous questions of its originality or sense of form.

This question of Delius' 'originality' has never been quite clear to me. Both Mr Cooke and Mr Burnett James have said that Delius owes nothing to other composers, and Ralph Hill writes: 'As a composer, he belonged to no school, nor did he derive from one; his style was practically the result of pure genius.' A listener who had never heard Delius might reasonably be excited by this promise of a remote and original kind of music; if he then put on a gramophone record of *Brigg Fair* or the *Hassan* incidental music, he would find it very difficult to understand all this talk about originality. He would hear a music that seems to owe much to early Debussy, and that often sounds not unlike Ravel, or even Sibelius (of *The Swan of Tuonela*). But above all, the *emotion* of Delius' music is thoroughly familiar. It is present in all late Wagner, particularly *Tristan* and *Parsifal*. (Thomas Mann's essay on *The Sufferings and Greatness of Richard Wagner* will make this parallel much clearer: Wagner's fatalism, his feeling that life is a 'dim, vast vale of tears' and that art is a disease that sucks life from the artist.) It is present in Mahler, particularly in the *Song of the Earth*, and in the Schoenberg of the *Gurrelieder* and *Verklärte Nacht*. But in Delius the apples of decadence have turned slightly more rotten. We may feel we hear this decadent, dreamy, world-hating Delius in his *Mass of Life* or *A Song of the High Hills*, but the 'programme' of the music inclines us to doubt our ears. (After all, Mussorgsky's preludes to *Khovanshtchina* and *Sorochintsy Fair* also sound dreamy and other-worldly, but acquaintance with the rest of his music soon puts them in perspective.) Then we hear the *Songs of Sunset*, settings of Dowson poems, and it is impossible to doubt any longer. Delius is the musical equivalent of Ernest Dowson. He finds that 'day is over-long', and believes that exhaustion and death are 'the end of every song man sings'.

And to understand Delius properly it is necessary to understand Dowson. It is true that, to some extent, Dowson can be dismissed as a mood that we all pass through in teens: later we are inclined to feel that Dowson threw in the towel too soon—in short, that he was a weakling. But this kind of generalization is dangerous, since it ministers to the favourite human delusion

of evolution and maturity. It is arguable that we have evolved
beyond the Victorians because *East Lynne* and the death of
Little Nell no longer make us cry; but there is an element of
self-complacency in applying the same argument to anything
and everything for which we have lost the taste. Because *King
Solomon's Mines* and *Treasure Island* give most pleasure to the
under-fifteens, this says nothing against them as self-complete
works of literature; to speak of outgrowing them is like speaking
of outgrowing primroses.

And certain poems of Dowson give the same sensation of
being unique, self-complete, even if we find it difficult to enter
into their mood. Their evocation of mood has reached a level of
skill where it is irrelevant to object to the mood as a condem-
nation of the poem. To enjoy them, we merely have to make the
'temporary suspension of disbelief' on which most aesthetic
enjoyment depends. We may not agree that:

> Out of a misty dream
> Our path emerges for a while, then closes
> Within a dream.

Still, we have to admit that the eight-line poem from which
these three lines come has found perfect cadences to express its
mood of sadness and resignation.

All Delius' music is conceived in the mood of Dowson; it is
as true of the *Florida* suite as of the *Song of Summer* (dictated
to Eric Fenby in the last years of his life). In a way, his least
characteristic music is to be found in *Hassan*, which has at
times a barbaric and most un-Delian quality; yet a closer consideration of *Hassan* only strengthens the point. Flecker's play
is a glittering work, brilliant, humorous, fantastic, cruel, a *tour
de force* full of assorted emotions, in which sadness plays only a
minor part. But ask anyone who knows the Suite to whistle
something from it, and they will almost certainly whistle the
tune that accompanies the words 'We take the Golden road to
Samarkand': that, or the Serenade (on which the above is a
variation), the tune expressing sadness and the hope of a
future in a fairy-tale country of dreams. Delius' music has
reduced *Hassan* to a kind of monochrome; it is clear that he
would have been more at home setting Yeats's early *Wanderings
of Usheen*.

127

The oddest thing of all, as Warlock pointed out, is that Delius professed to be a Nietzschean, and set *Thus Spoke Zarathustra* to music. What seems, on the surface, even odder, is that Delius was so much admired by that man of dynamic energy, Sir Thomas Beecham. And yet one only has to read Charles Reid's book about Beecham to realize that Beecham and Delius were alike in one basic respect: both were curiously immature split-personalities. Both were more interested in imposing themselves on the world than in trying to come to terms with life. It is significant that Delius was intolerant of all music but his own, while Beecham's taste in music remained unaltered over fifty years. In a certain sense, both men had put up shutters against the world. Great artists strike us as 'open' personalities; Mozart, Beethoven, Schubert, kept all their doors open and allowed the world to come in and out as it pleased. Delius and Beecham were egoists who were basically afraid of the world. We read of Beecham's famous sallies with amusement, but when we think more closely about them, and realize what it must have meant to be like that *all* the time, we see that there is an element of the childish in them, just as in many of the practical jokes that Reid mentions. We smile when we read of Beecham's constant rudeness—usually expressed in orotund phrases that could be rolled off the tongue like thunder—and then become aware that this constant playing to the gallery, this constant awareness of his effect on other people, is something that most of us leave behind with adolescence.

If the *enfant terrible* part of Beecham—his love of brilliant effects or, failing that, sheer noisiness—was his Mr Hyde, then his Delius side was Doctor Jekyll. In this respect, Beecham was like a man who drinks and swears for six days of the week, then goes to church and prays with genuine devotion on Sunday. The famous Beecham personality prevented personal expression of the emotional side of his nature. But to conduct *Paris* or *A Song of the High Hills* was like declaring in public that the world is basically a tiresome and unpleasant place, and that the spirit has its own values. It was a declaration of faith.

Delius' own personality was altogether more complex. The range of his music is not wide; it varies between the sadness of *Songs of Sunset* to the sensual, cat-like contentment of *Summer Night on the River* or *In a Summer Garden*. It never expresses

128

positive vitality. Even in *A Song of the High Hills*, where there are wordless cries (presumably of satyrs), Delius specifies that they should be 'distant cries'; nature must not be allowed to sound too exuberant. And yet Delius' personality, as described by Fenby (who was with him in the later years of his life) is the opposite of his music: harsh, intolerant, dictatorial, professing a barren stoicism about man and the universe, and hating religion with a startling violence. It would seem that, like Yeats, Delius created a mask, an anti-self, as a defence against the world. The hatred of religion might at first seem strange; after all, Dowson became a Catholic, and wrote movingly of Extreme Unction. Then one realizes that Delius would have been incapable of the surrender of personality demanded by religion, even the romantic, masochistic religion of *Parsifal*; the rejection was again a form of self-defence.

It is interesting and instructive to reflect on Peter Warlock's relation with Delius. Heseltine (who later became Warlock) discovered the music of Delius at fifteen, and the impact was tremendous. He heard *On Craig Dhu* in 1910; in 1914 he could still write: 'I am sure there is no music more beautiful in all the world; it haunts me day and night—it is always with me and seems, by its continual presence, to intensify the beauty of everything else for me.' This was no temporary adolescent passion, like Rupert Brooke's for Dowson. The admiration lasted several years beyond 1914. But Heseltine found his personality a burden; to live with Delius' attitude to life and the world, one must have a private income and live in seclusion. Heseltine came to hate his over-sensitivity, and deliberately developed an anti-self, the bearded, Rabelaisian Peter Warlock. Heseltine liked sweet liqueurs; Warlock drank only beer; Heseltine loved children; Warlock professed to loathe them; Heseltine was gentle and shy of women; Warlock roughly undressed them; Heseltine wrote dreamy and desolate songs to words by Yeats; Warlock wrote roistering songs about drink and sex. And yet Warlock, like Heseltine, lacked strength; a few disappointments and anxieties, and he committed suicide. Cecil Gray suggests that Heseltine chose this extreme method of destroying his Mr Hyde, but this seems unlikely; the motive was probably financial insecurity.

But what emerges from all this is that to soak oneself in

Delius' music for ten years is not the best way of preparing for life. Characteristically enough, 'Warlock' detested most of Delius' music, finding it spineless. We can understand, then, why Delius himself had to create his own 'Peter Warlock' mask —the Delius who shocked Eric Fenby by the bitterness of his attacks on religion (and probably even more by the narrow-mindedness revealed by them). This was the Delius who produced a dreary *Requiem*, of which Warlock wrote: 'With as much dogmatic self-assurance as the most bigoted Christian . . . the anonymous librettist denies the immortality of the soul and the survival of human consciousness as though there were something immoral and offensive in the very possibility.'

Listening to Delius' music, then, we have to recognize that it does not express an integrated personality. Still, this is by no means a final word against it. What can be said on the positive side?

I have said that all Delius derives from Wagner and Debussy. To its first audiences, the most startling quality about *Tristan* was its apparent formlessness. The music is sea-like; it rises and falls, and the climax of the 'Liebestod' makes us think of waves beating against a cliff. To a lesser extent, the same is true of Debussy's *La Mer*. Now, the point of this conception of music is that it tends to break away from the idea of 'movements', and also from specific melodies. It likes to start as a grumble in the basses, like the beginning of a storm, then rise slowly, mutteringly, to a climax, then again subside into a murmur. It is, one might say, a form of emotion, as distinct from the emotion of Mozart or Beethoven as delirium is distinct from exuberance. Sibelius also has this outlook, so that his music develops always towards unity; from tuneful and immediately appealing works like *En Saga*, *King Christian the Second*, and *Rakastava*, to the strangely formless and tuneless *Tapiola* and Seventh Symphony. Admittedly, Sibelius seems a far more vigorous and vital composer than Delius, and Mr Burnett James has discerned in his music a quality of stoicism, recognition of the hostile forces of nature. And yet when one listens to their music instead of thinking about it, the parallel becomes clearer. There is a strange similarity, for example, between the Delius and Sibelius violin concertos (particularly

Sibelius' first movement—the others were added later). In the thirties, Sibelius was regarded by many (Constant Lambert, for example) as the only truly great composer alive. Today, the reaction against him is based largely upon the perception of the narrowness of his range. The centre of his output is the symphonies, all tending to develop large structures out of melodic fragments; the tone-poems are minor symphonies. Even the songs are 'symphonic', as can be easily seen if they are compared with the songs of Schubert or Wolf. And the movement is always away from the artificiality of melody, towards something more like the sound of wind in the trees. Sibelius' brief excursions into opera and chamber music were unsuccessful —obviously because his temperament was pushing him towards the brooding, sea-like one-movement form. (Although the quartet is called *Intimate Voices*, it is in no way intimate or subjective, like the autobiographical quartets of Smetana or Janáček; it is too much the voice of nature—deep-breathing and slow-moving.) The truly great composer has many aspects: Mozart was equally at home in opera, symphony, concerto, song or chamber music. Sibelius is like Delius in that he has only one aspect, one emotion; once the listener has plumbed this, he has plumbed Sibelius to the depths.

I have deliberately raised this comparison with Sibelius because it shows us the way in which Delius should be approached, and because it throws light on what Delius was actually trying to do. His formlessness cannot be held against him, because formlessness was of the essence of what he was trying to do. The only objection that one might raise is that this particular emotion—the emotion that wishes to simulate the voice of nature—is that it tends to carry within itself the seed of its own decline. Having written the Seventh Symphony, Sibelius could go no farther; any new work would inevitably be a repetition of something he had done earlier. The same is true of Delius; the *Song of Summer* and the *Songs of Farewell* are inferior not merely because they are the work of a tired and sick man, but because they say nothing that has not already been said in earlier works. As far as Delius was concerned, there was nothing more to be said. It is surely significant that Sibelius' last work was the incidental music to Shakespeare's *Tempest*, which is completely uncharacteristic of Sibelius for the most part; it is Sibelius wearing a mask of Elizabethan music because he has nothing more to say with his own voice.

At the same time, there are dozens of other composers with only one thing to say—that is to say, minor composers: from Dowland to Webern—just as there are dozens of minor poets. It may be that one's favourite poems are by minor poets, and that one's list does not include a single short poem by Milton, Dryden, Wordsworth, or Browning. Poetry would be a barren landscape without the Campions, Herricks, Matthew Arnolds, and FitzGeralds. Delius should be listened to for what he has to give, and there is no point in trying to make merits of his defects. It is tired music, soothing music for exhausted nerves, a dreamy, introverted music that asks very little of the listener except that he should relax. It is also completely unpretentious; it does not ask to be judged as an important utterance. This is surely not the least of its merits.

8

SOME ENGLISH MUSIC

ENGLAND is a strange country, whose custom is to ignore its men of genius for as long as possible, and to denigrate them as soon as possible after their deaths. No one has ever explained this aspect of the English character satisfactorily; it would hardly seem to be true that Englishmen in general are more envious than other nations and therefore resent success more. Possibly it is connected with the Englishman's pride in his 'unemotional nature', his reputation for phlegm and caution. He views with a certain benevolent contempt the American tendency to worship success, to describe all their ducklings as swans. But most likely it is sheer philistinism of a peculiar kind. England specializes in a curious intellectual philistinism. In any other country the words would cancel one another out; not so here. The English intellectual—and I now have a number of contemporary figures in mind—is a strange figure who regards it as bad form to think too much. His intellectualism consists in having subtle emotions—usually based on a sense of defeat—and in being able to verbalize them brilliantly. He often explains frankly that he is uncreative because of the traumatic experience of going to a public school, or being a homosexual in adolescence. But he dislikes 'large questions' about life, human destiny, and so on, and is inclined to regard the people who ask them as fakes. Since most great music is somehow implicitly about the 'large questions', as is most good art or literature, his attitude towards it tends to be one of scepticism. It is not quite English to ask large questions, or expose one's ideas or emotions in public.

I believe this is the explanation for the curiously 'small beer' quality of most English music, as well as of the English failure to produce literature that vibrates as deeply as that of other European countries (it is impossible to imagine an English Dante, or Goethe, or Dostoevsky).

All the same, there has undoubtedly been an English musical revival since Elgar; and here again the Englishman seems determined to do nothing to encourage it. If you are a record collector and like modern American composers such as Copland, Piston, Riegger, Barber, you can import any quantity from America (or get a record shop to do so). If it is Russian or Czech or Hungarian or Polish music, again the records can be obtained directly from the individual countries: the Russians and Czechs in particular do very well by their own composers. But if you like English music, the best you can hope for is that the B.B.C. will broadcast it and enable you to tape it. There is nothing available here that is not available in any of the countries named above: on the contrary, there are many English works that are only in the American catalogues.

English music has a 'small beer' quality, and yet to say this is not to speak patronizingly of it. It is true of most countries in the world. Only Germany, Russia, Italy, and Czechoslovakia have produced a musical literature that compares in quality and variety with English literature; and in the case of the two last named, we must add a few qualifications. All French music has the 'small beer' quality, although the French are inclined to claim Debussy as a 'great' composer without qualification. (Great he undoubtedly was; but not without qualification.) So has the music of Scandinavia, Holland, Switzerland, Poland, and Hungary (in spite of the high claims of Erkel).

But English music has a flavour all of its own, and once the taste is acquired it is never lost. It is an indefinable quality that is present in musicians who seem to have little else in common— Elgar and Warlock, Delius and Britten, Butterworth and Tippett, Bliss, Bax, and John Ireland. Since I have said it is indefinable, I shall not attempt to define it. Let us look at some of the music.

I like to feel that the English musical revival began with Sir Arthur Sullivan. The music of the Savoy operas is completely and superbly itself. Sullivan's fertility and melodic gift were

134

surely as great as Rossini's. Twenty-five years ago, before the days of the long-playing record, the Sullivan items possessed by the average record collector no doubt seemed to justify the view that he was no more than a minor 'pop' composer, the 1870s equivalent of Jerome Kern. Now that the complete operas can be purchased at reasonable prices—one of the best recordings of *The Mikado* can be had for £2 as I write this—there is no longer any excuse for this snobbish attitude. The music sparkles on like a brook in the sunlight, most of it unfamiliar. The ballet suite that Charles Mackerras drew from Sullivan's music and entitled *Pineapple Poll* is every bit as good as any suite drawn from Rossini—*La Boutique Fantasque*, or Britten's *Matinées Musicales*. And one realizes that, without intending it, Sullivan caught some essential quality of his era; the best aspects of late-Victorian England are as clearly present in his music as Elizabethan England is in Shakespeare or Ben Jonson. There is the quality that I have referred to in speaking of Brahms, a feeling that the world is fundamentally an excellent place, even though it has its tragic aspects, the Victorian confidence in life and order and reason.

It is true that Sullivan derives from Offenbach, and was perhaps influenced by Lecocq (who ousted Offenbach from the Paris stage); but Sullivan was several degrees better than any of Offenbach's imitators—Hervé, Messager, Christiné, Hahn. Offenbach's music is delightful, but it is all froth and bubbles (except in *Tales of Hoffmann*, where it becomes magnificently romantic and outstrips Gounod and Massenet in one leap). Sullivan is light, yet there is often an almost Mozartian quality in his lightness. He has another dimension, that feeling of Edwardian optimism. Compare his music for a moment with Offenbach's—or with Kurt Weill's, for that matter—and this extra quality becomes immediately apparent. One feels that these men composed against a background of moral bewilderment, of fever and futility, a gaiety that somehow brings to mind the mood of *The Waste Land*. The background of Sullivan's music is the England of General Gordon and General Booth, an England whose lighter side can be heard on old recordings of Dan Leno, Arthur Roberts, and Henry Lytton (who also played the lead in many Savoy operas). This England is certainly moral, but by no means dull. Sullivan brought to the

Savoy operas a genius that has never been equalled in the history of light music, even by Johann Strauss. One has only to compare them with the 'operetta' successes that followed, for example, with *Merrie England* or *Chu Chin Chow*, to see that Sullivan is on an entirely different level. In *Cox and Box*, and in several of the later operas, Sullivan composed parodies of Handel, Rossini, Bellini—even Verdi—and expected his audiences to recognize the parody and chortle. German's *Merrie England* has none of this lightness of touch (which is found in abundance even in *The Yeomen of the Guard*); it is completely serious in its 'olde England' sentimentality. As to *Chu Chin Chow* (which, I believe, still holds the record for number of performances), it is already half-way towards the sickening, mindless confections that are offered in such quantities every year by Broadway. (Even the better ones, like *West Side Story* or *The Most Happy Fella*, have an overall atmosphere of 'writing down', the tacit assumption that the public is moronic.)

It was a happy accident that threw Gilbert and Sullivan into collaboration, even though one gets tired of Gilbert's wit far sooner than of Sullivan's music. He might have continued as a composer of sentimental drawing-room songs and boring oratorios, and been as totally forgotten today as Stainer or Parry. (Stainer's *Crucifixion*, which has recently been reissued on record, makes it clear that he deserves his obscurity.) Like Brahms, Sullivan had the mistaken notion that he was born to be a 'heavyweight', but without Brahms's capacity to support the idea with a *German Requiem*. As it is, there are parts of the Savoy operas that wear thin rather quickly—or have worn thin by sheer repetition—but when one counts the richness offered by a dozen operas (including *Cox and Box*), this is unimportant. Some music critic (I have forgotten who) once remarked that in any other country but England there would be a yearly Gilbert and Sullivan festival; as it is, they are considered unmentionable by any serious critic. Yet one only has to place a good recording of any of the operas on the turntable, and try to listen to it without preconceptions, to realize that there is no real foundation for this attitude. To patronize Sullivan is as stupid as to patronize Schubert or Tchaikovsky or Grieg.

When one comes to Elgar, it is easier to understand why so

many people can allow themselves to be patronizing. He is, in the completest sense, an English composer (Sullivan is not; I believe that if Gilbert's words could be well translated into European languages, Sullivan might well become the best known of English composers on the Continent). I mean 'English' here in a somewhat narrow sense of the word. No good composer can prevent his personality from coming through his music, so that the listener has a feeling of knowing him intimately in certain respects; Mozart and Schubert are always giving one this feeling that they are alive and in the room; so, in a quite different way, does Berg in the D minor interlude in *Wozzeck*. A minor composer may conceivably possess this gift in a greater degree than a major composer. At all events, Elgar's personality is as clearly present in his music as Mozart's is in the 'Jupiter' Symphony. This personality is that of a rather poetic, nature-loving English gentleman. Like so many English gentlemen, he is not in the least brilliant, has no quick sympathy for other people's moods, never dazzles, as Mozart does in every other bar, with some piece of musical juggling that amounts to magic. He also has no understanding whatever of sex or women; he has not even that rudimentary understanding of sexual attraction that Delius reveals in *Fennimore and Gerda*. One has a feeling that the sexual undercurrents of Wagner or Richard Strauss would make him clear his throat and blush. It is easy to underestimate him, to listen to that solemn marching opening of the A flat major Symphony (that sounds like all the British Empire marching to war) and to feel that this man is simply a musical Colonel Blimp. And, as Neville Cardus points out, his Falstaff is not Shakespeare's drunken, brothel-loving old scoundrel, but a Falstaff who has repented and confessed his sins. Yet when all this has been said he remains one of the most delightful of English composers, a lover of the countryside, of warm August afternoons, of that pastoral yet eminently English and respectable world that Rupert Brooke describes in 'Grantchester' and 'The Great Lover'; he recognizes that 'white cups and plates, clean gleaming' are as poetical as any goblin kings. He also brings to mind the Chesterton of such novels as *The Man Who Was Thursday* or *Manalive*, of whom Dixon Scott wrote: 'He has the poet's gift for seeing the most commonplace things—moons or men's faces, hills, street lamps and houses—with a startling freshness and suddenness, as though they had been but that instant made.' (The most famous, but by no means the best, example in Elgar is 'The Wagon Passes' from the *Nursery Suite*.)

Elgar has been compared with Richard Strauss, and even with Bruckner, but his closest musical relation remains the man who has obviously exercised the greatest influence on his music, Brahms. The Brahmsian melancholy is the Elgarian melancholy. It is surprising how much of Elgar's music has a certain 'dying fall'. The anti-Elgarians make much of this, pointing out that this imperialistic English gentleman with his pompous 'Land of Hope and Glory' was really a sad example of capitalist decadence, a man who secretly recognized that his beloved England, with its militaristic complacency and destiny for ruling and guiding less civilized nations, was on the way out. There is no real evidence for this view. What is more probably true is that Elgar found the burden of being the Great English Composer rather heavy. We tend to think of him as Sir Edward Elgar, the royal favourite, the rich country gentleman, forgetting that he was the son of a not particularly prosperous bookseller, who remained poor and unknown until well into his forties, and who never became anything more than 'comfortably off', even at his most successful. Perhaps the title is to blame for the false impression; for when we examine it more closely we can see that his career was hardly more 'triumphal' than Bruckner's. His persistent problem was lack of appreciation of his music. He was not well established until after 1900 (when he was nearly fifty), and by 1918 had become entirely unfashionable in a world that was arguing about Stravinsky, Schoenberg, and 'Les Six'.

The music itself shows that, as with Brahms, we are in the world of a miniaturist. Elgar is at his best in small works like the *Introduction and Allegro*, the *Serenade for Strings*, or the beautiful slow movement of the Quintet. That *The Dream of Gerontius* is his greatest work does not contradict this view; it is largely a work in a minor key, quiet, sad, frequently approaching the mystical. It is an enormously moving work (as far as I am concerned, its only really false step is the use of 'Praise to the Holiest in the Heights' at the end, but this may be because I came to detest hymn tunes at school). The two symphonies are at their best in the slow movements (that of the First Symphony contains some of his most beautiful music). I have always preferred the First to the Second. To my ear, the opening movement of the Second seems to be too obviously derived from the opening of Brahms's Third, while the slow movement actually sounds in places as if he is imitating Delius.

Most critics are inclined to place the *Enigma* Variations and *Falstaff* in the first place in Elgar's music. About *Falstaff*, I am totally unable to agree with the standard opinion, just as I have never been able to concede that *Till Eulenspiegel* is Strauss's finest tone-poem. I mention Strauss because I find *Falstaff* unsatisfactory for the same reason that I find most of Strauss's tone-poems. No doubt it could be very touching and moving if one followed it with a score and programme notes on what is supposed to be happening, or if one could listen to it while watching a coloured film of the events it depicts—rather like Disney's *Fantasia*. But without this, too much of the music is water vanishing under a bridge. The main Falstaff theme is not particularly striking, and for my ear, it is repeated far too often.

The *Enigma* Variations certainly deserve a high place as the first typical product of Elgar's genius; but for me the same objection applies to them as to so many works written in variation form, including Brahms's 'Haydn' Variations, Rachmaninov's Paganini Rhapsody and Britten's 'Frank Bridge' Variations: that is, that only a few of the variations appear to have much musical content or real feeling. In the Brahms, it is the last variation (the noisiest) that strikes one as having the real lyric flow; in the Rachmaninov, the famous inversion is the only point where the Rachmaninov of the Second Piano Concerto is visible. In the *Enigma*, only Nimrod has that sense of musical expansiveness, although the 'cello solo (Variation 12) is also completely typical Elgar. As for Variation 11, for example, it is difficult to imagine anyone enjoying it without being told that it is supposed to depict a bulldog falling into the water. The second part of the twelfth variation shows a defect of which one is frequently conscious in Elgar: it sounds as if it is music that has been written to accompany a documentary film about the countryside, but too little seems to happen in it for it to stand on its own as music. (I find that much of the Second Symphony also affects me this way—it ought to be accompanied by a film showing sunburnt farm-hands forking hay on to a cart, and then show the cart lumbering homeward through the evening sunlight.)

One has to accept that all Elgar's music is sad music when it is not being noisily extraverted, as in the *London Town* overture. This is another reason why I am inclined to reject Cardus's comparison with Bruckner. The countryside over which one floats in a Bruckner symphony is not sad; it is vast and open, and sometimes majestic. In Sibelius, we sometimes feel that the music has caught the true spirit of nature—immense, open, free, menacing if looked at from a merely human level, but far too impersonal to be truly menacing. In Elgar, nature is always seen through a slight mist of nostalgia, although it never reaches the point of real despair. There is something slightly sweet, heart-twisting about it, and it reveals that Elgar's vision of the world was small, intensely personal, 'human, all too human'; there is no sense of vastness, of impersonal forces, of the greatness of heaven and earth; it is almost as cosy as *Our Village* or *Goodbye Mr Chips*. Still, that is Elgar, as English as Delius, and as full of gentle melancholy. We might hope that one day there will be a really great English composer who will show in his music some of the England that Wordsworth and Blake show in their poetry. Until that time, Elgar is about the best we have to offer—and let us make no mistake about this, he is plenty to be grateful for.

It would be impossible to write about English music without at least mentioning one of the most striking and original composers we have produced—Gustav Holst. And yet it is impossible to do much more than mention him, since so little of his music is known. This is undoubtedly due to the fatal popularity of the *Planets* suite, which seems too immediately impressive to be the work of a profound composer; the *Perfect Fool* music and the *St Paul's* suite add to this impression. And yet one has only to listen to *Egdon Heath* or the *Hymn of Jesus* (both issued in this country on record in 1962) to recognize that here is a composer with a strong and unique personality, who deserves to be more fully represented in the record catalogues. There are at least a dozen important works that should be recorded, including two operas (*Sāvitri* and *At the Boar's Head*), the Choral Symphony, two concertos, four songs for voice and violin, the Choral Fantasia,* an *Ode to Death*, and several works for chorus and orchestra.

Holst's health was even worse than that of Delius, with the result that many of his works are short—an advantage, since several could be packed on to one record. He made a virtue of necessity, and learned to concentrate his musical thinking so that a great deal could be said in a few pages. If Holst had been a German, this characteristic would have led to a Holst vogue, with many pupils trying to outdo the master in pregnant brevity. As an Englishman, he does not even receive the tribute of an occasional performance on the B.B.C. Worse still, pleasant but comparatively unimportant works like *The Planets* and *The Perfect Fool* are overplayed so as to give the impression that he is no more than a minor late romantic of no particular individuality—an impression that is quickly dispelled by a single hearing of the *Hymn to Jesus* (which, although it reminds us of Delius' *Mass of Life* in places, is an altogether tougher-minded work).

My own favourite among English composers of the pre-1914 years is George Butterworth, whose song cycle *A Shropshire Lad* is surely the most beautiful in English. On the evidence of this, it would seem that Butterworth was a kind of English Schubert. The songs are all melody and simplicity.† It is said that Housman was totally unmusical, and used to flee from the room with his hands over his ears if anyone tried to play him a setting of one of his poems. This is a pity, for he would have probably found that Butterworth caught his intentions perfectly. This completely English poetry is set to music that also seems perfectly English. It is instructive to compare Butterworth's setting of 'Is my team ploughing?'—a dialogue between a dead man and his best friend, who has inherited the dead man's sweetheart—with that of Vaughan Williams in the cycle *On Wenlock Edge*. Vaughan Williams scores his setting for voice

*Promised by World Record Club for 1964.
†There used to be an excellent recording, sung by John Cameron, on HMV DLP 1117, which is worth searching the second-hand shops for.

and string quartet, and aims at dramatic effects. The last stanza
goes:

> Yes, lad, I lie easy
> I lie as lads would choose.
> I cheer a dead man's sweetheart
> Never ask me whose.

This poetry is moving because of its simplicity. Vaughan
Williams has the tenor declaiming 'Yes lad! yes lad!' while
after 'Never ask me whose' the strings shriek dramatically.
Butterworth has no repetitions, and no more musical effects
than in any of the other verses, except that 'Never ask me whose'
is sung quietly, and followed only by a few dying notes on the
piano. Every one of these eleven songs by Butterworth is a
minor classic, and could be written about at length. The best-
known of the cycle is 'Loveliest of Trees', upon which Butterworth based the orchestral poem which is his most popular
work. Butterworth's death is, for me, the most regrettable
tragedy of the 1914 war—even allowing that T. E. Hulme,
Wilfred Owen, and Rupert Brooke were, in many ways, more
important figures. Butterworth's output was small; apart from
the works already mentioned, he composed two more orchestral
poems: *The Banks of Green Willow* and *The Cherry Tree*, and
another song cycle on poems by Henley which, to the eternal
disgrace of the record companies, has never been recorded.

I may well state here that the accidental acquisition of the
Shropshire Lad cycle was the foundation of my own taste for
English music, about which I had been inclined to be patronizing.
The English works that are most popular in the concert hall
tend to give an immediate impression of romanticism and
superficiality—Bax's *Tintagel*, Vaughan Williams's *Wasps*
Overture, Elgar's *Serenade for Strings*, Holst's *Planets*. During
the war various variety programmes on the radio would punctu-
ate the show with the B.B.C. Variety Orchestra playing someone
or other's arrangement of 'Baa Baa Black Sheep' or 'Old King
Cole'. As a small boy, I was inclined to feel that these 'arrange-
ments' only enfeebled an already feeble tune. Subsequently, I
came to feel that much English music has the insipid flavour of
the B.B.C. Variety Orchestra playing an arrangement of a
nursery tune. Undoubtedly, there are certain 'English' har-

monies—the *Wasps* overture is full of them—and possibly the B.B.C. arrangers made too much use of them, producing a prejudice against them. Elgar is full of these harmonies; no doubt this is why so many people instinctively dislike his music. In Butterworth the 'Englishness' has a fine, clean quality, in no way cloying. For this reason I would recommend *A Shropshire Lad*, either the songs or the orchestral poem, to anyone who has a prejudice against English music. It may lead to the discovery of other English songs—there are usually a number of excellent anthologies in the record catalogue—and to such fine minor composers as Ivor Gurney, Gerald Finzi, Herbert Howells, and T. W. Southam. Some of Finzi's settings of Hardy poems are of the same high quality as Butterworth's *Shropshire Lad*; for light-heartedness, his 'Budmouth Dears' is one of the most delightful English songs ever written.*

The greatest composer of English songs is undoubtedly Philip Heseltine (Peter Warlock, of whom I have spoken elsewhere),† whose suicide was a great tragedy for English music. Warlock was a strange man, a dual personality; he escaped his own over-sensitivity by acting the part of a kind of Elizabethan rake. His songs divide into two groups, as if written by different aspects of his personality. One may doubt Cecil Gray's theory that it was the conflict of these two personalities that finally drove him to suicide; many poets have been self-divided in the same way without ill effect. John Millington Synge seems to have been a divided personality in this sense; so does Robert Burns. Even the work of Blake shows that he possessed a Rabelaisian *alter ego*.

Warlock's 'Rabelaisian' songs are often more successful than more directly emotional songs. 'Captain Stratton's Fancy', 'Yarmouth Fair', 'Away to Twiver', and 'Jillian of Berry' will always be favourites at tenor recitals, whereas a curious work like 'The Fox' makes little impact on first hearing, and later may be found to be too bare and gloomy. It is a matter for conjecture whether the many Elizabethan songs should be

---

*Available on a Jupiter recording, JUR 00A5, sung by Wilfred Brown—a record whose standard is so high that it should be a collector's piece. It also contains Southam's lovely setting of a Durrell poem, 'Nemea'. Other fine records of English songs are: Saga XIP 7011 (John Shirley-Quirk, baritone); I.W 5241 (Peter Pears, tenor); and Saga XIP 7013 (Janet Baker, contralto).
†See Chapter 7, 'Delius'.

regarded as 'Warlock songs' or 'Heseltine songs', but most of them catch the curiously English flavour that is somehow peculiar to Warlock. This cannot be easily described. Warlock is a subtle composer—he might be regarded as a kind of English Hugo Wolf—so we seldom get the obvious English effects that are found in certain songs by Ireland or Vaughan Williams. So while the songs are unmistakably English, their subtlety raises them above the folk-song type of nationalism that so often spoils Vaughan Williams or Holst. Of all English composers, Warlock is the one who is most likely to make an international appeal to music lovers. It is therefore regrettable—but in no way surprising, knowing the record companies—that only about a dozen of his hundred songs are recorded. Luckily his finest work— 'The Curlew',* written to words by Yeats—has been available for several years. Like Vaughan Williams's *On Wenlock Edge*, it is scored for tenor and string quartet with an added flute and cor anglais. In my own opinion, this is possibly the finest piece of English music written in the present century. On a first hearing it sounds bleak and chilling, but on a second hearing one can only wonder at the subtlety of the writing. One might expect from the words—early Yeats of the dreamy period— that it would show obvious traces of Delius' influence. But this music is more icy and remote than anything Delius could have written. At a particularly effective point, the instruments stop playing, and the voice speaks the lines:

> No boughs have withered because of the wintry wind
> The boughs have withered because I have told
>   them my dreams.

It increases the effect of desolation, as if the voice is too exhausted to waste time singing any more. The quality of this music explains why Warlock was capable of suicide; he was more capable of despair than any other composer of his generation.

We return to the 'mainstream' of English music: Vaughan Williams, Ireland, Bax, Bliss, Walton, and Britten. Vaughan Williams I find the most difficult of composers to assess. By sheer longevity he came to dominate British musical life. He

*Argo RG 26, which also includes a dozen of the songs.

composed nine symphonies, and the mere number leads one to feel that he must be in the major composer class. One cannot, as with Elgar, accuse his music of expressing complacency; yet in some way one feels that his musical language is as confined as that of Elgar. In his last two symphonies there is a great deal of key feeling, and a liveliness of scoring that at times reminds us of Russian music. But the first seven all have the same tendency to indeterminacy, the modal feeling, as if their chief desire was to undulate along without being forced to make any definite statements. The kind of open, flat statements of theme that we get, for example, at the opening of Beethoven's 'Pastoral' Symphony, or the Sibelius Second, or Strauss's *Heldenleben*, are completely foreign to Vaughan Williams. It would seem that this is mixed up with a mystical intention, if we accept that his key works are the Fifth Symphony and the opera *The Pilgrim's Progress*. In this latter work the sinuous modal melodies give one the feeling that the world is a 'dream-crossed twilight between birth and dying' (to use Eliot's phrase), and the trumpet-like sound of Christian's words, 'I will arise in the name of the Lord', seems to state: 'Here lies meaning.' This makes the opera one of Vaughan Williams's finest works. But this modal quality, and the tendency to keep his themes to a few notes within a narrow range, give most of his works a sense of arriving nowhere, being afraid to come out and state flatly what they mean. It is inevitable for one to have a suspicion that they mean nothing, or that they are bullfrogs trying to make themselves as big as cows. We are reminded of the technique that Sibelius uses in so many of the symphonies, of keeping things indeterminate, fragmentary, until one's interest is aroused, and then suddenly knitting everything together and coming out with some sweeping tune. But as often as not Vaughan Williams never gets to the sweeping tune. It is all mood music, as in Delius—but then, Delius did not compose nine symphonies, so we take it for granted that he is a miniaturist.

Vaughan Williams was, of course, as completely immersed in folk song as Bartók, and this explains a great deal about his music, since many folk songs date from the days of modal music. But this does not explain why he stuck so persistently to this type of music throughout a long career. Obviously, the need to avoid definite keys without sounding actually atonal corresponded to some psychological need. In certain early works, like *Toward the Unknown Region* and *The Lark Ascending*, it seems that the intention is similar to that of Delius, poetic evocation of nature. But then, Vaughan Williams somehow does not strike us as a 'nature composer', as Bruckner does. There is infinitely less of nature in his *A Pastoral Symphony* (No. 3) than in Beethoven's, or in Bruckner's Fourth. Instead, we are in the Vaughan Williams world of half-lights, of melodies that seem to want to delay the unpleasant moment when they must sound as if they have arrived somewhere.

A glance at the nine symphonies shows that they can hardly be classified with Beethoven's nine, or even Mahler's. The first is actually a sprawling tone-poem about the sea, set to words by Whitman. Vaughan Williams once put himself on record as feeling that the last movement of Beethoven's Ninth is a let-down. In this I agree with him—but is this not because Beethoven somehow tried to make words do the work that should have been done by music? Vaughan Williams seems to fall into the same trap in many of his works. *Towards the Unknown Region* strikes one as being somehow naïve idealism in that it tries to express its mystical emotions by making the words do as much work as the music. But as words are usually inaudible in a choral work anyway, one only has an impression of some idealistic sentiment being sung in an exalted manner. The same kind of thing goes for *A Sea Symphony*. As the opening chorus sings emphatically: 'Behold the sea', one feels inclined to say sarcastically: 'No, *you* behold it!' One feels that music ought to carry the feelings along, not try to hold them up in this 'stand and deliver' manner.

A London Symphony hardly deserves the title of a symphony, it is a fantasia on the theme of London, and as such has some of that unfortunate quality of the 'arrangement' by the B.B.C. Variety Orchestra. It is fine music, pleasing music, but not a symphony. The same seems to me to be true of *A Pastoral Symphony*, which is an over-long Delius tone-poem rather than a symphony.

These objections do not apply to the Fourth or the Fifth. It is significant that neither of these works is programmatic (although the latter became the basis for *The Pilgrim's Progress*).

146

In No. 4 he seems determined from the beginning to sound the harsher note, to be genuinely symphonic. It has a touch of Hindemith in it, and reminds us that Vaughan Williams shares Hindemith's tendency to keep the melody moving within a relatively narrow range. In other respects this symphony is reminiscent of Walton's First (which struck many of its first hearers, in 1935, as being the first real 'post-war' musical statement, a picture of tension and ragged nerves). But Vaughan Williams's attempts to sound urgent and contemporary only keep reminding us that his natural pace is a slow amble—and, in fact, the Finale lapses into one of those long, sleepy passages. Still, like the Fifth, this is a remarkable symphony, perhaps the best of the nine. The Fifth I have already mentioned: its content seems to be religious in the manner of *The Pilgrim's Progress*, and gives the impression that he has decidedly turned his back on his brief flirtation with modernism. Its first movement is one of the most effective in all Vaughan Williams's work; although it has the usual modal feeling, there is a power and certainty about it that gives it the quality of an affirmation.

The Sixth Symphony sees the complete return of the introspective Vaughan Williams. There is a tradition that its pianissimo final movement is meant to be a description of the bomb ruins of London lying in the moonlight; to think so certainly helps one to appreciate the composer's intention. And yet one experiences a sense of disquiet on listening to this symphony, disquiet on the composer's behalf; he seems to be running into the same problem as Sibelius, the music becoming slower and quieter until it comes to a halt. The Fourth expressed his fears about the modern world, the Fifth his religious faith; the Sixth sees the fears realized, but manages to end with a sense of great calm. Where can a composer go from there? The answer would seem to be: nowhere. For the Seventh Symphony is no more than a rehashed version of the sound-track of *Scott of the Antarctic*. As one would expect from music that expresses the frozen South with its icy wastes, its unending winds, the constant blizzards, this music exaggerates Vaughan Williams's quality of getting nowhere; at times it sounds like Delius' muezzin in *Hassan*, at others, simply like the moaning of the wind, which one would not expect to show any feeling for key centres. It seems to confirm what one had long suspected: that part of the intention of Vaughan Williams's music is, so to speak, to make the flesh creep, to give a sense of the alien, the non-human. If so, it usually fails because so much of Vaughan Williams's music sounds as if it had been written for organ, and it would be difficult for an organ to sound 'alien'—we associate it too much with churches (although Messiaen succeeds in *L'Ascension*).

In the final two symphonies Vaughan Williams seems to have decided to try to abandon his persistent mannerism; they are hardly recognizable as his music. They have been described, accurately, as 'extraverted'. There are still a number of the Vaughan Williams fingerprints, but the old unwillingness to allow a melody to sound conclusive seems to have vanished.

On several hearings I have not been able to decide whether either of these works is truly a symphony; in spite of their brighter colouring and sense of light and air, they do not give a sense of developing symphonic thought. I personally find them preferable to most of the other symphonies because the old sense of the church organ has gone. But then, I must confess to finding the *Fantasy on a Theme by Tallis* a most unsatisfying piece of music, inconclusive and somehow stifling; I welcome the gongs and bells and blaring brass of the Eighth and Ninth.

Obviously, all this is a matter of taste. I do not like the things Vaughan Williams generally does with an orchestra, unless he is being straightforward, as in the two last symphonies or the *Old King Cole* music. I do not doubt that there is genuine religious feeling and love of nature underlying the music, but I do not like the solemn, slightly Elizabethan way in which he expresses it. On the other hand, a song cycle like *Songs of Travel* seems to me wholly successful; it has great variety of feeling; it is more heavy-footed than Butterworth, but it has as many melodies. Setting short poems by Stevenson, Vaughan Williams is under no temptation to drone off into one of his indeterminate melodies; he is forced to stay unpretentious. A song like 'Youth and Love' shows more ability to write sheer melody than anything in the symphonies.

When one turns from Vaughan Williams to Sir Arnold Bax one confronts another of those problems whose answer may be

148

obvious to future ages, but that seems unanswerable today: why the one should be held in high regard and be so well represented on record, while the other is ignored. Bax is the composer of seven symphonies that are in many ways as remarkable as those of Sibelius; of a large number of fine piano works, with four sonatas; and of many tone-poems, including the popular *Tintagel*, and the less well known but equally fine *Garden of Fand*. Bax's music is romantic and colourful, which is admittedly enough to make it unpopular with the musical cliques; even so, his romanticism is not of the broad, sweeping variety of Tchaikovsky; it is delicate, subtle and intelligent.

One reason for Bax's current neglect becomes apparent as one listens to his Third Symphony—one of his finest works. Although this is romantic music, it has none of the easily remembered melodies of Sibelius or Tchaikovsky. It has to be recognized that Bax was not a great melodist. There *are* melodies—plenty of them—but none that one whistles after hearing a single performance. This means that Bax does not make an immediate appeal to the kind of unsophisticated listener who knows each composer by his best-known melody—Handel by the Hallelujah chorus, Bach by the Air on a G string, Mozart by *Eine Kleine Nachtmusik*. Even *Tintagel*, fine and exciting as it is, only has one romantic melody, and that is unwhistle-able after its first two bars. Since romanticism is intellectually suspect today, Bax has lost his natural public—discerning and intelligent listeners. All this would seem to answer the question why Bax is ignored while Vaughan Williams is known to every music lover. But it does not explain why there is so little of him on record, or why his work is never heard on the radio. Admittedly, the four piano sonatas have been recorded by Frank Merrick, who is certainly one of the finest pianists in England today; and the best of them, the second, has the benefit of two recordings. This is a recent development at the time of writing, and one hopes it may lead to some renewed interest in his orchestral works. But the main question, how a composer of such importance can be consigned to something like total oblivion, still remains.

This question applies in an even greater degree to a number of English composers of the twentieth century. For example, although I have frequently seen the name of Lord Berners, and of Bernard van Dieren, I have never actually heard a piece of music by either of them, and I doubt whether anyone else of my generation has. (Van Dieren came to exercise a considerable influence on Warlock after his early infatuation with Delius; he was apparently a more 'intellectual' composer than Delius, and no doubt an acquaintance with his music would help to explain some of the peculiar, cold quality of *The Curlew*.) This may be because their music lacks all merit; but this does not seem to be the opinion of *Grove's Dictionary*, or of many other musical authorities.

E. J. Moeran is another example of incomprehensible neglect; his Symphony is a fine work, although it shows much of the influence of Sibelius; but his Violin Concerto and his piano music (some of which has been recorded by Iris Loveridge) show a remarkable and individual musical personality. Moeran is also a romantic—the Violin Concerto is full of Celtic melancholy. This melancholy apparently led to his downfall, for he was an extremely heavy drinker in his last years. The neglect of his music may also have contributed to his sense of defeat.

Bax's name is usually associated with that of another post-Elgarian romantic, John Ireland. Those who love Ireland love him above all other English composers; he is an addiction. Since his only readily available work is the Piano Concerto, many listeners will find this difficult to understand. But Ireland is at his best as a composer for the solo piano, and his finest music is to be found in various piano works: *Sarnia*, *An Island Sequence* (perhaps his finest), the Piano Sonata, *London Pieces*, *Decorations*, *Green Ways Suite*. The beautiful second Violin Sonata (which brought Ireland fame)* is in some ways reminiscent of César Franck, and makes one aware that Ireland has much in common with that great French master, as well as with Debussy, Ravel and Fauré. His work is all delicate, a matter of pastel shades. It would be an over-simplification to speak of him as an English Fauré, and yet the description would indicate the quality of subtlety and delicacy that makes such enthusiastic converts to his music. It is intensely English music, but not as aggressively English as so much of Vaughan Williams, and the harmonies are thoroughly post-Debussy. (His music sounds extremely simple, yet a pianist friend has told me that he is the most difficult of

*All these works are now available on record.

English composers to play; this is somehow typical of Ireland's musical personality.) Like Fauré, Ireland can never become a popular fashion; but, again like Fauré, he will always have a band of admirers for whom his music is unique. He is a curious blend of romantic (he wrote many pieces based upon the work of Arthur Machen) and restrained intellectual.

The music of Sir Arthur Bliss has been somewhat better served by the gramophone companies, although much of it is no longer available. He is one of those musicians about whom the fashionable critics are patronizing, although when one listens to the music it is difficult to think why: perhaps because some of his orchestration brings Elgar to mind. His best-known work is the March from the film *Things to Come*, although the Children's Ballet from that work is finer and more characteristic music. He has produced two concertos on a large scale, one for piano, one for violin, both of which are works that deserve a high place in the repertoire. They are warm, colourful, and often noisy. The Violin Concerto has an emotional quality that is reminiscent of Ernst Bloch, and at times of Max Bruch; the Piano Concerto is as much a bravura work as Rachmaninov's Second. But Bliss is also at home in the medium of chamber music, and some of his finest music is to be found in his Clarinet Quintet, while the Oboe Quintet and String Quartet, No. 2 are delightful works that can form the basis of a permanent addiction to the composer's work. After the *Things to Come* March, his most popular work is the Elgarian *Music for Strings*, one of his most openly romantic works. But a recent song cycle, *A Knot of Riddles*, commissioned by the B.B.C., reveals an astringent quality that reminds us that some of his earlier music, such as *Conversations*, made its impact by its wit—and occasional sarcasm. This was played in a Third Programme concert which is usually devoted to the most *avant-garde* music obtainable, and revealed that Bliss can hold his own even in the company of Boulez and Thea Musgrave. Like Bax, Bliss seems fated to fall between two stools; he is ignored by the fashionable critics, but has no compensation by way of being popular with the public of unsophisticated music lovers. This must be an irritating position for a composer of such brilliance, and is another example of the casual way that England treats its artists and composers. Bliss is not a great composer; but, musically speaking, he is at least the equivalent of Khatchaturian in Russia, or Samuel Barber in America. (He has much in common with Barber.) Neither of these composers suffer anything like the neglect that Bliss suffers. It is a hard business being a composer in England, particularly when one's music misses the fashionable trends.

The name of Sir William Walton also brings with it a question mark, but of a completely different nature from the one associated with Bax or Bliss. Even today, thirty years after it was written, Walton's First Symphony sounds urgent and modern, a voice for its time. Walton also has some of the Prokofiev quality of the *enfant terrible*, as capable of wit and sarcasm as of lyricism. So there is no question that Walton would have been able to hold his own among the *avant-garde*. Yet for some reason Walton has written very little music, and nothing of the same standard as the First Symphony, even though the Violin Concerto, 'Cello Concerto and Viola Concerto are all fine works in their different ways.

The early music of Walton has a quality that we associate with the period of *entre deux guerres*: full of nervous tension, astringencies, and a kind of musical wit that is somehow a counterpart of what Coward was doing on the stage. He also showed a formidable degree of talent, an ability to make a success with anything he touched. The Symphony has power; *Belshazzar's Feast* is the most dramatic oratorio in existence; the Violin Concerto has steely brilliance and drive; the *Façade* music, and the setting of certain Edith Sitwell poems have a breath-taking, jaunty charm. If Walton had possessed staying-power to match his talent, he would certainly have been one of the most important composers of this century.

What happened to Walton, then? One is cautious about dismissing the later work of any composer; he may confound everyone by coming up with a masterpiece. But it seems regrettably true that Walton has produced no music since the war that compares with the Viola Concerto or *Belshazzar's Feast*. A quartet that has been widely praised has a certain seriousness of purpose, but is not particularly striking music. Its first movement has much of that jerky, nervous music that one hears in the First Symphony, and one suspects that Walton writes this kind of music when he decides to be serious. This seems to be confirmed by the Second Symphony, which has an urgent opening theme that brings to mind the jerky rhythm of morse code. After several hearings, this symphony still shows no kind of development from the First, while much of its musical material is far less interesting. Many critics made the occasion of its first performance an excuse for writing epitaphs on Walton as a composer, which is unfair. The symphony may not reveal any new facet of Walton's personality, but it is by no means a negligible work. Still, one can understand the feeling of disappointment. Walton had produced no work of real importance since before the war; a 'cello concerto proved to be somewhat uninteresting after the two earlier concertos, while the opera *Troilus and Cressida* has an air of romantic eclecticism. There was hope that the Second Symphony would reveal that Walton was still in the running as a major European composer, and it certainly failed to do this.

The opera is a puzzling work. There was little in Walton's earlier output to suggest that he would find opera a natural expression of his peculiar qualities, so it was looked forward to with some curiosity. Would he, perhaps, accept the necessity of moving closer to experimentalism and produce a work in which his characteristic tensions would find vocal expression, in which case it would be hard to see how he could avoid sounding like *Wozzeck*? Even the choice of subject was a curious one, since *Troilus and Cressida* is fundamentally an unromantic story—a kind of Graham Greene-ish subject, full of human viciousness, pettiness, and betrayal. But Walton has written a romantic opera in which some of the characteristic airs (like 'How can I sleep?') have a flavour of *Porgy and Bess*. There is no feeling at all of compelling self-expression. Since Walton decided on a romantic mode of expression, he certainly loaded the dice against himself by choosing this story. Even Shakespeare's play is an artistic failure because Cressida is neither heroine nor villainess, and the final effect is one of ambiguity. In Walton's opera (based on Chaucer rather than Shakespeare) this only underlines the sense that the composer is not quite sure what kind of music he should be writing.

The most likely explanation of Walton's failure to emerge as a major composer is that the English cultural soil is too thin.

More than any other English composer since Elgar, Walton was an 'internationalist'; Prokofiev is a fairly close musical relative. If Walton had been forced to live out of his own country, like Prokofiev, his musical personality might have been nourished by the challenge of new ideas. The prevailing musical atmosphere encouraged him to become a conservative to avoid experimentation. His coronation march *Orb and Sceptre* is a saddening experience for the admirer of Walton's earlier music. Its main theme is a slight variation on the opening bars of Mendelssohn's Wedding March, and the whole thing has not even the virtue—like Bliss's *Things to Come* March—of being a rousing piece of music; it actually manages to be nondescript.

This explanation (the thinness of England's cultural soil) may well be the wrong one. Most major composers tend to be prolific. Walton has always worked with painful slowness. The development of a musical personality is a matter of more difficulty than that of a literary personality, since ideas, words, can be examined more clearly than the 'content' of a symphony or quartet. It seemed, in the First Symphony, that Walton had a personality worth expressing. But as one listens to the later music the suspicion dawns that Walton was a phenomenally clever composer with nothing in particular to say. No doubt England's cultural deadness is also to blame—the English loathe ideas, and are no more capable of original thought than of turning back somersaults—but at this stage it is impossible to decide. All that seems unpleasantly clear is that Walton has remained static as a musical personality.

The case of Benjamin Britten seems to demonstrate that it *is* possible to develop as a composer in the English cultural atmosphere, although one might raise the question of exactly how far Britten *has* developed since the days of *A Boy Was Born*. The reason for Britten's superior staying-power is revealed on the most superficial acquaintance with his music. The characteristic of cultural life on the Continent, at least in France and Germany, is a certain complexity, a tension of ideas. The artist is therefore lowered into a saturated solution of traditions, and attempts to work out his own synthesis according to his character. England has no tradition of ideas or of experimentalism, so a composer of Walton's type is a fish out of water. Now, Britten is in no sense a composer of ideas, and he shows no tendency at all to experiment. His music is all innocence. He is a kind of musical counterpart of J. D. Salinger, looking back wistfully to lost childhood. He favours the comparison of his art with that of Mozart; and indeed the comparison is not too wide of the mark in a certain sense. Britten is prolific, and his musical personality has a simplicity that is reminiscent of Mozart. But, as I have remarked elsewhere, the simplicity often degenerates into a sickening *fausse naïveté*, like Peter Pan asking his audience 'Do you believe in fairies?' His opera *The Little Sweep*, for example, has some delightfully fresh music—like 'Sammy's Bath'—but it is incredible how any serious composer could have condoned some of the trashy sentimentality of the libretto, and underlined it with his music (as in the passage where the children sing 'Dearest Rowan, dearest dearest Rowan'). Once one has become definitely irritated with this kind of thing, one begins to hear far too much of it in his music. The passage 'Spring, the sweet spring' from the 'Spring' Symphony has this same quality. Nowadays it is difficult to stomach some of the 'sweet innocence' that the Elizabethans found perfectly natural—all the 'Hey nonny nonny' and 'Birds do sing, Hey ding a ding ding' (which no English bird has ever been known to do). Kingsley Amis hits out at this in *Lucky Jim*, the middle-aged gentlemen in absurd shorts performing Morris dances on the vicarage lawn, waving ribbons on the end of a stick. Britten takes this all too seriously, and is encouraged in it by Peter Pears, for whom so much of his vocal music was written. Pears is a superb musician of great intelligence—it is impossible to doubt this—but his voice has a strangled quality that makes it easy to parody. (Dudley Moore does it with deadly effect in the 'Little Miss Britten' number of *Beyond the Fringe*.) Far too many of the songs that Pears is inclined to sing, with Britten at the piano, are about childhood and innocence and 'little pretty boys' (to quote the words of Ireland's 'I have twelve oxen', which Pears sings on a recital record). This non-stop emphasis on innocence has persisted in the thirty years since Britten wrote *A Boy Was Born*, and leads one to suspect that there has been no real development in his work. The *War Requiem* certainly shows a prodigious cleverness —but this was already apparent in the oboe quartet that he wrote at eighteen. But does the *War Requiem* reveal the development of Britten's total musical personality? It is undeniably an impressive work; but when one has listened to it several times one becomes more aware of the echoes of other composers— what Britten has learned from some of Shostakovich's noisy marching climaxes (like the one in the first movement of the Eleventh Symphony, for example) or from Stravinsky's *Canticum Sacrum*. This is the sort of cleverness and eye for dramatic effects that Walton revealed in *Belshazzar's Feast*—another influence that is clearly present. But the persistent theme of his music continues to be innocence, the innocence of young boys. (In *The Turn of the Screw*, Miles emerges far more clearly as a personality than Flora, his sister.)

There is no reason, of course, why innocence should not be a valid theme for music; but to dwell on it for thirty years argues a certain arrested development, a tendency to turn one's back on complexity. The 'Pickled Boys' episode of *St Nicholas* is typical; St Nicholas warns some travellers not to eat their dinner, as it is the pickled flesh of three boys, killed by the butcher. Nicholas then brings them back to life, and they depart singing. Everything is solved by a miracle; the real problem of the world's evil, and the complexity that is the necessary accompaniment of evolution, are ignored.

All this is not, of course, to deny that Britten is the most important English composer of this century. Like any other prolific composer, he has many long, dull passages, particularly for the voice. Also, the talk about his gift for melody is greatly exaggerated. In all Britten's output there is not a single melody that sticks in one's head like the third theme of the first movement of the 'Jupiter' Symphony, or even the opening of *Eine Kleine Nachtmusik* (although there is a charming waltz in *St Nicholas* and another in *The Little Sweep*). The aria 'Now the Great Bear and the Pleiades' in *Peter Grimes* is written on little more than one note, although it is perhaps the most important in the opera. In spite of all this, Britten shows a more natural gift for melody than any composer since Puccini; one can put on a record of *Peter Grimes* or even the *War Requiem* as background music and be continually arrested by delightful effects that seem to have the naturalness of the singing of a bird.

In view of this, it is surprising that so few of Britten's songs are memorable. Too many of them have a quality (which again,

Dudley Moore catches in his 'Little Miss Britten' parody) of melodic arbitrariness; the voice swoops or soars abruptly, or sings some phrase that seems deliberately ugly or characterless. One of the few exceptions is his setting of 'Down by the Sally gardens', but here the tune is based on Irish folk melody. The setting of Hardy poems in *Winter Words* compares badly with Finzi's Hardy settings, and Britten's songs altogether lack the delicate individuality of those of Butterworth or Warlock. Britten comes into his own as a song writer when he uses an orchestral accompaniment, as in the *Serenade* for tenor, horn and strings or the *Nocturne*. The lack of 'tunefulness' is unimportant compared with the beauty of the orchestral colouring and some of the fine poetic effects. (There are very few songs in either cycle that one could detach from its setting and sing to a piano accompaniment.) This is also, in the main, true of the operas. They are full of fascinating orchestral effects, 'mood music', as in the scene between Billy Budd and the novice, or the opening of the third act of *Billy Budd*, with its 'misty morning' music. The Passacaglia of *Peter Grimes* reveals his ability to write powerfully moving music, as does the *Sinfonia da Requiem*. The early *Variations on a Theme by Frank Bridge* also has some beautiful orchestral writing, but tends to lose itself in rather barren cleverness. The Piano Concerto and Violin Concerto reveal a Britten much under the influence of Prokofiev; but the latter has some beautiful music, and deserves to be heard more often. The same is true of the Left Hand Piano Variations, written for Paul Wittgenstein. His Second String Quartet is undoubtedly one of the finest that has been written by an Englishman, and repays repeated hearings.

Altogether, then, it seems rather a pity that Britten has devoted himself more and more to vocal music since the success of *Peter Grimes*, even though none of the operas he has written subsequently has had anything like the same power. The reason is partly that *Peter Grimes* had a certain richness of subject, a full-bloodedness, that has not been attained since. *The Rape of Lucretia* is written to a taut, intellectual libretto by Ronald Duncan, and this only emphasizes that Britten is not an intellectual musician; in retrospect it seems that too much of the opera is taken up with rather sweet choruses for women's voices. From the drama and scene painting of *Peter Grimes*, and the tension

157

and austerity of *Lucretia*, the operas descend a step to *Albert Herring* and *The Little Sweep*; the Maupassant comedy is transposed to England, and becomes a knock-about farce with village policemen, vicars and autocratic ladies with rich fruity voices. *Billy Budd* does not succeed in returning to the level of drama in *Peter Grimes*; it also labours under the disadvantage of an undramatic plot. Melville's short novel has become fashionable in the last fifteen years, since Melville has acquired the reputation of being a writer whose fundamental concern was good and evil. (This is untrue; Melville was a teller of tall stories with a penchant for German metaphysics, rather like Coleridge; there is little real moral insight in his work.) Even if *Billy Budd* had possessed the moral profundity that some American critics have claimed for it, it is doubtful whether Britten would have been able to convey it in music. As it is, it is just a rather unsatisfactory story, in which an innocent man dies through a stupid accident which stretches one's credulity (he 'accidentally' kills the mate with one blow of his fist). It lacks the material of real tragedy, and the unsatisfactoriness of its plot only emphasizes the unsatisfactoriness of Britten's obsession with innocence.

Britten has written two full-scale operas since *Billy Budd*— *Gloriana* and *A Midsummer Night's Dream*. The first of these suffers from the same disadvantage as *Billy Budd*, but to an even greater extent. The plot is episodic, and one does not feel that the downfall of Essex is an inevitable tragedy. Since Britten was writing about Elizabethan times, one feels that he could have allowed himself some tuneful Elizabethan music, which might have saved it from failure. In the Choral Dances (which are available on record) one is again aware that the writing of simple, memorable melody is not Britten's strong point; he is best at delicate orchestral colour, which is hardly suitable for a pageant opera. He is more at home in *A Midsummer Night's Dream*, where the lightness of the music matches the lightness of the subject.

There are also two smaller operas, *The Turn of the Screw* and *Noyes Fludde*. In both of these we are again in the kingdom of innocence and naïvety, and one's reaction to them depends on whether one enjoys this aspect of Britten. *Noyes Fludde*, written largely for children's voices, is as simply tuneful as Carl Orff's *Music for Children*, and even has touches that are reminiscent of

Ravel's *L'Enfant et les Sortilèges*. *The Turn of the Screw* is another story that is supposed to be about pure evil. The critics who believe that it reveals Henry James in a Graham Greene mood find it difficult to explain why the Master called it 'a fairy-tale pure and simple', but usually put it down to irony and contempt for his readers. If it had any undertones of evil, they vanish under Britten's treatment, which emphasizes everyone's innocence. Even Peter Quint sounds innocent as sung by Peter Pears. It is usually stated that this opera is Britten's best since *Peter Grimes*; but it has nothing of the universal appeal of *Peter Grimes*, and has never been revived.

To summarize: in my own opinion, Britten is at his best when writing orchestral music. The comparison with Mozart reveals the narrowness of his range in writing vocal music. Mozart can write about innocence, as in *The Magic Flute*, but he is equally at home conjuring up the light-hearted and lecherous Don Juan, or the violently jealous Electra (in *Idomeneo*). To enjoy completely much of Britten's vocal music, one must abandon oneself to a rather effete, unmasculine world. This can be pleasant in small doses, but one soon finds oneself longing for the cheerful scoundrelism of Don Juan or for the violent passions of Verdi's Otello. To hear Peter Pears singing 'Winter Words' or 'Now the Great Bear' is to feel that there is something rather cliquey and narrow about Britten's world. Most of the real world seems to be missing. One feels that if Britten ever lands up in hell the devil could not devise a better torture than to make him set Fleming's James Bond stories to music.

Britten makes one more clearly aware than ever of the problem of British music. If it is to be truly English, to have its roots in the English cultural tradition, then it must be 'small beer' music. Perhaps this is because the English temperament is phlegmatic and empirical, or because British scenery is usually green and unspectacular. It is surely significant that most of the Elizabethan plays portraying great passions are set in foreign countries.

The unnourishing nature of the British cultural tradition can be seen in two of the most interesting of Britten's contemporaries, Michael Tippett and Humphrey Searle. Musically speaking, Tippett seems to be a curious misfit who has never found his feet. Like the early Walton, he feels the need for deeper cultural soil than England can provide; but this attempt to escape his own Englishness seems to have robbed him of creative impetus. The oratorio *A Child of Our Time* is significant in that it attempts to write a politically conscious work; its use of negro spirituals reveals a tendency to experimentalism that reminds one of early Walton. Even so, one has a feeling that it fails to come off; it does not achieve its aim. It does not sound like a completely natural expression of Tippett's feelings; it seems to be rather an attempt to express what Tippett feels he ought to feel about Nazism and persecution.

The opera *The Midsummer Marriage* reveals even more clearly that Tippett is thoroughly dissatisfied with the English tradition, and wants something profounder, more complex; but again, it fails to achieve this. The plot is a complicated farrago with many interwoven allusions to *The Waste Land*. There is a character called Madame Sostrosis, and the 'villain' is called King Fisher. There is a great deal of symbolic action, all centring around the relations between a young couple. (At times one wonders if Tippett meant to write a Lawrencian opera.) But one feels that Tippett is a naturally unsophisticated person who is trying to graft an additional dimension—of intellectualism—on to his character. One can respect the intention, so foreign to English music; but it seems doomed to failure from the beginning. Most of Tippett's other music has a knotty, difficult character; it is somehow very hard to get to grips with it. In view of *A Child of Our Time* and *The Midsummer Marriage*, one wonders whether he is not aiming at something more complicated than comes naturally to him, and whether this is not the reason for his extremely small output. It would be wrong to speak of insincerity; but there are moments when one feels that he is straining for effect—in the *Magnificat and Nunc Dimittis* for example, where the organ emits sudden high squeals that sound as if Dizzie Gillespie has accidentally got into the church.

The music of Humphrey Searle reveals this same dissatisfaction with the English tradition, the desire to do something more profound. Although Searle was a pupil of Webern, his music is closer to that of Berg. 'Bergian' certainly describes the turbulent moods of the First and Second Symphonies. His Fourth Symphony is completely Webernian—that is, a few arbitrary notes are spaced over a long period, and the conductor seems to have more to do than the orchestra. In view of the Bergian content of the first two symphonies, and Searle's acknowledged admiration for Liszt (which some critics profess to detect in the symphonies), one cannot help wondering whether Searle is not being untrue to his own musical inspiration in an attempt to be *avant-garde*. (He has always shown a penchant for *avant-garde* subjects; he has set parts of *Finnegans Wake* and Edith Sitwell's *Gold Coast Customs*.) Certainly one of his most moving works is the strongly Bergian *Poem for Twenty-two Strings* (1950).

This suspicion is deepened by Searle's two recent operas, one based on Gogol's *Diary of a Madman*, the other on Ionesco's *Photograph of the Colonel* (*The Killer*). The atonal music adds nothing at all to the Gogol. Where the Ionesco is concerned it becomes clear that Searle is looking for a text that will serve as his own *Wozzeck*. But where Büchner's *Wozzeck* is a disguised social tract, Ionesco's play is a piece of shallow pessimism, written in his favourite manner of humorous grotesque. It is a Kafka-esque dream about a perfect garden city where a killer lures people to a pond by offering to show them the photograph of a colonel, then pushes them in. The hero, Beranger, finally meets the killer, and finds that he cannot be influenced by any arguments, and is indifferent to all human aspiration and human sorrow; Beranger allows himself to be killed. Presumably the killer is supposed to symbolize death. The point of the play is obscure, unless we assume that Ionesco takes three acts to say that all men must die. It is certainly intended to make human effort seem pointless, and human life grotesque and delusory. What it really amounts to is a highly polished cynicism, expressed in the casual, allusive way that Büchner was the first to use in *Wozzeck*. To this Searle adds music that is frequently reminiscent of *Wozzeck*, including a jangling café piano. The question one asks at the end of it is whether the composer has added anything to the play by setting it to atonal music. Berg's music, with its feeling of nightmare, of unconnectedness, added to Büchner's play; for the human passions underlying it are still quite recognizable, though seen through a distorting glass. One is also aware that the grotesqueness is really a grimace of Swiftian fury at the cruelty and stupidity of human beings, and Berg makes this clear by the pity that breaks out in the D minor interlude at the end (which sounds at times very like Delius).

161

Ionesco's play has no such underlying feeling; one does not even feel that it is a serious presentment of man's predicament. By deliberately using a dream technique, it has thrown overboard its true centre of gravity, the reference to human life and its values. In *Wozzeck*, the expression may be ambiguous, but the underlying meaning is clear: pity. Ionesco's play is all ambiguous. Consequently, Searle's atonal music only deepens the ambiguity. But a work of art cannot be ambiguous fundamentally, or it is simply unsatisfying. Searle's opera leaves behind the impression that the composer and playwright have got together to preach a sermon on the futility of human life. But the desire behind it all is not to say something of importance, but simply to write an opera. At the closing heavy chords, as the killer strikes, one is reminded of Tolstoy's comment on Andreyev: 'He keeps shouting Boo, but I am not afraid.'

It seems to me that this work of Searle's reveals even more clearly than Tippett's *Midsummer Marriage* the fundamental dilemma of the English composer. If he is not satisfied with the tradition of Elgar and Vaughan Williams, he has only two alternatives: to try to become a part of the Continental mainstream, or to try to create his own tradition. (Blake wrote: 'I must create my own system or be enslaved by that of another man'; and Tippett's music reminds one of Blake's strenuous efforts to patch up a mythology and system of ideas.) Both alternatives are self-defeating. An English composer cannot really become a part of the Continental tradition unless he moves naturally and freely in the Continental cultural milieu, and feels as happy reading Goethe or Dostoevsky as Shakespeare. This is much to ask of a musician, for ideas are the only true *lingua franca*, and music does not deal with ideas. On the other hand, the attempt to create one's own tradition involves so much mental effort that one's flow of creativity is bound to be affected.

This is the problem. It is likely to remain insoluble until England can cease to be a backwater, as far as ideas and art are concerned, and move into the centre of the main current. This is by no means as unlikely as it sounds. During the nineteenth century England produced no important music because England was insulated from the rest of the world; it was as stagnant and fixed in its ways as the society depicted in Ibsen's plays. It is significant that the first real English music was produced towards the end of the nineteenth century, when the period of disquiet had already commenced—with the Crimean War, the Zulu War, the first Boer War. Since that time British insularity has been swept away bit by bit, until now there is very little of it left; England is no longer a world power, but only another small country trying to defend its chances of survival. This is the situation in which England could conceivably take the intellectual lead away from the rest of Europe—or at least become a fruitful part of the European cultural tradition instead of a tiny separate entity. Whether this will happen will depend, of course, upon individual artists and thinkers. All that we can say is that the chances seem better than ever before.

9

SOME NOTES ON OPERA

I N OCTOBER 1959, Mr Peter Harrison, the music
critic of *The Twentieth Century*, reviewed Dallapiccola's opera *The Prisoner* and Carl Orff's *Die Kluge*.
Predictably, he thought *The Prisoner* magnificent, and dismissed
Die Kluge with a few words about cheapness and banality. I wrote
a letter to *The Twentieth Century*, arguing that operas that have
dramatic force without memorable tunes may be worth-while
theatrical experiences, but cannot be regarded as the legitimate
heirs of Wagner, Bizet, and Verdi. Mr Harrison did not agree
with me, as his irritable counterblast the following month
showed. Yet I feel that my point was worth making. Because
Dallapiccola's opera is obviously more serious than Orff's, does
this necessarily mean that it is a better opera? If we were discussing novels, or even plays, the answer might well be yes; we
take it for granted that *Pickwick Papers* or *Harry Lorrequer*,
though excellent of their kind, cannot be seriously compared
with *Crime and Punishment* or *Moby Dick*. That a good light
novel may often be better than a bad heavy novel is beside the
point. Opera is a different matter. To begin with, there is a
certain element of necessary absurdity about it, as Johnson
pointed out. It is like a musical comedy in which the characters
burst into song at every dramatic moment. I can remember how
I used to hate these interruptions as a small boy; I resented the
suspension of the action, and also felt instinctively that this was
cheating. Watching a play requires a 'willing suspension of
disbelief'; but if the play is to be interrupted for music, then it
demands a second act of faith. I felt that one was enough.

Since opera depends upon absurdity, is it not possible that
there might be a fallacy in assuming that an opera that aims at

realism and seriousness ought to be better than a light opera? This seems to me to apply particularly to twelve-tone operas. Berg's *Wozzeck* and *Lulu* are exceptions for a simple reason: the emotion that Berg wanted to convey demanded an unfamiliar kind of music, a tortured music of the nerves. It is, in a sense, literary music; it depends upon the reader's knowing something of the original play. The last (unfinished) act of *Lulu* is typical. Lulu has come to the East End of London and has decided to take to prostitution. A jangling barrel organ sets the mood. But her first customer is Jack the Ripper, who carries her off into the bedroom. Wedekind describes the killer as 'a thick-set man with a pale face, red-rimmed eyes . . . a drooping moustache . . . and fiery red hands with bitten nails. He keeps his eyes on the ground.' But when he staggers out of the bedroom, 'sweat drips from his hairy face . . . his eyes are popping out of his head'. And his next words are: 'I was always a lucky fellow.' This is one of the most hair-raising lines in twentieth-century literature. He is like a cat that has emptied a bowl of cream; he is gorged, exhausted; he feels the gods have been kind to him. As the climax of Wedekind's great play of sex-obsession, this is unsurpassable. Berg catches this nightmare quality in the music, and then uses a master stroke for his own climax: a scream. No one can listen to this last act of the opera (or rather, the last movement of the *Lulu* Symphony, which is always played in place of the last act) without feeling that subject and music have here achieved a remarkable unity.

The music of *Wozzeck* and *Lulu* had to be like this. One has only to compare *Lulu* with Phyllis Tate's Jack the Ripper opera *The Lodger*, written in a tuneful 'popular' style, to recognize that Berg was 'inside' his subject, and Miss Tate was not. If one is going to write an opera about a sex murderer, then it had better be done like this. Tunefulness would be out of place.

But this does not mean that a serious opera must be atonal. I have spoken in Chapter 8 of Humphrey Searle's Ionesco opera, and of my feeling that Searle's music adds nothing whatever to Ionesco's play. My feelings are much the same about most of the other atonal (or twelve-tone) operas that I have on record. The American composer Hugo Weisgall, for example, has produced atonal operas based on Strindberg's *The Stronger* and Wedekind's *The Tenor*. The first is simply a monologue sung by a woman; as far as I am concerned, Weisgall might as well have left it alone. It is difficult to understand what he thinks he has added to the play by setting it to music that sounds completely arbitrary, as if he had written it by closing his eyes and sticking a pin into a sheet of music paper. In *The Tenor*, a light comedy, this music sounds altogether out of place; its one really delightful moment is the tenor's aria 'Packing clothes is quite an art', that has something of a tune and seems to be intended as a parody of the big first-act aria in conventional opera.

It remains true that each opera must be judged on its own merits. Before *Wozzeck* no one would have believed it possible that a completely atonal opera could be a moving work and take its place beside the great operas of the nineteenth century. Schoenberg's *Moses and Aaron* also comes close to being a success; like Berg, he had the same sure instinct for the dramatic, and recognized that a twelve-tone opera must rely on the libretto as much as on the music. But I am not at all sure that *Ewartung* and *Die Glückliche Hand* are the masterpieces that ardent Schoenbergians claim them to be; the former seems to me a curiously barren *tour de force*, and I cannot accept for a moment the contention of Donald Mitchell that it is a finer work than *Wozzeck*.

I would suggest that it is probably a general truth that the modern idiom cannot be successful in light opera, or any opera with a strong element of comedy. Even Rolf Liebermann's *School for Wives*, which has moments of great lyricism, strikes one as an uncomfortable hybrid. Stravinsky's *Rake's Progress* seems to me to belong in the same class. But in many cases I feel that the modern idiom is not suitable to 'heavy' opera either. Nicholas Nabokov's Rasputin opera *The Holy Devil* is an example. The murder of Rasputin ought to be an excellent subject for opera. But somehow it is the wrong kind of drama for an opera. The murder of Rasputin is dramatic enough to read about, but as soon as it is set to music the music only robs it of its brutal impact, translates it to the level of a fairy-tale. This is the problem that Phyllis Tate encountered in *The Lodger*.

It is tempting to argue that there is no natural form for twentieth-century opera, and that its continuance is an anachronism. Opera is at its best, its most natural, in the 'heavy' works of the nineteenth century: *The Huguenots, Tristan, Faust, Carmen, Aida.* Puccini seems to be the last of this line. Meyerbeer and Halévy had the right idea: opera was meant to be noise and spectacle. One was not expected to take the plot too seriously; this was often little more than an excuse for providing music and pageantry. Mérimée's *Carmen* is one of the finest pieces of realistic writing of the nineteenth century; Bizet's opera is hardly more realistic than *The Pirates of Penzance.* No one expects it to be, and no one objects because it is not. *Cavalleria Rusticana* and *I Pagliacci* may have struck contemporary audiences as *verismo*; today, they seem no more realistic than Verdi's *Il Trovatore*; we listen to them because they are melodious, because they are all that we mean by Italian opera.

I am sometimes inclined to believe that the decline began with works like Dargomizhsky's *Stone Guest*, Verdi's *Falstaff*, and Puccini's *Gianni Schicchi*; these attempted to be realistic in a different sense. The music critics, as usual, explain that *Falstaff* and *Gianni Schicchi* are masterpieces; but how many opera lovers can say honestly that they prefer *Falstaff* to *Otello*, or *Gianni Schicchi* to *Turandot*? Not myself, certainly. What is more, if Verdi and Puccini had started their careers by writing this type of opera—in which music is little more than accompaniment to the dialogue—I doubt whether they would have had careers. We are willing to accept *Falstaff* as the masterpiece of Verdi's old age because it *ought* to be his masterpiece, and because it is an honest attempt to do something entirely different from the operas that made him famous. How far we are influenced by such extra-musical considerations I cannot say; but probably more than most music critics would admit.

I have called this chapter 'Some Notes on Opera' because short of writing a book on opera, I can think of no way of getting my thoughts about it into any sort of order. I have remarked in the Introduction that my first real experience of opera was a performance of *Carmen* at Coventry. Before this, I had occasionally listened to operas on the B.B.C., but I was secretly inclined to agree with Dr Johnson that it was an absurd form of entertainment that demanded more suspension of disbelief than a sane man should be prepared to make. It was *Carmen* that showed me that opera is partly supposed to be a *magic* spectacle, the adult's equivalent of the pantomime. When I began collecting operas I realized that I was still looking for this magic and tunefulness. The first time I played side one of *Faust* the music suddenly brought an intense feeling of well-being, the desire to chuckle aloud. I have felt it again many times since: with Flotow's *Martha*, with Adam's *Postilion of Longjumeau*, with Offenbach's *Tales of Hoffmann*, with Cilèa's *L'Arlesiana*, with Boieldieu's *La Dame Blanche*, with Charpentier's *Louise*, with Orff's *Der Mond*, with Douglas Moore's *Ballad of Baby Doe*, with Barber's *Vanessa*. In the introductory scene of *Tales of Hoffmann*, Hoffmann starts to sing the song of Kleinzach, and then, as he speaks about Kleinzach's features, goes off into a daydream about his mistress, Stella. No one could call this passage about Stella great music; yet it is passionate music, beautiful music, some of the finest Offenbach wrote, and it has a lyrical flow that makes one feel that Hoffmann might rise off the ground and float towards the ceiling. This is what opera is supposed to do: to sing like a bird, to convey a feeling of almost supernatural affirmation. Puccini is always doing it. The aria 'Mi chiamano Mimi' from *La Bohème* begins like any number of other arias in modern Italian opera; it might have come from Leoncavallo's *Bohème* or from an opera by Cilèa or Giordano. But when Mimi comes to the words 'ma quando vien lo sgelo' (but when the thaw comes) the music also seems to expand like the spring; it rises upward with the ease of an aeroplane taking off, into pure lyricism. This is what Cilèa and Giordano could never do. Their operas are like Puccini without these moments. There are many such in Puccini: another of my favourites occurs at the end of 'In questa reggia' in *Turandot*. Puccini may not have been a great composer, but he had a gift that might be the bitter envy of many greater composers. Some writer on music uses the phrase 'a tune like a fragment of heaven', which seems to me to describe exactly that quality possessed by Puccini, as well as by Tchaikovsky.

This tradition has been continued in the twentieth century, but it is no longer taken seriously. Carl Orff decided that there was no future in writing operas that would only appeal to a few highbrows, and produced *Der Mond* and *Die Kluge*. The former is my favourite, although, for some reason, most critics rate *Die Kluge* (*The Wise Woman*) higher. *Der Mond* is a fairy-tale about how, in the days before the moon existed, a German village had a 'moon' hung on a tree in the village square, fed by oil. Four villains from another village stole the moon, carted it off in a wheelbarrow, and took it to their own village. When they died each one had his quarter share of the moon placed in the tomb with him, and when the last of them died the other three woke up, clapped their quarters of the moon together, and lit up. All the dead then woke up and proceeded to play bowls, until God silenced them with a thunderbolt, and sent St Peter to collect the moon and hang it up in the sky. This absurd and delightful fable is an unending flow of gay tunes—there are times when one is reminded of Mozart. The tomb scene, ending with the whistle and tremendous crash of the thunderbolt, is particularly lively.

Die Kluge is also tuneful, although I find it slightly less so than *Der Mond*. Its drinking song is one of the most catchy in opera. Both these works were written immediately after his best-known work *Carmina Burana*; after this, Orff's inspiration seemed to flag. His largest opera, *Antigone*, is a strict setting of Sophocles' play, but seems as rhythmically repetitious as Ravel's *Bolero*; also, it has no good tunes.

One of the minor operas of this century which deserves to be better known is *Tiefland* by a Scotsman, Eugène d'Albert. This is somewhat Wagnerian (and is in German), but also has its own individual melodic quality.

Richard Strauss is at the moment a composer about whom there is little disagreement; everyone seems to feel that he was over-rated in his own day, and that his work ceased to be interesting after *Der Rosenkavalier*. This is the opinion expressed by Brockway and Weinstock in their *Men of Music*. There is a basis of truth in it. Strauss never had a great deal to 'say' as a composer. As Wagner's major follower, he was not really qualified to carry on the tradition of the master; for that, he would have needed an adventurous temperament closer to that of Scriabin. Strauss was a bourgeois with an unadventurous mind—and yet a great musician. It is true that he never surpassed *Der Rosenkavalier*; but what I find even more astonishing is that, for the remainder of a long life, he wrote so much music that was so little below the standard of his earlier masterpieces. *Ariadne auf Naxos* is generally conceded to be one of his most beautiful works. But his next opera, *Die Frau ohne Schatten* (*The Woman without a Shadow*), is in some ways even better. It and *Ariadne* are my two favourites among Strauss's operas. The story is absurd and extravagant, and demands all kinds of extraordinary effects, such as the earth opening up, and a flood bursting through the wall of a house. But it would probably be ideally suited to the medium of the screen. (A film of *Rosenkavalier* that was made in recent years only convinced me that, in spite of many beautiful moments, that opera is far too long, and does not deserve its reputation as Strauss's masterpiece.)

Two other late Strauss operas are available on record as I write this: *Capriccio* and *Arabella*. I find them both delightful in quite different ways. What is certain is that these operas seem made for the gramophone and the long-playing record. Critics have objected to the static nature of the plot in *Capriccio*, and to the immensely long string quartet 'overture', which goes on for about twenty minutes. If one is sitting in an opera house, no doubt this makes itself felt; in one's own sitting-room one can relax and allow the music to flow on gently; it is beautiful music, if a little uneventful—like Strauss's last work, the *Metamorphosen* for string orchestra (which, according to legend, was an elegy for the death of Hitler). In these two works, *Capriccio* and *Arabella* (a kind of sequel to *Rosenkavalier*), Strauss could be described as an operatic Bruckner. Still, if one likes Bruckner, this is no objection. In the final analysis, I am inclined to rate Strauss as a great composer; not because any one of his works is as great as *Tristan* or *Otello*, but because he produced such an enormous volume of very good work, from the early tone-poems to the *Metamorphosen* and *Four Last Songs*.

One of the few operatic composers who has successfully imitated Strauss is Italo Montemezzi, whose *Love of Three Kings* is deservedly one of the most popular of twentieth-century Italian operas. Perhaps it is unfair to accuse Montemezzi of imitating Strauss; but the music has an over-all rich German flavour that keeps bringing Strauss to mind. It has no great arias, but a delightful, warm, lyrical flow that brings to mind *Cavalleria Rusticana*. Archibaldo's aria 'Son quarant' anni' in the first act is typical of the opera's quality; it has no music that sticks in the mind like 'Vesti la giubba' or 'Nessun dorma', and yet anyone

170

hearing it without knowing what it was would recognize that here is a composer of some stature. (The fact that Archibaldo has some of the most magnificent basso music since Wotan may contribute to this effect.)

There are a great many Italian operas of the twentieth century that should be known to opera lovers in England and America, and fortunately many of them are recorded on Cetra labels. The standard of recording is often low, but the pleasure of discovering new music may compensate the listener. Zandonai is one of the Italian composers whose music is hardly known outside Italy. His first great success was with *Conchita*, which again has some of the qualities of *Cavalleria*. (Zandonai was a follower of Mascagni.) Two of his other operas that are available on record repay investigation: *Francesca da Rimini* and *Romeo and Juliet*. The love music in the former makes little secret of its indebtedness to *Tristan and Isolde*, even to the whispering of the lovers' names: 'Paolo', 'Francesca'; but the music itself is so attractive that this can hardly be held against it. The *Romeo* music has this same quality of attractiveness; again one is tempted to say that it is Puccini without memorable tunes. Other Italian opera composers who are available on record are Wolf-Ferrari, Giordano, and Cilèa. Wolf-Ferrari is best known for the one-act opera *Susanna's Secret* (Susanna's secret was that she smoked cigarettes); but his *Quattro Rusteghi*, issued by Cetra, is a delightful comic opera. Cilèa and Giordano have both been well treated by the record companies, and fine stereo recordings of *Adriana Lecouvreur* and *Andrea Chénier* are available. Both these operas have crowd scenes that come over admirably in stereophonic sound, and help one to understand why they achieved such popularity on the stage.

I have often thought that the careers of Mascagni and Leoncavallo are typical of an odd kind of tragedy that seems peculiar to the twentieth century, although I suppose there are examples to be found in earlier centuries. Both began with an enormous success, and then had a lifetime of failure, as if the initial success had made everyone determined to right the balance. Puccini had a similar experience with *Madame Butterfly* which came after the tremendous success of *Manon Lescaut*, *La Bohème*, and *Tosca*. The public and critics seemed tired of his success; they wanted to see it varied by a flop; so the first-night audience of

171

CHORDS AND DISCORDS

Madame Butterfly at Milan noisily demonstrated its contempt. Edward Greenfield points out that the general public 'was glad that Puccini had had a failure'. What is the psychology of this? It seems to be more general in our century than in any previous one—probably because the rewards of success in our century *can* be so enormous, and so out of proportion to the merit of the piece that produces them. There is a positively destructive delight now in declaring that the second book of a successful author, or the second play of a successful playwright, reveals that he (or she) has written himself out.

Puccini had the satisfaction of seeing *Madame Butterfly* go on to become his most successful opera. It must have given him a feeling of gleeful malice to look back on the criticisms that appeared after that first night in Milan. Neither Mascagni nor Leoncavallo had any such satisfaction. The story of their early success is well known. Both were poor young men, struggling hard. Mascagni wrote his one-act opera for a competition; it made him world famous within a few months. Leoncavallo deliberately set out to imitate *Cavalleria*, and reaped the same success. Both of them went on to write many more operas—Mascagni died at the age of eighty-two in 1945—but neither ever again had a real success. Mascagni was probably the more gifted of the two; his *L'Amico Fritz* shows a desire to write a good opera of a quite different kind from *Cavalleria*. He succeeded; *Fritz* is a gentle, pastoral opera with no violent emotions, and it is entirely successful. I find it extremely difficult to choose between it and *Cavalleria*.

A fair amount of Mascagni is available on record from Cetra, including the complete *L'Amico Fritz* and the later *Il Piccolo Marat*, and a record of excerpts from *Isabeau*, an opera based on the Lady Godiva legend. These make it difficult to understand why Mascagni is rated so low nowadays. (I have, in any case, never belonged to that group of blasé critics who find *Cavalleria* cheap and tiresome; I think it one of the most splendidly tuneful of all Italian operas.) Brockway and Weinstock declare that after *Cavalleria* the fount of melody ceased to flow for Mascagni; the briefest acquaintance with any of the other operas on record disproves this. The interlude in *Isabeau*, for example, is very nearly as effective as the one from *Cavalleria*. It lacks finesse admittedly; it sets out to be striking; but then, one does not go to Mascagni for finesse but for melodiousness. Even *Il Piccolo Marat*, which is somewhat more Wagnerian than most of Mascagni—that is to say, it is more of a music drama, without set arias—has plenty of the melodiousness that distinguished *Cavalleria*.

Leoncavallo died in 1917, so had not quite so many years in which to regret the fame that vanished with *I Pagliacci*. His *Zaza* has some pleasant music in it, if one is to judge by the half-dozen or so arias that are obtainable on recital records, but nothing as striking as 'Vesti la giubba'. His *Bohème*, produced a year after Puccini's, reveals why he never gained the same secure hold on the Italian public as his rival; the music simply bears no comparison. Leoncavallo is pleasant, but indistinctive; he has also plagiarized plentifully from Puccini, as Edward Greenfield has pointed out in his book on Puccini, not to mention a very obvious echo of *Tristan* at the opening of Act III. But the main thing one realizes from the comparison is that Puccini had a gift for melodies that stay in the mind after a single hearing; there is not one in Leoncavallo's *Bohème*.

While on the subject of Italian opera we might well speak of Gian Carlo Menotti, whose case, unfortunately, bears some relation to that of Mascagni and Leoncavallo, although he may well produce more work as striking as *The Consul*. Menotti's first opera, written in his twenties, was *Amelia Goes to the Ball*, which already reveals his lightness of touch; it is almost Rossinian. His first great success was scored in 1946 (when he was thirty-five) with a double bill, *The Telephone* and *The Medium*. These operas show perfectly Menotti's gifts and his limitations. *The Telephone* is a light piece about a man who cannot manage to propose to a girl because she keeps making telephone calls, so that he is forced to go out and propose to her over the phone. The music is light and pleasant; the girl's aria, sung over the telephone, is altogether original in opera; the piano used here is an inspired touch, and so are her exclamations of 'Aha' to indicate that she is listening. It is all very delightful . . . and yet there is something rather silly and trivial about the whole idea. One cannot help wondering whether the man must be mad to want to marry such an obviously empty-headed girl, or how one can be expected to be interested in two people so obviously commonplace. There is a disturbing element of naïveté about Menotti, a touch of the Britten quality. It is difficult to believe that he could ever be more than a light-weight composer. This is confirmed in the Piano Concerto, written at about the same time as *The Telephone* and using one of its themes in the opening.

The Medium is an attempt at a new kind of *verismo*, the kind of *verismo* that one might find in a Sunday scandal sheet; it deals with a fake medium and with her customers—particularly a man and woman who have lost their child. Yet here again there is something subtly wrong with it all, something faked about its seriousness, as if *A Farewell to Arms* had been rewritten by Enid Blyton. It ought to be tragic and horrifying, but one cannot take the artist's seriousness for granted. And yet it is very nearly successful, and the fact that it remains in the current repertory and has been filmed shows that its slight touch of 'phoniness' is hardly noticeable to the opera-going public.

Substantially the same criticism applies to Menotti's most successful opera *The Consul*. And here, for the first time, one realizes that Menotti's chief mistake is to write his own libretti. He writes English as if it were Italian; the emotions are a little too over-ripe and high-pitched, and the effect is always on the edge of bathos. Menotti is an atrocious librettist, and it is a great pity that the critics did not do him the service of telling him so at an early point in his career. Instead, they have been inclined to flatter him; even a recent book by Joseph Machlis on contemporary music declares that his words and music are inseparable halves of the same dramatic conception. A good English libretto should be colloquial and pitched in a low key, like that of *Peter Grimes*; overstatement is fatal. It is unfortunate that Menotti also produced a libretto for *Vanessa* by his friend Samuel Barber—in many ways a more talented composer than Menotti; *Vanessa*, which has some most effective music, might otherwise have been one of the finest of modern operas.

The Consul, although it sets out to be a serious political opera about oppression in a fascist state, already shows that Menotti is fundamentally a composer of light music or film music. The whole of the first scene—in which a man arrives home from an illegal political meeting with a bullet in his leg—has effects that have come straight from Hollywood, including a thoroughly tiresome mother who seems to have no other role than to moan and complain. If one compares *The Consul* with a work like Koestler's *Darkness at Noon*, one can see at once what is wrong with it; Koestler's work is in deadly earnest, and convinces the reader of this within a few pages; Menotti never manages to convince the listener that he is really in earnest about his political protest; when the baby dies and the mother commits suicide, we feel that it is all a bit too close to *East Lynne*.

This same objection applies to the television opera *Amahl and the Night Visitors*, which has a depressing Brittenish naïvety, and to the two larger works, *The Saint of Bleeker Street* and *Maria Golovin*. The religiosity of *The Saint* is nauseatingly unconvincing, and the libretto is so appalling that it is surprising that no solicitous friend explained to Menotti that he was ruining his operas by clinging to this mistaken notion that he was a writer and a dramatist as well as a composer. It has one excellent aria that might have been written by Puccini, Michele's 'I know that you all hate me'; but even in the title of the aria one can see Menotti's tendency to write in violent primary colours. *Maria Golovin* is about a blind man who falls in love with a woman who thinks she is a widow; again one feels that, in his choice of subject, Menotti is trying to tug at the heart-strings; consequently one refuses to have them tugged.

All this is a pity. As a musician, Menotti is excellent; but he should stick to music. Britten has always been sensible enough to choose intelligent libretti or poems to set. If Menotti had been equally sensible, he would probably now be rated as one of the world's most important composers. There is no great originality there, but there is a gift of melody, and a prodigious cleverness. By writing his own libretti he has exposed the calibre of his intellect in public. No one doubts that his heart is in the right place; but in Anglo-Saxon countries one does not wear it on one's sleeve to that extent. I personally get a great deal of pleasure from Menotti's music, and am irritated when I have to wince at some awful platitude in the libretto.

It is easy enough to understand why so many people believe that opera has reached the end of its tether in the twentieth century. On the one hand, we have 'modernistic' works that can never be expected to appeal to a wider public, except, perhaps, for 'scandal' reasons (like Pousseur's *Elektra*, which manages to achieve a nervous tension and horror even greater than Strauss's by the use of electronic effects); on the other hand, there are various traditional works that seem to be hang-overs from the previous century, and to offer no possibility of fresh development. This is not to say that such works may not be good operas in their own right; Marc Blitzstein's *Regina*, Barber's *Vanessa*, Moore's *Ballad of Baby Doe*, Menotti's *Consul*, Gershwin's *Porgy and Bess*, are all artistic successes on a certain level—and posterity may decide that their level is not far below that of most of the operas of Gounod, Massenet, Thomas, or even the early Verdi. France has also produced some good traditional opera. Poulenc's *Breasts of Tiresias* and *The Carmelites* deserve special mention. The first owes much to Ravel's *L'Enfant et les Sortilèges*, but it is a masterpiece for all that, full of gaiety and tunes that lift the heart; *The Carmelites* is less successful, on a bigger scale, but has at least one scene that is quite overwhelming: the Finale, where the nuns march to the guillotine singing a 'Salve Regina', and their voices are cut off one by one by the horrible thuds of the blade, until only one voice is left—and then a final thud cuts it off. For sheer dramatic effectiveness, this must be one of the finest scenes in modern opera. Poulenc's only other opera, a setting of Cocteau's *La Voix Humaine*, is, in my own opinion, a boring failure, consisting mainly of recitative; the music adds nothing to Cocteau's words, which are maudlin enough anyway. Another recent French opera well repays a hearing by record enthusiasts, particularly as the French critics gave it anything but a kind reception: Gilbert Bécaud's *Opéra d'Aran*. This work, by a man who is best known as a comedian, owes much to *Porgy and Bess*, but some of the music is as emotionally effective as Puccini. The plot concerns a braggart called Angelo who is cast up on the Aran Isles and steals a girl from her lover by means of grandiose lies. In the last scene of the opera he admits that he is a liar, and he and the girl sail off into a sunset that is already dark with a rising storm. A man rushes down to call them back, but his cries of 'Angelo' are blown away by the wind. It is typical of the absurdity of opera that they should have to sail away into a storm; but the last scene, with the shouts of 'Angelo', is remarkably moving for all that. (Opera composers have never been noted for displaying a critical sense about libretti; I once asked Britten why Peter Grimes has to sail out to sea at the end and

pull the plug out of his boat—no one but a fool would do it—
and he admitted that he was not sure.)

And yet there are operas of the twentieth century that are
neither modernist nor traditionalist, and that show that authentically modern operas do not have to fall into either category.
There are, to begin with, the operas of Leoš Janáček, whom
many consider to be the greatest of Czech composers. Janáček
remained unknown until he was in his sixties (in 1916), when
his early opera *Jenufa* was performed and made him famous. In
the few years left to him he composed a large number of astonishing works. Many critics consider that his finest opera is his
second, *Káta Kabanová*, based upon a heavy tragedy of little
merit by the depressing Russian playwright Ostrovsky; it is
certainly a work of great power. He also wrote a fantastic opera
based on a Čapek play, *The Makropoulos Affair*; a delightful
comic opera, *Mr Brouček's Excursions*, which is one of my own
favourites; a fairy-tale opera, *The Cunning Little Vixen*, which
is the best thing of its kind since *Hansel and Gretel*; and finally
a curious and nightmarish work, more cantata than opera, based
on Dostoevsky's novel *The House of the Dead*, about a Siberian
prison camp. Janáček's music is fundamentally romantic, but has
an astringent quality. The prelude to *The Makropoulos Affair*
gives an idea of all Janáček's qualities in the briefest time. It has
some jarring repeated figures, that produce a tense effect like
that of morse code, but also a broad, flowing melody; but the
melody is not allowed to flow for more than a few bars; it keeps
being stopped with a jerk while the orchestra makes morse code
noises, as if Janáček is ashamed to allow his lyric inspiration to
flow. It is like a man in a powerful car, who keeps suddenly
applying the brakes every time he has got up a good speed.

Janáček relies a great deal upon repetition: the prelude to
From the House of the Dead consists of the same bars repeated
over and over again; yet the repetition is not irritating, as it so
often is, for instance, in Carl Orff. In the *Concertino*, for example,
the same phrase repeated over and over again produces a kind
of hieratic effect; one feels that the repetition is serving some
purpose that one cannot define; it is a kind of development in its
own way. Janáček is a limited composer; there is a sameness
about all his best music; but he is undoubtedly one of the most
individual voices of the twentieth century; his music is as

immediately identifiable as that of Bartók, Hindemith, or Stravinsky. There are also moments in his work where he keeps the brakes off, so that the music is allowed to expand into romantic beauty—as, for example, in the last scene of *Mr Brouček*, describing the earth after Mr. Brouček gets back from the moon, or in the final scene of *The Cunning Little Vixen*.

Another opera composer of equal individuality is Sergei Prokofiev. His first opera, *The Gambler*, was not of remarkable quality, if one is to judge by the suite taken from it; but his second, *The Love of Three Oranges*, is a splendid work, greatly superior to the well-known suite, absurd, noisy, at times cacaphonous, always breezy and vital; it reveals Prokofiev at his most mischievous.

There is something of a tragedy connected with Prokofiev's greatest opera—and one of the greatest operas of this century—*The Fiery Angel*. Prokofiev had left Russia after the revolution, and hoped to make his home in the West; but neither America nor France showed much appreciation of his work, and he might well have starved if it had not been for various commissions. *The Love of Three Oranges* was performed in Chicago in 1921, but even this evidence of abundant genius failed to gain him recognition in America. In disgust he went to Paris, where he wrote *The Fiery Angel*, based upon the masterpiece of Valery Briussov, a novel of witchcraft and obsession. It was never performed in the western world, and when he returned to Russia the Russians were not interested either; so one of the greatest operas of this century remained unknown for a quarter of a century after its creation.

The Fiery Angel is the story of a knight, Ruprecht, who meets a possessed girl, Renata, falls in love with her, and agrees to help her search for an angel with whom she used to play as a child. The opera includes a scene with Faust and Mephistopheles, a duel (in which Ruprecht allows himself to be wounded at Renata's intervention), and a finale in a convent in which all the nuns become possessed and Renata is sentenced to be burnt by an Inquisitor. The subject is perfectly suited to Prokofiev's torrential genius; it has moments of lyric tenderness, and moments when he can make full use of his driving, machine-like rhythms. One of its most exciting scenes takes place when Ruprecht goes to interview Cornelius Agrippa to ask the magician's help. Agrippa denies that he is a magician, and explains that he is only a philosopher; as he says this, two skeletons suspended from the ceiling leap up and down and shriek 'Liar!' The music is wild, nervous, hysterical, and very powerful indeed. This work is, in my own view, Prokofiev's masterpiece. Luckily, an excellent French recording exists, and enables listeners to judge for themselves whether modern opera has to be either conventional or incomprehensible.

After his return to Russia, Prokofiev smoothed the asperities out of his music, and produced a number of other operas, including *The Duenna* (based on Sheridan), *War and Peace*, and *A Story about a Real Man*, based on a trashy novel about a Russian airman. *The Duenna* is mostly recitative, and does not allow Prokofiev much opportunity for lyricism, although it has many fine moments. *War and Peace* must be judged as an opera, not as an attempt to translate Tolstoy into terms of music. Like much Soviet opera, it owes much to Mussorgsky, which is particularly apparent in Kutuzov's fine aria on the eve of battle. This is not great opera, it sets out a little too obviously to be popular; but it contains much fine music, and deserves a place on the record shelves beside *The Love of Three Oranges* and *The Fiery Angel*. (There exists a good American recording.) His last opera, *A Story about a Real Man*, met with opposition from the censor, and was not performed until many years after Prokofiev's death. Apparently this was no great tragedy; the critics found it to be a little too blatantly full of communist propaganda. This does not mean, of course, that it could not be a masterpiece; but Prokofiev was never at his best when he had one eye on Stalin's approval. He was naturally a rebel.

Shostakovich's opera *Lady Macbeth of Mtzensk* also deserves mention; it was recently performed for the first time in England, and showed itself to be another 'Prokovian' work—witty, tuneful, and sharp. It certainly deserves to take its place in the standard repertory as a major twentieth-century opera that can appeal to the audiences who enjoy Wagner and Verdi.

Shaporin's *The Decembrists*, while no masterpiece, is another recent Soviet opera that is worth getting to know. Again, it is heavily indebted to Mussorgsky, but has a tunefulness that makes it appeal on first hearing. Other modern Russian composers who have produced conventional but tuneful operas are

179

Dankevitch (*Nazar Stolola* and *Bogdan Kmelnitsky* are recorded), Tigranin, an Armenian (whose *Anush* and *David-Beg* are also available), Hulak-Artemovsky, and Stekenko. These seem to prove that Russia can carry on indefinitely producing operas on nationalistic subjects that have at least as much immediate appeal as Verdi's *Lombardi* or Erkel's *Hunyadi László*.

Opera *is* based upon absurdity. We might wish that the plot of *Il Trovatore* was a little less improbable, but it does not really hinder enjoyment of the music. Realism *can* add to the effect; we are moved by the chorus of freed prisoners in *Fidelio* because we believe in them more than we believe in the Count di Luna. But belief is not essential. I have seen a friend of mine moved to tears by the wife's waltz song in Poulenc's *Breasts of Tiresias*, although it occurs in a completely farcical situation. This seems to indicate that there is a fallacy in the idea that twentieth-century opera should go one further than *Wozzeck* in realism. Yeats expressed the objection in a poem that really applied to the realistic novel:

> Shakespearian fish swam the sea, far away from land;
> Romantic fish swam in nets, coming to the hand;
> What are all those fish that lie gasping on the strand?

That is to say that Shakespeare created objectively, using material that was anything but personal; the romantics became more subjective, and made personal honesty a criterion of artistic value; many modern writers have tried to carry subjectivity and personal honesty to an extreme, but have consequently dammed up all possibility of creative development—for, as Yeats says elsewhere, poetry is telling lies. ('What! be a singer born, and lack a theme?') The innovations of Hemingway and Joyce can be exciting; but when innovation is accepted as an end in itself—as by the French anti-novelists, for example—the result is a kind of constipation.

Opera was meant to be Shakespearian; its plot, the human situations, are excuses on which to hang music; its *raison d'être* is musical beauty, a Mozartian flow of musical affirmation. In the greatest opera the music unites with the human truth of the situation to move us more than the music could alone. This happens usually in love scenes or death scenes—as in *Tristan*, the love scene of Fibich's *Sarka*, the final scene of *Otello*. But the human situation can be a mere sketch, a peg on which to hang the music. The truth is that *Wozzeck* and *Moses and Aaron* are not so much operas as plays with music, a single stage more 'unified' than Kodály's *Háry János* (which is no more than a play with incidental music). The play of *Wozzeck* is just as moving as the opera, for although the opera gains something from Berg's music, it loses something of the impact of Büchner's chilling casualness. (The last line of the play is the police chief's comment, 'A nice little murder, a very nice little murder. . . .')

I believe, then, that Orff was right in theory when he decided that he would write operas with whistle-able tunes. Twelve-tone music is *not* suitable for operatic expression, except in special cases where the composer wants to produce a music of nightmare or nervous tension. (Even so, to my own ear the 'Dance round the Golden Calf' from *Moses and Aaron* has never sounded like orgiastic dance music.) If a composer has individuality, it will appear in his music without any attempt to impose a 'system'. I sometimes feel, perhaps unfairly, that a young composer who finds it necessary to adopt serialism or one of its variants is like a man who takes elocution lessons because he is ashamed of his local accent and his origin. It indicates a desire to be different without making the effort of self-discipline that will *make* one different.

But the point of these notes is not to argue against serialism, but to say that the talk about 'exhaustion of the operatic language' is far from true. In the twentieth century we have operas as different as Janáček's *From the House of the Dead*, Busoni's *Doktor Faustus*, Prokofiev's *Fiery Angel*, and Britten's *Peter Grimes*—all in a more or less conventional idiom—to prove that a composer with individuality can produce a good opera without going far beyond the resources that were available to Wagner or Verdi. The problem, and this applies to music in general as well as to opera, is really a problem of conviction, which makes for individuality. There is no such thing as 'pure music'—certainly not in our own age. Music *says* something, even if the something could not be translated into words. I find it as difficult to imagine music without some underlying conviction as to imagine the poetry of Shelley or Blake without its content of ideas.

Let me repeat my own conviction about the art of the twentieth century: it has become enfeebled because it has come to place emphasis on the means of expression rather than on content; and it has placed emphasis on the means because it is difficult to have any deep religious or philosophical convictions in an age of scepticism. Science destroyed man's belief in his uniqueness as a special object of God's attention, and then destroyed his belief in his uniqueness as a biological organism. Contemporary science and contemporary humanism have done much to alter this; once again, in a fashion, man is the centre of the universe, the evolutionary spearhead. Researches into 'mind-changing' drugs and extra-sensory perception may turn the last part of the twentieth century into a new age of discovery —this time of interior discovery. But so far these changes have only reached biology and touched the edge of philosophy (the latter is still pessimistically oriented). Most of our art still flounders in the wastes of cultural nihilism. But its problems are problems of content (or rather, lack of content), not of exhaustion of language. If we should enter a new musical golden age, it will not be because the theories of Schoenberg or John Cage or Edgar Varèse have given us a new key to the problems, but because our culture has again become healthy enough to start sustaining new Mozarts and Beethovens. It would become clear that there was never any question of the novel coming to an end after *Ulysses*, or music after Schoenberg. Music is content; the means of expression are a by-product.

10

AMERICAN MUSIC

'**I** s a y, with all this passionate love of music amongst you Americans, *Where are your American composers?*' It was the philosopher Whitehead who fired this question at his Boswell, Lucien Price, in March 1936. And Price remarked: 'If we had had any undeniably of the stature of the great Germans, he would not have asked it. What I did find to say was that this art of symphonic orchestration has been imported into America at the very peak of its complexities, and that our composers, instead of beginning back where the Europeans began, in simplicity, have begun in complexity, and tried to make it more complex. It is perhaps too soon to know whether this is a success or a failure.'

If Whitehead had asked the question thirty years later, Price might have felt less embarrassed. America in the 1960s can boast at least as many composers of world stature as any country in Europe. The question of whether America now has a music of its own must be left until later. What we can at least say is that America now has a musical *history* of its own—and an extremely interesting one it is.

In fact, the story of modern American music had already begun when Whitehead asked his question. And if Lucien Price had been less shy of the great man, he might have mentioned Roy Harris as a young American composer who was probably slated for world renown. For by 1936, Harris was already *the* American composer, and his powerful and original First Symphony had been played some dozens of times. That was the trouble with Harris's career: his send-off was too good. It is a typically American story: feverish public enthusiasm, followed by a kind of outraged indignation on the part of the

183

public that their idol is failing to live up to all the advance publicity. (Conductors like Werner Janssen and the Englishman Barbirolli could tell the same rather bitter story.) By the mid-1940s, Harris was a back number—at least, according to his critics. There are certain weed-killers whose effect is to fertilize the weed so powerfully that it immediately grows to twice its height—then promptly dies of the effort. The publicity treatment has the same effect on artists.

Still, the Harris boom wasn't entirely a disaster, except for the unfortunate Harris himself; it created a genuine public interest in American music. Americans tend to be culturally modest, as Whitehead remarked; the result, up to about 1930, was to prevent them from believing that their own composers might have anything to say; so a certain way of ensuring that a concert lost money was to include an American work on the programme. To a large extent, it was Harris who changed all this. Musical historians of the future will also doubtless be tempted to add the name of Gershwin to those who rescued American music from the doldrums. This would be musically true but historically false. Gershwin possessed authentic musical genius (as Arnold Schoenberg pointed out), but the Piano Concerto, the *Rhapsody in Blue* (1924) and *Porgy and Bess* (1935) were not regarded as a real contribution to American music. (Nowadays, some critics have gone to the opposite extreme, and tend to regard them as the realest contribution so far.)

Still, the history of American music begins at least half a century before Harris placed it on the map. And it would be a great deal more creditable if Americans *had* been less culturally modest and had paid more attention to their composers, for they had a number of fine ones who could easily have ranked with the best in Europe. (And it must be remembered that 'the best in Europe', at this *fin de siècle* period, meant Grieg, Elgar, Ravel, Debussy, Mahler and Rimsky-Korsakov.) The stories of MacDowell, Griffes and Charles Ives are artistic tragedies, tragedies of neglect and stupidity. At the time when Finland had granted the thirty-two-year-old Sibelius a pension that amounted to around $5,000 a year, America was allowing Edward MacDowell to go insane from overwork and over worry. A decade later, the same fate was allowed to overtake Griffes.

Edward MacDowell's name is hardly known in England; to judge from the record catalogue, it is hardly better known in the country of his birth. I came across him by accident, when the Chávez recording of his two piano concertos was issued in England. I knew 'To a Wild Rose', and that didn't endear him to me. However, I bought them out of curiosity, and put the first on the turntable. (This is the one that is never played, and has only been recorded once; the second is slightly better known.) The thing delighted and charmed me. A friend who came in while it was playing said, 'Good heavens, what's that?' I told him to try and guess. After a minute, he said: 'It's obviously some imitator of Rachmaninov, but I can't for the life of me think who it could be. Some modern Russian?' It was a pleasure to point out that it had been composed a good fifteen years before Rachmaninov's Second, and ten years before the First.

His mistake, of course, lay in choosing Rachmaninov instead of Grieg. It is the latter who is the major influence on Mac-Dowell. And in my own view, the two piano concertos are every bit as good as Grieg's. It is a mystery why these are not regularly played in concert programmes, because they both have the highly popular quality of the Grieg A minor and the Rachmaninov Second—nostalgia, simplicity and warm, flowing melodies.

Grieg's physical health made him a minor composer. It took him several years of sweat to write the *Peer Gynt* music, and he would have been physically incapable of a symphony, or even a full-scale piano sonata. MacDowell had abundant physical strength. He went to study in Europe at the age of fifteen, and nine years later bought a small house in the woods near Wiesbaden. If he'd had the sense to stay in Europe, he would have undoubtedly gone on to produce a lifetime of fine work. Instead, he allowed himself to be persuaded to return to America (in 1888—back to a young and noisy country, a country whose Wild West was still alive and kicking, whose Chicago and New York were exploding cities already dominated by gangs. It was vital, vulgar, materialistic and bone-headed. For seven years Mac-Dowell was relatively successful. He produced the works for which he is best known—the Second Piano Concerto, the *Woodland Sketches* (which contains 'To a Wild Rose'), *Sea Pieces* and several piano sonatas. The small piano sketches contain some of his most beautiful music, heavily influenced by Grieg. (I am among those who consider that Grieg's finest work is to be found in the *Lyric Pieces* that he produced throughout his career.) But MacDowell found America frustrating; he felt as though he was working in a vacuum. So when Columbia University offered him an appointment in 1896, he accepted eagerly. This looked like being his opportunity to influence the younger generation, to watch his artistic idealism producing its effect on young minds. It was a fatal temptation—so like the one that led Dickens to kill himself by reading his works aloud. It was all overwork and frustration, with plenty of the kind of unpleasantness and petty opposition that had wrecked Smetana's health in Prague only twenty years earlier. Eight years of this was enough to destroy all his optimism and resilience. He resigned, and tried to go back to the countryside and creative work. It was no good; he was overtired and hopelessly discouraged about American music. For the last three years of his life he lived in a mental twilight, although his physical health was still excellent. America had broken his creative mainspring.

So MacDowell remains one of the might-have-beens of art. Even so, the music that exists can give a great deal of pleasure. The piano sonatas are well worth the trouble of getting to know them. He gave them all romantic names—the 'Tragica', the 'Eroica', the 'Norse', the 'Keltic'. James Huneker called the 'Tragica' the greatest contribution to piano literature since the Brahms F minor. It certainly isn't that. The Brahms work is great music that can stand comparison with Beethoven or Schumann; the MacDowell sonatas lack the architecture of greatness. A better standard of comparison would be those two beautiful Rachmaninov sonatas for two pianos, especially the Second.

No, MacDowell is no Brahms. But he is at least of the stature of Grieg or Rachmaninov. The half-dozen LPs of his work that I possess are among my most played records.

The story of Charles Tomlinson Griffes is so like that of MacDowell that it would be unbearable to go into detail. Twenty-three years MacDowell's junior, he went to Berlin at the age of nineteen to study under Humperdinck. At twenty-three,

186

he returned to New York and became a teacher. Hack work and discouragement killed him by the time he was thirty-six.

In certain ways, Griffes was a finer musician than Mac-Dowell. He was influenced by Debussy, and his compositions have a complexity and sophistication that we do not find in MacDowell. But the mood is basically the same. His greatest work, a piano sonata, completed three years before his death in 1920, has precisely those qualities that MacDowell's sonatas lack—richness, complexity and architecture. It probably deserves the praise that Lawrence Gilman lavished on MacDowell's 'Tragica': the most important contribution that an American composer has made to musical art. Since 1930, there have been a great many major contestants for this prize, but I imagine that the Griffes sonata is still well in the running. It has been alleged against a number of American composers that they tend to be imitative of European models, and it is obviously true of MacDowell and Griffes, as of the early Ives. But in a sense, Griffes went beyond his master Debussy; architecturally the sonata surpasses any of Debussy's piano works.

Griffes was an extremely slow worker. His return to America was an even bigger mistake than MacDowell's because he had no 'popular' side; he was all sensitivity and intelligence. Griffes's compressed style has led to his being slightly better served by the record companies than MacDowell; most of his best works are available: the *Roman Sketches* for piano, an extremely beautiful work that can easily become a passion; the two poems for orchestra, *The White Peacock* (from the *Roman Sketches*) and *The Pleasure Dome of Kubla Khan*; and the Poem for Flute and Orchestra. All three of these orchestral works show Griffes's taste for the exotic and his kinship with the Debussy of *L'Après Midi* and the Delius of *Brigg Fair*, as well as with Rimsky-Korsakov. The Poem for Flute is perhaps the most immediately beautiful and striking of Griffes's works.* (In parenthesis, it might be remarked that any lyrical composer who writes for the flute gives himself an unfair advantage, since the sound of the instrument can be so beautiful and unearthly; the flute sonatas of Debussy and Prokofiev underline this point.)

*There exists an excellent recording of it by the Cleveland Orchestra which also includes the equally ravishing *Night Piece* by Arthur Foote, one of the New England school of composers, which included George Chadwick and Frederick Converse and the much underrated Horatio Parker.

CHORDS AND DISCORDS

The American composer whose work now commands most respect is Charles Ives. Although he lived to be eighty, his effective creative life lasted a mere twenty years. He composed little during the last forty years of his life, shattered by the effort of making an impression on American philistinism. It is arguable that Ives is the most important composer that America has produced, and certainly probable that he is its nearest thing to an original genius in music. It is a pleasant thought that Ives received a reasonable amount of fame and recognition in the last fifteen years of his life (he died in 1954), and he's a lesson to artists that dying of discouragement and neglect isn't worth while.

There is something baffling about Ives's genius. While Schoenberg and Stravinsky were still writing rich nineteenth-century harmonies, Ives was banging out jarring discords on the piano and writing for the voice with a tonal freedom that would have made Scriabin or Mahler green with envy. This is a strange phenomenon. How on earth did it come about? How did a contemporary of MacDowell—and a New Englander at that—manage to discover the atonalism of Schoenberg for himself in the first decade of this century?

I am not competent to answer this question. Even at this stage, when there is an increasing literature on Ives, we do not possess enough information about his personality and its conflicts. But a part of the answer can be given immediately, and it is somehow typically American. It is that Ives was a man with a rich sense of humour, who did not believe in taking art too seriously. So his approach to atonalism was quite unlike the tight-lipped fanaticism of Schoenberg. Ives's artistic personality was closer to that of Mark Twain. The odd thing is that he possessed a musical intelligence as acute as any in Europe at that period. (It is to Schoenberg's credit that he recognized Ives's genius at an early stage.)

Ives is an incredibly difficult composer to assess. More than the music of any other American, his makes an impression of powerful individuality. To listen, for example, to a song like 'The Cage', written in 1906, or the *Three-Page Sonata* (1905) is to be astounded that any musical mind was thinking in terms of these clear, powerful dissonances as early as this. (Schoenberg's radical Piano Pieces, op. 11, were not written for another four years.) One has only to listen to a few minutes of the early *Symphony: Holidays* to recognize that one is in the presence of a musical pioneer, a close relative of Thoreau and Emerson. And yet the problem keeps presenting itself: How far is this real creative pioneering, and how far is it musical extravagance and eccentricity for its own sake? There is more than a touch of original Beecham about Ives, the *enfant terrible* who wants to startle. And as far as Ives's personality goes, a comparison with Erik Satie would not be too far-fetched (although their writing for the piano could not be more different). But Satie was a musical light-weight *because* of his fundamentally unserious personality; he could not keep the twinkle out of his eye for long enough to develop real musical *conviction*. (And this, after all, is what is at stake.) And this is what bothers one about Ives. Everyone who discovers his music goes through a honeymoon period of delight: a major American composer at last! Then the doubts begin to set in. Yes, he is original; that is self-evident. But *why* is he original? One has to know. Listening to Schoenberg's quartets in their numerical order, one can see why he had to develop as he did, and this feeling of inner logic increases one's respect for the composer. With Ives, one is never sure whether he isn't a kind of musical exhibitionist.

Studying his life and development (in the excellent biography by the Cowells, for example) fails to answer these questions conclusively. Ives's musical leanings were inherited from his father, a bandmaster. At fourteen he was church organist, and at twenty he entered Yale and studied music with Horatio Parker. At this point, he seems to have faced the same choice as Hanslick at that age: had he the stamina to be a first-rate musician and to devote his life to music? Like Hanslick, Ives decided against it. His reason was no doubt quite different: the reason, in fact, that according to Van Wyck Brooks made Mark Twain deny expression to his serious talents and concentrate on humour: the American go-getter ethic. Ives became an insurance agent, just as Wallace Stevens did, and by the time he was forty-two, he was the head of the biggest insurance agency in America. He demonstrated conclusively that he was no suicidal romantic of the early Yeats variety. During his years as a businessman, he composed all his best music in his spare time. In 1918, he had a breakdown due to overwork; after that, he

189

composed very little music, although there are a few remarkable songs and chamber pieces.

Now a real artist is a man who must devote his life to individual creation, whether he likes it or not. No matter what problems and disappointments it seems to offer, no other way of life is possible. An artist may feel slightly ashamed of his youthful *Sturm und Drang* period later, but this is because it has become so completely a part of his inner nature that he no longer has to verbalize it. The fact remains that to decide to devote one's life to the cause of mind, of imagination, is as radical a step as entering a monastery, and gives one a feeling of being set apart from the rest of the world. The idea of poverty and loneliness, while not exactly attractive, is not at all discouraging, any more than her lover's poverty is discouraging to a woman in love.

At the time when Ives began to write music, this 'high priest' attitude to art was very much a part of the atmosphere of the day. One has only to listen to a few bars of a symphony by Mahler or Bruckner, or a song by Wolf, to know that we are quite conclusively in that world of mind, of imagination. Joyce's *Portrait of the Artist* dramatizes the feeling. In the past forty years or so, it has become somewhat unfashionable again; we are inclined to think of art in its relation to society. But this is hardly a matter for fashion. Even if he is ashamed to admit it, the true artist *is* a kind of high priest, and he begins his career by making a mental act of dedication. If the symphonies of Mahler are at present almost as popular as those of Beethoven, it is because, in spite of their self-pity, we recognize this near-religious spirit in them, and welcome its seriousness.

Now if we listen to the Second Symphony of Ives (excellently recorded by Bernstein), we immediately become aware that here is a man whose imagination is at home with the great Germans. One could be unkind and call this a monstrous German pastiche—of Bach, Beethoven, Brahms, Bruckner Mahler and Wagner. (Ives actually quotes bits of Beethoven, Brahms, and even a few bars of the *1812* overture.) But in spite of all this, the symphony is far more than pastiche. It reveals that, at the age of twenty-eight, Ives had the true Romantic temperament, the strange contemplative detachment from everyday existence that makes the artist. The slow opening bars may be Brahmsian (with echoes of Bruckner and Mahler), but one thing is beyond doubt: Ives is really expressing something that *he* feels.

It is this that makes the symphony a strange case—and a nutshell presentation of the Ives problem. Although there is hardly a bar in it that is not an echo of somebody else, it is obviously a sincere work of art. Only a major artistic personality would have had the stamina to produce nearly an hour of derivative music of this kind. It proves that Ives *could* have devoted his life to music. Unlike Hanslick, he really had the inner stuff of the artist.

Yet we can also see why Ives lacked the courage to take the step. Right at the end of the Mahlerian opening passage, he drags in a quotation from 'America the Beautiful'. And from then on, there are almost as many quotations from American songs—'The Star-Spangled Banner', 'Turkey in the Straw', 'Camptown Races', etc.—as from European composers. The intention is partly to Americanize the pastiche. But one also becomes aware of a strain of uncomfortable self-mockery, as if he wants to anticipate the charge of wearing his heart on his sleeve. And in spite of all this, one is still inclined to agree with Leonard Bernstein that this *is* a great symphony, or very nearly so.

Still, when one has listened to this symphony, and to the early song 'Ich grolle nicht' (which might be straight out of the *Knaben Wunderhorn**), and to the Largo of an abandoned Trio, and to the four sonatas for piano and violin ('harmless little pieces', Ives called them), one begins to get an inkling of why Ives developed the atonal percussive style. When the music is not actually derivative, it is pleasant and nondescript. It would be very difficult to guess who had written the Largo, or most of the violin sonatas (if it were not for the American songs). Nothing is more irritating to the genuine artist than to feel that he has no individual voice. It is a feeling that we have considered several times elsewhere in this volume, in connection with Schoenberg and Bartók and Stravinsky. I am not suggesting that Ives decided to write dissonances because they sounded less insipid than his neo-romantic manner; there was almost certainly a deeper impulse. But it is surprising how often early

---

*This does not mean that I assume Ives knew Mahler; at this period he almost certainly didn't; but the spirit is identical.

CHORDS AND DISCORDS

Ives piano music sounds like the Bartók of *Mikrokosmos*, for example (like the 'Hawthorne' movement of the *Concord Sonata*). This leads one to suspect that the same kind of complex *personal* history may lie behind it.

What all this amounts to is that the young Ives did violence to his own development. His mind was too impatient. He tried to create an individual voice overnight by brooding on how to sound original, and the result often strikes us as 'inauthentic'.

And yet what is important is that, in spite of this, Ives *did* end by creating an extremely individual voice. It can be heard in the *Symphony: Holidays*, in the *Concord Sonata*, in the Second Quartet, in the Third Symphony and *Three Places in New England*. This latter is typical Ives, and gives rise to some interesting reflections. Its most striking movement is the second, with its famous effect of two brass bands passing one another in the street. And one becomes aware of an element in Ives that distinguishes him completely from any of his European contemporaries. In a strange way, one feels that he is a kind of musical novelist. He is like a man who has got tired of the sentimental stuff that passed for literature in the second half of the nineteenth century and decided that he would actually capture the flavour of reality in his work. It is an American reality, as distinctly so as the atmosphere of Lewis's *Main Street*. This, I feel, is one of the most important elements in Ives's personality: the realistic novelist. In a very straightforward and obvious way, this can be heard in a piece like the 'Decoration Day' movement of the 'Holidays' symphony, which is a descriptive tone poem complete with programme, in the manner of *Danse Macabre* or *Pacific 231*, with blaring brass bands at its climax. But this is not a good example of the novelist element in Ives; the 'Thanksgiving' movement of the same work is a better one. It combines the brass band texture with a rich, polyphonic complexity that provides a highly satisfying musical experience. And at the end, when a chorus bursts into a hymn tune, one does not wince at the naïvety, for somehow the slightly dissonant accompaniment emphasizes that the tune is simply another colour on this abstract canvas. Ives's best music is 'popular' and abstract at the same time.

Still, this is not to say that his attempts at collage are always successful. In the *Concord Sonata*, for example, the first movement ('Emerson') is a completely successful piece of atonal music which has the austereness of Schoenberg; but in the second movement ('Hawthorne') he cannot resist dragging in the brass band tune that is also used in *Three Places*. The effect here is one of bathos.

The quickest way to get to know the best of Ives in the shortest possible time is to listen to the song 'William Booth's Entrance into Heaven', written in 1914. It is a setting of a Vachel Lindsay poem of the 'hot gospeller' variety. Here Ives gives the poem drive with a jazzy-sounding hymn tune, 'Are you washed in the blood of the Lamb?', and at the climax of the poem, this becomes an orgy of shouting of 'Hallelujah'. The dissonant accompaniment contributes just the right degree of detachment and irony to the whole thing. But even in this song, which is a *tour de force*, we have a touch of the Ives tendency to overdo it. The second section of the song describes how Booth leads his mob of cripples and criminals in a circle in the court-house yard, and how Jesus appears and turns them into angels. Lindsay wrote that Booth led his queer ones 'round and round the mighty court-house square'. But Ives has to change this to 'round and round, round and round, round and round', repeated for what seems half an hour. As it happens, both versions of the song have been recorded; Corinne Curry sings the 'round and round and round' version, while Donald Gramm sings the words as Lindsay wrote them. The latter is by far the more satisfactory version. (It is true that, in any case, this is hardly a song for a woman; its delivery needs too much energy and sheer volume.) One can only speculate on why Ives decided to make this absurd and irritating change. One always feels, with Ives, that one can never rely on his artistic judgement and discretion. He never seems to know when he has written something unique and powerful, and when he has lapsed into dreariness or bad taste.

Ives began to come into his own about 1939, when a recording of the *Concord Sonata* became a highly unlikely best seller. Now he is most satisfactorily represented in the American record catalogue (although hardly at all in the English one, a sign that his vogue has not crossed the water). There is the inevitable tendency to overrate him; a recent book on American music by Wilfrid Mellers devotes twenty-seven pages to Ives, while most of the other composers have to be contented with three or four (a notable exception being Elliott Carter). It will be some years before we can see Ives in perspective and judge his stature in comparison with that of his European contemporaries. The final verdict may well be that he is a kind of American freak who fails to fit in anywhere. Although he lived to be eighty, one has a feeling that his life was an artistic tragedy, and that, in this case, the tragedy was about fifty per cent his own fault.

All this at least helps us to define the problem of modern American music—the problem that embarrassed Lucien Price. Charles Ives shows us what is wrong. He was a real artist, and he had the ideal background for a real artist—the small town, with its hard-headed traditions, its insularity, its way of taking itself for granted. Most of the major artists of the past century have sprung from a similar kind of background. Auden once said that the aim of education was to produce neurosis. Presumably he meant that education aims at making people creative— or ought to—and that creation is impossible without a certain tension, a certain compression. Cordite in a bullet is highly exposive; lit in the open air, it burns only a little more vigorously than paper. Russia's highly repressive regime of the nineteenth century produced great novelists, poets and musicians by the dozen. If we consider the case of English literature in the present century, we discover that all the minor writers are those with a fairly well-to-do background and a university education— Walpole, Maugham, Galsworthy, Mackenzie. It is as if the sheer healthiness of the environment, the lack of claustro- phobia, prevents the build-up of the kind of creative tension we find in Shaw, Joyce, Yeats, Wells, Bennett. A claustrophic, neurosis-producing background acts as a kind of pressure- cooker, it would seem. The drearily provincial Ireland of Joyce, or Austria of Musil and Rilke, or 'Combray' of Proust, or Bromley of Wells, or Novgorod of Gorki, fulfills Auden's con- dition of producing the right amount of neurosis ('as much', Auden said, 'as the pupil can stand without being permanently damaged'). Ives was a major composer because he was a provincial in this sense. Now in modern America, this kind of provincialism becomes increasingly rare. Almost anyone can get to a university; and a university with ten thousand or so students can hardly be described as a 'pressure-cooker'. The most individual voices in twentieth-century America have been men from neurosis-producing backgrounds, like Henry Miller and Richard Wright.

Most of the musicians of twentieth-century America have been men who went to music school, then did a few years in Europe studying with Nadia Boulanger or some other celebrated teacher, then returned to write commissioned symphonies for various subsidized orchestras. This is not the atmosphere in which real music is created. So while many American composers strike one as having individual voices—Piston, Sessions and Riegger, for example—they fail to impress as *creative* individuals.

The sheer number of composers who deserve to be considered in a chapter on American music makes the task extremely difficult: Menotti (whom I have already discussed in Chapter 9), Piston, Copland, Barber, Sessions, Riegger, Harris, Schuman, Hanson, Thomson, Mennin, Bergsma, Moore, Cowell, Chanler, Blitzstein, Ruggles, Carter, Weisgall, Bernstein . . .; the list could easily be extended to twice this length. But the problem can be simplified if we consider that much of this music falls into types. There is, to begin with, a certain kind of *Gebrauchsmusik*, a kind of music written because there is a demand for it, because an orchestra wants a new symphony by an American composer. This kind of music may often be extremely impressive on a first hearing, and may even stand up to repeated listenings—and yet one has no feeling that it is created out of inner compulsion, an urgent need to express a certain artistic sensibility, the kind of need that, in spite of its borrowings, we *do* feel behind the Ives Second Symphony.

There have been certain American symphonies of this type that I have discovered with considerable pleasure and played through half a dozen times before I have begun to feel a certain lack of content. A case in point is Roy Harris's Third Symphony, which most critics declare to be his best, and which one writer assures me is still the finest symphony to come out of America. On a first hearing, one says: 'Ah, here is a true American symphony, with broad American themes'. But with successive hearings, it becomes less and less satisfactory; if one tries to think of it as a *totality*, it becomes elusive. One finds oneself concentrating on particular aspects of it: the American 'flow' of the melody, or the imitation Bach that constitutes most of its second half.

I have found the same sort of thing in Peter Mennin's Third Symphony, which made his reputation at the age of twenty-three. The first ten minutes give the impression of a man who has something to say and intends to say it forcefully. But after another ten minutes, one has discovered that he is like a good actor with an excellent delivery, but no important lines. The same kind of thing goes for the Third Symphony of William Schuman (a pupil of Harris), particularly its last quarter of an hour, with its Hindemithian fugal passage. One can perfectly well understand why its first audiences were so enthusiastic and why it had so many subsequent performances. And yet it leaves a final impression — of manufactured music, almost as if a Hollywood producer had said: 'Write me half an hour of powerful, exciting music for a technicolour Western'. Howard Hanson's Third Symphony leaves something of the same impression on me, although I find his frank romanticism and warm colouring almost as attractive as MacDowell's. (It is a pure accident that I happen to be concentrating on third symphonies; it seems to be a coincidence that most eminent American composers have scored a success with a third symphony.) On the other hand, Walter Piston's Third Symphony strikes me as somehow solider than most of these, although I still find its idiom not sufficiently individual.

I am not suggesting that a lot of American music, particularly symphonies, can be dismissed as a kind of *Gebrauchsmusik*. There is no question of dismissal. In a sense, America is in the midst of a kind of musical golden age comparable to the eighteenth century in Europe. We do not dismiss Vivaldi and Locatelli, and the various children of Bach, and Corelli and Scarlatti and Couperin and Rameau and Albinoni and a dozen others simply because the casual listener finds it hard to tell them apart. But we might hope that the present period in American music is only a prelude to an age that will produce its American Mozart or Beethoven. For a week before the writing of the present chapter, I listened constantly to records of American music. I often found that, if my attention wandered, I could not remember what I had got on the turntable. Was it a symphony by Harris or Hanson or Schuman or Mennin or Barber or Piston or Riegger or Moore; or could it, perhaps, be one of the lesser-known composers recorded by the Louisville Orchestra and whose name had escaped my mind? No doubt this was partly my own fault, but it conveys my point all the same. The same thing could happen with certain English composers, particularly the younger ones: I might easily forget whether I was listening to Maxwell Davies or Racine Fricker or Elizabeth Lutyens or Alexander Goehr; but then, most of these are committed to a vaguely twelve-tone idiom that would make the mistake understandable. The American composers I have mentioned all write in a more or less 'universal' style which is supposed to appeal to any musical audience. If I were listening to British composers of more 'universal' appeal, I would certainly not mistake Walton for Tippett or Britten or Bliss. And this, I think, explains why audiences outside America have not bothered to acquaint themselves with much American music, in spite of its variety and vitality. Except for Charles Ives, there is a lack of the one thing worth looking for: the clear individuality, the musical personality, that distinguishes a Sibelius from a Stravinsky or a Poulenc or a Berg or a Hindemith or a Prokofiev or a Britten with a few bars. I may have misgivings and reservations about most of these composers, but I cannot doubt their intense individuality.

A case in point here is Aaron Copland, whom most Americans would now recognize as the representative composer of his generation (Harris having failed to live up to his promise). Copland certainly has an individual texture. But it is still not the texture of a major composer. Again, we might consider his Third Symphony as a typical work. (One writer describes it as 'his magnificent Third Symphony'.) Anyone who knows *Billy the Kid* quickly recognizes the Copland fingerprint in the opening bars—those remote-sounding woodwinds suggesting night on the open prairie, that slightly Vaughan Williamsy melody which is nevertheless characteristically American. But from this point on, one gets increasingly the impression that the music was commissioned for a Western travelogue. In the second movement, there are passages that could be mistaken for Prokofiev, or possibly Shostakovich. The last movement makes

197

use of another short work by Copland, the *Fanfare for the Common Man*, which is exactly what it says: a fanfare, an exciting brassy noise that arouses interest and expectation, and then stops at the very point where one is hoping for development. But the Fanfare lasts for only a few minutes; as used in the Third Symphony, it becomes a major theme, and here its unsatisfactory, expectation-arousing character becomes more obvious. One feels that this symphony would have been better if it had begun with the fanfare and gone on from there.

All this, of course, only indicates that Copland may not be a natural symphonist. If we study Copland's development, this becomes more obvious. His music teacher tried to influence him against 'modern' music, which naturally had the opposite effect. His first symphony was so uncompromisingly modern that the conductor remarked that a man who could do this at twenty-four should be ready to commit murder in the next five years. But a 'jazz' piano concerto, written not long afterwards, revealed a warm and emotional Copland (the 'jazz' element is extremely small) with a gift for melody. In 1930 came the 'difficult' Piano Variations, which later became a set of Orchestral Variations (1957). (The latter sounds at times like an odd collaboration between Webern and Copland.) Another 'difficult' work is the Piano Sonata of 1941, but it is notably more melodic than the Variations. For by this time, Copland had decided that there was no point in keeping up this 'difficult' front, that he was naturally a composer of warmth and melody. The usual version of this change of heart, in books about American music, is that Copland decided that he wanted to 'reach the people' and cease to sound intellectual. But a leopard does not change its spots just like that. The truth was that Copland had never genuinely been an intellectual composer.

So Copland's most characteristic work can be found in the delightful *American Folk Songs*, in the Danzón Cubano, in the Clarinet Concerto he wrote for Benny Goodman (which, all the same, has less melody than one has a right to expect), in *Billy the Kid, Rodeo*, and the somewhat overrated *Appalachian Spring*. The last work is pleasant enough, but it is certainly not, as one critic has stated, the finest orchestral work to come out of America; its pleasantest theme is the Shaker hymn "Tis the gift to be simple', which Copland has set so well in the

American Folk Songs. He has gone on record in recent years as saying that he considered his *Connotations* for orchestra his most significant work. This work is not recorded (at the time of writing), but I managed to lay my hands on a tape of a B.B.C. performance and played it through eagerly. My suspicions were confirmed: it is Copland trying on his intellectual hat again, and producing nothing that deserves to be called a major work. Whether a study of the score would reveal unappreciated depths I am unable to say; but two careful hearings failed to detect any.

All of which is to say that Copland is fundamentally a warm and colourful composer in the American tradition. But since the American tradition in the twentieth century is a melodiousness that we tend to associate with film music, it is difficult to consider Copland quite simply as a serious composer, the Piano Sonata and Orchestral Variations notwithstanding. His work may be easier to recognize than, say, that of Piston; but one feels that, in spite of this, it is Piston who may possess the heavy-weight creative personality.

Another frequently suggested candidate for the laurels of the true American composer is Carl Ruggles. I have already quoted Ruggles's statement, 'Music that does not surge is not great music'—a sentiment that would gain the assent of Ayn Rand. It is extremely doubtful whether Ruggles's music would arouse her enthusiasm. The adjective that suggests itself for *Men and Mountains* is 'Bergian'. And herein lies the incongruity. Berg's atonal music has this tense, nervous, surging movement because it expresses a certain view of life, a view not far from that of Eliot's *Waste Land*, a feeling of pity, horror, tragedy, futility. Aldous Huxley, under mescalin, said outright that it was pure self-pity. Atonal music is ideal for this purpose because it suggests the dislocation of the human emotions. Just as a flowing melody has the effect of concentrating and directing the emotions, so atonal music—particularly when used for operatic purposes—has the effect of suggesting the opposite: horror, tension, the *alien* breaking into man's private universe. This is why, apart from *Wozzeck*, one of the most successful of atonal operas is Blomdahl's 'space opera' *Aniara*, which is about the confrontation of human emotions with the emptiness and

199

indifference of space, the certainty of the extinction of a few human beings in a lost space ship. Atonal music is particularly adapted to suggesting the alien because its feeling of logical progression through a sequence of notes is opposed to the arbitrary feeling that comes from lack of melody, so one gets the feeling of some non-human monster stumping along.

Now Ruggles is concerned to express a kind of life-affirmation, a heroic feeling, caught in the quotation from Blake:

> Great things are done when men and mountains meet.
> This is not done by jostling in the street.

Wilfrid Mellers includes Ruggles in a chapter with Roy Harris as a 'religious primitive'. Now it can be seen that Harris's 'heroic frontier' emotions are basically opposed to the Bergian feeling; so there is a fundamental conflict, in the nature of a self-contradiction, at the heart of Ruggles's music.

This is not to say, of course, that it is entirely unsuccessful. Surging atonal music can, to some extent, express mysticism, in fact, is ideally adapted to it, since mysticism is also about the alien, the other-worldly. So the 'Lilacs' section of *Men and Mountains*, scored for strings, has a certain emotional fierceness that carries conviction. But the very height at which the whole thing is pitched means that it is incapable of development. Like the technique of understatement in literature—in Hemingway, for example—it is able to carry intense emotion, but at the cost of being unable to express anything else. And Ruggles's extremely small output, like Hemingway's, is the penalty of trying for this kind of intensity. One might also sense in a later work like the *Organum* for orchestra (1945) the same kind of decline as in the later Hemingway. Having committed himself to always expressing himself with aphoristic pregnancy and an air of immense significance, he is forced to go in off the top diving board. The result is a feeling of inauthenticity that is not unlike the badness of Hemingway's *Across the River and into the Trees*, or some of Faulkner's later works.

In my own view, Ruggles is certainly among the most interesting of American composers, but for what he attempted rather than for anything he achieved. In Ruggles's story there is the story of the intellectualizing of twentieth-century art, the attempt to abandon the common daylight of the Victorians for a new intensity. An essay on Ruggles would probably be forced to consider at some length the development of artists as unlike as van Gogh and James Joyce—both, however, aimed at a certain 'mystical' intensity. But if I put 'Lilacs' or *Portals* on my turntable, my immediate response is a kind of nervous cringing. It depends on my mood whether those shrieking violins sound like intensity or hysteria.

Consideration of Ruggles leads naturally to the intellectualist faction among modern American composers, whose chief representative in the older generation is Sessions, and in the younger, Elliott Carter. This is also, perhaps, the point at which to mention a remarkably individualistic composer of the Sessions generation, John J. Becker (born 1886). Becker seems to be one of those composers about whom one is tempted to use words like 'rugged' and 'pioneering'. The only work of his to be found in· the American catalogue at present is a piano concerto that recalls the Ives of the *Concord Sonata*—atonal, yet in a tough and individual manner, owing little to Schoenberg. It seems strange that this arresting composer should be so generally ignored in America. (Apparently there has been no recording of his work since 1930, excepting the present one, although there was some hope when Bernstein conducted his Third Symphony in 1958; this apparently came to nothing.) One wonders whether the Americans will allow Becker to die before he is 'rediscovered' like Ives.

Roger Sessions is a composer with whom I have always found it somewhat difficult to come to terms. A pupil of Horatio Parker and Bloch, and later deeply influenced by Schoenberg, his outlook has been called 'internationalist'. But this sounds like one of those adjectives that people use when they have no idea of what else to say of a composer.

Like most of the composers of his generation, Sessions is formidably accomplished technically. The note one always seems to miss is that of deep feeling, the kind of thing one finds in the Ives Second Symphony. His First Symphony bounces along powerfully and brightly, like a more cheerful *Rite of Spring* or like long passages of the English composer Tippett. In fact, it is finally Tippett whom Sessions brings to mind—an angular, intellectual kind of texture, and a tendency to let the mind do the work of the heart. The Violin Concerto opens promisingly in a rather Schoenbergian idiom, and one has a feeling that this is a man with something to say and the knowledge of how to say it. But after twenty minutes or so, one feels less happy about it. The one thing this lacks is the thing that the Schoenberg and Berg concertos contain: passion, intense *subjectivity*. It is an objection that can be made to so much American music. If we bear in mind what Kierkegaard meant when he said, 'Truth is subjectivity', then it can be seen that this is precisely what so much American music lacks: the 'inner direction' that David Riesman speaks about. I certainly feel this strongly when listening to one of Sessions's major works, the *Idyll of Theocritus* for soprano and orchestra. The work should, in fact, be a small opera, a monodrama in the manner of Schoenberg's *Erwartung*. The 'plot' is powerful enough: a girl invokes the moon goddess to help her recover the lover who has abandoned her (he is a wrestler) and describes how she seduced him. It is about hysteria and nymphomania rather than about love, and the girl's vengefulness, her determination to kill the man by magic rather than lose him, makes it an ideal subject for monodrama. Why, then, does it fail to move the listener? Perhaps because he feels that this is a rather late attempt (1954) to imitate the *Erwartung-Wozzeck* type of opera, rather than a work of original impulse. The libretto seems to cry out for tonal music. The Strauss of *Elektra* would have made an admirable job of it. But as one listens to the girl describing how she felt sick with lust at the sight of Delphis and almost died (the fleshly, slightly nauseated atmosphere is reminiscent of Akutagawa's *Kesa and Morito*), the carefully atonal music sounds somehow phoney, an affectation. I much prefer the more personal, less ambitious Sessions of the short piano pieces *Pages from a Diary*, written in 1940.

Elliott Carter would seem to be one of the most powerful talents that has come out of America since Ives. His later music is as uncompromisingly atonal as Sessions's, but it seems naturally more subjective, more personal. This is something that cannot be explained, but which stands out immediately when one hears some of the music. A musician friend of mine who had never heard of Carter happened to switch on the B.B.C. music programme late one afternoon when a programme of modern American chamber music was being broadcast. His attention wandered until Carter's Sonata for Flute, Oboe, 'Cello and Harpsichord (1952) came on. This, in my own view, is not one of Carter's most satisfying works; yet my friend said he immediately made a note of Carter's name, feeling: 'This is a real musician'.

Carter's early work hardly indicates that he would develop into an important composer. The First Symphony is pleasant and inoffensive, showing the influence of Stravinsky and of the Copland-Harris school. An earlier work still, the ballet *Pocahontas*, is noisy and driving in the manner of Prokofiev's *Scythian Suite* or Bartók's *Mandarin*. The early Carter could be fairly called an eclectic. The individual Carter begins to appear in the fine Piano Sonata of 1946, written when Carter was thirty-eight. It is an 'experimental' work, that requires great skill to perform; but the listener who expects the kind of experimentalism found in the Boulez or Barraqué sonatas is in for a pleasant surprise, for this is no *avant garde* sonata; it is primarily melodious and pianistic. In fact, it shows something that one had almost given up hoping for in American music: a talent that is at once intensely personal, capable of melody, and yet also highly intelligent.

Carter's sudden emergence as a composer on the international scene came with his first String Quartet (1951). This is a powerful and Bergian work, full of the 'subjectivity' that one has missed in so much American chamber music. Wilfrid Mellers, who devotes several pages to it in *Music in a New Found Land*, waxes lyrical about it, talking about 'whirling atomization', 'telescoped dissonances', 'stellar spaces', and says that the scherzo 'flickers whimperingly to nothingness'. This is perhaps going rather far, as is the comparison of the work with the late Beethoven quartets. Still, there is less nonsense here than one usually finds in bursts of musicological hysteria. When Hodeir tells us that Barraqué's Piano Sonata is the most supreme work since Beethoven's Opus 111, and has, in fact, ended the piano sonata as a form, one knows he must be talking nonsense because Barraqué was in his early twenties when he wrote it, and a man of that age could not possibly have anything to add to Beethoven's Opus 111. (And, in fact, the work strikes me as a bad example of meaningless *avant garde* show-off.) But Carter was approaching fifty when he wrote the quartet, and had come through a long and interesting development. Mellers's point has a certain validity, for here is certainly a work of concentrated emotion and subjectivity. Mellers evokes Beethoven in order to remark that the late Beethoven works pass through chaos and conflict to a kind of synthesis, a *Paradise Regained*. All that this really means, translated out of these literary metaphors, is that the quartet is a neurotic work that stays neurotic throughout. This is true, and it perhaps explains the unsatisfactoriness of Carter's subsequent development. Never does one feel more clearly than here that music is more than sounds and technique: that it is the living spirit of a composer. Beethoven's music achieves greatness because he was a great man. Opus 111 and the late quartets move us because they are genuinely about a conflict that has been resolved through stubborn vitality and faith. The music actually conveys something Beethoven has learned about life through living it *and fighting it*. In comparison, so much American music seems to be music of total inexperience or of conventional gestures. Harris gained his early following because those breezy gestures of the early symphonies were so obviously genuine, a true expression of vitality and optimism. (And when this same vitality expressed itself in the *Folksong Symphony*, No. 4, its shallowness became painfully evident, for only a totally unsophisticated person could have called this medley of American folk songs a symphony.) Carter's quartet strikes us as genuine music because it is intensely personal, a kind of diary written without thought of an audience. But as a diary, it has much in common with Amiel's *Journal* or Barbellion's *Journal of a Disappointed Man*: that is to say, to put it politely, it is the diary of a sensitive and tormented soul, not of a Beethoven. So Mellers's talk about Beethoven and Milton is supremely irrelevant in the last analysis.

And now, it seems to me, Carter found that he had put his head into the same kind of noose as Ruggles. He had become known for intensity and atonality, and had to keep going in that direction. Being a superb musician, he has been able to make something of these conditions. The Double Concerto for

Harpsichord and Piano with Two Chamber Orchestras (1961) and the Sonata for Flute, Oboe, 'Cello and Harpsichord (completed just after the quartet) are both fine and arresting works, rather unearthly in sound (due to the harpsichord). But the much praised Variations for Orchestra (1955) seem to me merely an interesting exercise in orchestral sonorities, like some of Messiaen's work, and oddly disappointing as a piece of self-expression.

Mellers devotes almost as much space and enthusiasm to Carter's second String Quartet (1959) as he gave to his first. I find the Second Quartet disappointing also. In this work, Carter has the four musicians sitting in four corners of the room, and tries to give each instrument an individual temperament: first violin, bravura; second violin, anti-lyrical; viola, expressive; and 'cello, rhapsodic. Ives had done something vaguely of the same sort in the Second Quartet, where one of the instruments is timid and conventional, and shocked by the experiments of the others; but Ives was chuckling ironically as he scrawled encouragements to the timid one on the manuscript. Carter is completely serious—as one would expect from the First Quartet—and the result sounds rather gimmicky. Even Mellers obviously has some misgivings, for he writes: 'One's only doubt is that the tension generated out of its very nature is so great as to seem incapable of relaxation'—the trouble with Hemingway-type prose and Ruggles-type music. Perhaps this is also what Constant Lambert meant when he said that twelve-tone music cannot convey humour. Music cannot exist on this high, tragedy-queen level all the time, and if it makes the attempt, it comes to sound either over-dramatic or merely abstract.

This sounds perhaps unfair, but there is a genuine problem here. T. E. Hulme remarked about Byzantine art that this kind of abstract art is the ideal way of expressing intense religious emotion, because it doesn't really try. It seems to say: 'I know this cannot be expressed in ordinary language, so this abstraction is a token of an inexpressible meaning'. And an artist who tries hard to achieve greater and greater intensity always ends by spilling over into this kind of abstraction, which you are asked to accept as a token of the inexpressible, of the realms beyond ordinary language. The music of Ruggles is a case in point. But then, it is easy for this kind of intensity, which, by its very nature, lacks humour and lyricism, to spill over into the phoney. An excellent example in literature can be found in the Russian pessimist Andreyev, who always claimed to be concerned with Big Questions, God, the Universe, Death, metaphysics, etc. And in his later work, all this seriousness has become a mere gesture, an actor's trick of dropping his voice and rolling his eyes.

In short, unless a composer makes immense efforts of self-development, and manages to get beyond the merely personal, beyond self-pity and neurosis, his atonalism is bound to end as an empty form. The path of development that Carter has chosen since the Piano Sonata is as steep and difficult as the Purgatorial mount. By its very nature, it leads to silence. It might be called anti-musical, since the nature of music is lyrical, life-affirming. One senses that Britten has come to face this problem in his later music, such as the 'Cello Symphony and Curlew River: a dehydration that is owing not to a drying up of talent, but to radical changes in the personality (in Britten's case, one sometimes suspects an increasing sense of pessimism and futility). If Carter's First Quartet already inhabits these 'icy stellar heights', what possible development can be expected? Either Carter must resolve his spiritual problems in the manner of a Beethoven, and learn to express some new vision of reconciliation, or become steadily less authentic as he continues to express his old personality in a language that is pitched too high. The Double Concerto of 1961 is full of strange silences that seem to indicate that Carter has faced the nature of his problem; but what happens next is anybody's guess.

Carter seems to me to have an importance quite beyond that of his music. (While the First Quartet and the Double Concerto impress me, I could easily live without them; the Piano Sonata is almost his only work that I replay for pleasure.) He proves that it is possible to become a first-rate composer by making a long and continual effort: that one can remain an interesting eclectic up to the age of thirty-five or so, and *then* strike an individual note. Artists nowadays are far more aware than they used to be of the problems of tradition and individuality; at the age of twenty, they can produce a hundred good reasons why it is impossible to write a great novel or a great symphony in the twentieth century. There is a fundamental error here. While a great novel or symphony can obviously be analyzed down to questions of technique and content, this does not mean that its composer started off saying: 'Well, this is what the content is going to be, and this is the technique in which I propose to say it'. One feels with so much modern music that the composer has studied Webern, Stravinsky and Messiaen, and then asked himself: 'How do I go on from here?' A twenty-year-old poet worries about how he can sound distinctive, original, in a poetry magazine with thirty other contributors. This is to approach the whole thing the wrong way round. Carter underlines the point. He is a good composer not because he set out to find a language that would distinguish him from Schoenberg, but because he allowed his personality to develop until he had something to say. In fact, it would be hard to explain how his language *does* differ from that of various atonal contemporaries. His music just sounds different because he has a real personality to express. Sessions's music does not sound 'different' because there seems to be so small a sense of urgency and compulsion.

It seems to me that there are about a dozen different ways of being artistically inauthentic, compared to the one single way of being authentic; and American music offers examples of most of them.

Consider the example of George Antheil, who began his career as a member of the Ezra Pound group of revolutionaries in Paris, and whose *Ballet Mécanique* made his reputation. This work, with its deliberate use of extraneous noises (including the roar of aeroplane engines) is amusing, but almost non-existent as music. Antheil went to Hollywood in the thirties and composed film music. This is apparent on hearing his 'war symphony', the Fourth, which is noisy, romantic, and more or less empty. The Fifth is subtitled 'The Joyous', which means in effect that it is unashamed imitation Prokofiev, with a few actual quotations from the Russian composer. A short opera, *The Wish*, is morbid and maudlin, with appropriate tuneful music. Here is obviously a case where revolutionary beginnings were the worst possible send-off for a composer.

Antheil happens to be a particularly flagrant example of

what can happen to a composer who merely wants to be a well-known composer and has nothing to say. It may, of course, be doubted whether Antheil could ever have been a good composer, whether or not he had started off as 'music's bad boy'. All we can tell from his music is that, if he can be called a serious composer at all, he is a minor. If he had gone about it in the right way—that is, quietly and intelligently—he might have been a very good minor composer, of the stature, say, of Theodore Chanler (of whom I shall speak in a moment). As it was, he has never composed anything worth respect.

The same kind of thing seems to me to be true of John Cage and Harry Partch. Cage, I feel, has tried to take the short cut to musical celebrity, deliberately creating strange noises. A work like *Construction in Metal*, written when he was twenty-seven (1939), is the kind of thing one expects a bright young rebel to do—music made by striking various metal objects. But to continue to do this kind of thing for another quarter of a century reveals an inability to see through one's own self-deceptions. Cage has produced a kind of musical testament on two records called *Indeterminacy*, in which he tells Zen-type anecdotes which are punctuated by electronic noises. It is an attempt to raise his music and musical theorizing to the level of a religious mystique. The best that can be said for *Indeterminacy* is that it is good light entertainment; it is on this level that Cage must be taken.

Partch is in some ways a better composer, but he has marched off up the same road of musical inauthenticity. He is obsessed by micro-tones (tones less than a semitone) and has produced a scale with forty-three notes to the octave. He has spent much of his life building complicated machines that will play all these notes and writing compositions for them. And listening to the only commercial recording of his music that is available, one feels that it is all rather like engraving the Lord's Prayer on a pinhead—challenging, but hardly worth the effort. The tinny, bell-like tones of which he is so fond give the music a vaguely oriental cast—in fact, Partch seems to have started an American sub-department of the Messiaen school of orientalism. A short work like *The Letter* reveals the Partch virtues in the shortest possible space; a beatnik-style letter from an ex-convict is chanted in a monotonous, railway-train rhythm to a whiny mandoline and some Indian-sounding instruments. Its effectiveness is largely the extra-musical effectiveness of the letter itself ('I think I have a job starting the 12th of October and I truly hope my dear little wife is dead by then'). The whiny mandoline only emphasizes the trouble with this micro-tonal music: that, in practise, it merely sounds out of tune. (The same thing can be observed in the slurred quarter-tones of the Bloch Piano Quintet.)

There is another tradition in American music, which produces rather better results than revolutionary experimentalism: the Peter Pan tradition of innocence and refusing to grow up. Of composers like Samuel Barber and Virgil Thomson, one can at least say that they are not fakes; as someone remarked at Poulenc, 'When he has nothing to say, he says it'. In temperament, if not in manner, Barber is the nearest thing America has produced to Benjamin Britten. The early First Symphony is a surging, tuneful work that seems to express the vitality of young America more effectively than Harris. It is light-weight, but it does not pretend to be much more than that. The First Quartet, from which the famous Adagio for Strings is taken, shows the same tunefulness and deftness, and leaves no doubt that Barber is a genuine musical talent. The Adagio is very close in spirit to the beautiful Adagio for Strings by the Belgian Lekeu, a pupil of Franck who died in his early twenties, and this similarity tells us fairly clearly what to expect of Barber: unashamed musical romanticism expressed in a kind of musical watercolour technique: clear, transparent shades. And this is what one finds in the best of Barber: in the fine *Hermit Songs*, set to words composed by anonymous Irish monks, and in the beautiful and delightful *Excursions for Piano*, op. 20. The *Hermit Songs* express the essence of Barber—a sad, early Yeats kind of romanticism, a desire to turn back to the past:

> Ah, to be alone in a little cell
> with nobody near me;
> beloved that pilgrimage
> before the last pilgrimage to Death.

The sentiment is close to the Mahler of the *Song of the Earth*.

CHORDS AND DISCORDS

But Barber can also be tempted into trying larger forms—a Violin Concerto, a Piano Concerto, the opera *Vanessa*, a Second Symphony. One might expect a romantic like Barber to be at home in the medium of the violin concerto and to produce something moving; in fact, his concerto is disappointingly light-weight, like diluted Max Bruch. The Piano Concerto is an example of Barber at his worst. He has nothing to say in this medium and lacks the courage to produce something brilliant and light-hearted in the Poulenc manner. (And the *Excursions* reveal that he would have been quite capable of it.) He writes a virtuoso concerto, technically brilliant and quite unmemorable. The Second Symphony is usually regarded as a great advance on the first one. This may be true as far as form is concerned—the First Symphony is little more than a short rhapsody—but it seems to me to have far less to say; it is again Barber striving to fill a larger form than suits him.

The 'innocence' of Virgil Thomson is less nostalgic and youthful than Barber's. (Barber's early photographs seem to express the essence of his musical personality: good-looking in a shy, sensitive, Young-Woodley kind of manner.) His music is always straightforward and diatonic. *Four Saints in Three Acts* is an astonishing feat. The Gertrude Stein libretto, like everything she did, is meaningless and pretentious; it would have been more suited to a setting by John Cage. Thomson has set it with non-stop melodiousness, and the contrast of meaningful melody with meaningless words is deliciously piquant. The trouble is that it all goes on too long; about a quarter of an hour is enough. Even the condensed version that is available on LP—which plays for only about forty minutes—is far too long.

This is perhaps the trouble with Thomson; in extended works, his simple idiom tends to be a little boring. One critic said of his 'Cello Concerto that there is not a dull spot in the whole thing. This is not quite true; there are several, and the last movement, with its 'Yes Jesus Loves Me' theme, will not bear more than one hearing. Still, it is a tuneful and pleasant work. The same can be said of his Second Quartet and the suite from the opera *The Mother of Us All*, while the short suite from the film music of *Louisiana Story* is a classic. Thomson excels in short works, such as the Sonata No. 4. The diatonic simplicity is not *fausse naïveté*, but a preference for the melodic tradition of

Mozart and Haydn. Parts of the Second Quartet are almost Mozartian, although not in an imitative way.

The other American composer whose name should be linked with Barber and Thomson is Theodore Chanler, who died in 1961. Chanler was an example of a minor talent that is not ashamed of its smallness, and produced some almost perfect things. In certain respects, he resembles the English composer George Butterworth. Two short songs, 'The Rose' and 'I Rise When You Enter', are surely among the most delightful songs that have come out of America. Chanler's major work in this line is the cycle *Epitaphs*, taken from very short poems by Walter de la Mare. They have all his best qualities: wit, humour, flowing melody, a sadness that is genuine and quite unmawkish.

The short Chanler opera *The Pot of Fat* is an example of Chanler at his best and worst. It is based on a Grimm fairy tale about a mouse and a cat who set up house together, and the cat deceives the mouse until he ends by eating her. The music is sometimes slightly Stravinskian, in the manner of *Renard*, but is always gay and melodious. And yet it is not a work to which I want to return, because one becomes so clearly aware of the negative side of Chanler's innocence. It is all a little too naïve, a musical J. D. Salinger; the tragedy is a little too facile. It reveals that, for all his lightness of touch, Chanler was basically rather a silly and defeated man. Because *The Pot of Fat* is a nasty little story, with a moral of cruelty and mistrust. For any fairly cheerful and healthy-minded person, it is impossible to enjoy this tale of deceit, with its element of sadism. Since one can hardly believe that Chanler was a sadist, one can only conclude that he was saying: 'Well, this is what life is really like.' If that is so, then I for one find it hard to sympathize with him.

There remain a great many American composers whom I am not qualified to discuss because I do not know enough of their work: Randall Thompson, Norman Dello Joio, Ben Weber, Leon Kirchner, William Bergsma, William Flanagan, Lukas Foss, Harold Shapero, Leo Smit, and a dozen others. This is partly the fault of the record companies. I have heard single works by all of these composers, but not enough to excite me to go to great trouble to hear more. This certainly does not mean that a composer is not worth getting to know better, as I have often discovered from experience. An example is Marc Blitzstein. Several years ago, I bought his *Regina* on record. It struck me as pleasant and melodious, partly imitation Gershwin, and not worth much attention. When *The Cradle Will Rock* was issued on record, I was delighted to discover that I had made a mistake. Here is a matter on which I cannot agree with Haggin, who, in *Music Observed*, dismisses the opera scathingly as 'the crudest agit-prop falsification suited to an audience of readers of the *Daily Worker*'. This is surely beside the point. The same is true of Weill's *Threepenny Opera* and *Mahagonny*, but we enjoy these things for their musical vitality, just as we enjoy Offenbach or Gilbert and Sullivan. Good light music is not so abundant that we can afford to allow extra-musical considerations to bother us too much. Blitzstein is in the Weill tradition, but not quite as good as Weill. He resembles Weill in that he is prone to perpetrate agonizing sentimentalities. (I have never quite understood how the composer of *The Threepenny Opera* could sink to the sham-folksy rubbish of *Down in the Valley* or some of the sentimental songs from *Lost in the Stars* and *Street Scene*.) The germ of *The Cradle Will Rock* was apparently the prostitute's song 'The nickel under your foot', which led Brecht to encourage Blitzstein to write the opera; in spite of its social subject, this song is painfully sentimental. The same goes for most of the 'serious' scenes of the opera (or operetta, or whatever it is) including the final one, which is supposed to bring the house down. But the satire scenes are superb: the scene on the lawn of Mr Mister's house, in which the editor sings 'Have you been to Honolulu?' to Mister Junior, and the scene between the two sham artists and Mrs Mister. (I presume Blitzstein must have had a feud with Heifetz, since one of the fake artists is called Jascha, and there is a pointless quip: 'What she doesn't know about music would put Heifetz back on his feet'.)

Blitzstein's trouble is sentimentality and bathos—in fact, the trouble with most musical comedy, particularly when it tries to be something more than just entertainment. (There is just as much in *West Side Story*.) The very scene that Mellers cites approvingly—the drugstore scene in which the honest worker is about to be framed and murdered—is one of the worst. It is obvious that somebody flattered Blitzstein into believing that portraying love between 'workers' was his forte. It isn't, as the 'Franny' scene from *No for an Answer* also demonstrates most conclusively. Blitzstein's was a light-weight talent that was at its best when combining political satire with jazzy music. He can be best enjoyed when not taken too seriously. (For example, we can chuckle about the song 'There's something so damned low about the rich' provided we don't think about it too closely and see what nonsense it is.)

The subject of Blitzstein provides the opportunity of raising again the matter of America's chief contribution to musical entertainment, the Broadway musical. On this matter, I am entirely in agreement with Haggin, who points out simply that all the high claims made for musical comedy fall down when we consider that, by its very nature, it is expressing nothing of importance. *The Most Happy Fella* may be an unusually subtle example of musical comedy, but judged by any serious standard, it does not begin to rate. Even as musical comedy, it falls into the usual pit of sentimentality.

The talent of Leonard Bernstein is sometimes cited as an example of the 'shifting frontier' between serious music and musical comedy. In fact, when considered closely, it proves nothing of the sort. It is true that *Candide* is first-rate musical comedy on a highly intelligent level, and that Bernstein's music for it very nearly reaches the level of Sullivan. The same thing goes for the conscientiously trivial opera *Trouble in Tahiti*, which is dedicated to Blitzstein. But as soon as Bernstein moves into a larger canvas, the lack of staying power becomes apparent. *West Side Story* is obviously strongly influenced by Blitzstein, and it is capable of the same excruciating bad taste. (For example, the music in the 'Maria' song for the lines: 'Say it loud and there's music playing; Say it soft and it's almost like praying'.*) And this seems to be the rule with Bernstein's music. When it is unambitious, it is excellent. (Even the incidental music he did for a children's record of *Peter Pan* shows how good he can be.) As soon as he tries to be serious, music lovers blench and duck. Of the three symphonies, for example, the first, the *Jeremiah*, is little more than noisy technicolour film music. The second, *The Age of Anxiety*, which includes a piano, is far better, but this is partly because he now

*Copyright 1957, 1962 by L. Bernstein and S. Sondheim.

borrows so frankly from Prokofiev and Shostakovich. But to understand the lower depths of which Bernstein is capable, it is necessary to listen to the Third Symphony, the *Kaddish*, dedicated to the memory of President Kennedy. If a world poll is ever taken to decide on the worst piece of music ever written, I imagine this symphony would stand pretty high in the results. The symphony is for speaker and orchestra, like Schoenberg's *Survivor from Warsaw* and Bloch's *Sacred Service*, and it is bad for the same reason that these works are bad. It does not merely wear its heart on its sleeve; it wears its liver, bowels and intestines there as well. I have heard it suggested that 'Kaddish' should be spelt with a C, since the chief object of the work would seem to be to cause acute embarrassment in its listeners. I find it difficult to imagine how the members of its first night audience succeeded in looking one another in the face afterwards.

A survey of the American music scene only seems to underline the points that emerge from the survey of the European scene. America has not yet created a unique culture of its own, although it may be in the process of doing so. And like Europe, it is inclined to believe that the good music of the next fifty years must somehow be several steps further on than the good music of the past fifty. So a lot of consideration is given to the problem of how to sound original, how to sense the direction that cultural history is taking. There is consequently a great flurry of artistic activity, and not a great deal to show for it.

Seen from the 'historical' point of view, the problem looks insoluble. In the thirties, when Harris was the promising light, it seemed that the direction for a 'true American music' lay in a kind of nationalism, a counterpart of the Russian nationalism of the 'five', or the Finnish nationalism of Sibelius. But then Russia and Finland did not have a flourishing musical comedy and film business to cheapen the national tradition, and America very definitely has. It is not a very long step from Copland and Harris to Ferde Grofé's *Grand Canyon Suite* or Dimitri Tiomkin's soundtrack music for *Giant*, and this almost certainly means that there is no future in the Harris tradition. The experimentalism of Cage and Partch is obviously a dead end; so, for more complex reasons, is the atonalism of Ruggles and Carter. It would seem that there is no way forward—at least, if the situation is to be analyzed in this objective manner. In fact, what will happen is that small and intensely honest talents like Chanler, or men of integrity like Ives and Carter, will continue to work out their own musical salvation, and in doing so will create the American tradition of the future. If there is one lesson to be learned from Ives and Carter, it is that the individual needs the courage of inner-direction, of forgetting that he is an 'American composer' and recognizing that he is a particular kind of human being called an artist, whose business is with human evolution.

Lightning Source UK Ltd.
Milton Keynes UK
UKOW05f0448091217
314080UK00021B/303/P